ICFA Continuing Education
Asset Allocation in a Changing World

Proceedings of the AIMR seminar "Asset Allocation in a Changing World"

April 1–2, 1998
London, United Kingdom

Paul Duncombe
D. Don Ezra
Khalid Ghayur, CFA
William A.R. Goodsall
Martyn Hole, CFA
Ronald G. Layard-Liesching
Stephen Lowe

Patrizio Merciai
John Morrell
John C. Stannard, CFA, *Moderator*
Mark Tapley, CFA
Roger Urwin
Daniel Witschi
James R.C. Woodlock

> To obtain the *AIMR Publications Catalog,* contact:
> AIMR, P.O. Box 3668, Charlottesville, Virginia 22903, U.S.A.
> Phone 804-980-3668; Fax 804-980-9755; E-mail info@aimr.org
> or
> visit AIMR's World Wide Web site at **www.aimr.org**
> to view the AIMR publications list.

©1998, Association for Investment Management and Research

All rights reserved. No part of this publication may be reproduced, stored in a retrieval system, or transmitted, in any form or by any means, electronic, mechanical, photocopying, recording, or otherwise, without prior written permission of the copyright holder.

ICFA Continuing Education is published monthly seven times a year in May, May, June, June, August, December, and December by the Association for Investment Management and Research, P.O. Box 3668, Charlottesville, Virginia 22903, U.S.A. This publication is designed to provide accurate and authoritative information with regard to the subject matter covered. It is sold with the understanding that the publisher is not engaged in rendering legal, accounting, or other professional services. If legal advice or other expert assistance is required, the services of a competent professional should be sought. Periodicals postage paid at the post office in Richmond, Virginia, and additional mailing offices.

Copies are mailed as a benefit of membership to CFA® charterholders. Subscriptions also are available at US$100 for one year. Address all circulation communications to ICFA Continuing Education, P.O. Box 3668, Charlottesville, Virginia 22903, U.S.A.; Phone 804-980-3668; Fax 804-980-9755. For change of address, send mailing label and new address six weeks in advance.

Postmaster: Send address changes to the Association for Investment Management and Research, P.O. Box 3668, Charlottesville, Virginia 22903.

ISBN 0-935015-29-9
Printed in the United States of America
December 1998

Editorial Staff
Terence E. Burns, CFA
Book Editor

Maryann Dupes
Editor

Jaynee M. Dudley
Manager, Educational Products

Christine E. Kemper
Assistant Editor

Lois A. Carrier
Diane B. Hamshar
Composition

Contents

Foreword v
    Terence E. Burns, CFA

Biographies vi

Overview: Asset Allocation in a Changing World 1

The Forecasting Pyramid 5
    Roger Urwin

Are Global Market Returns Converging? 14
    Khalid Ghayur, CFA, and Paula Dawson

Global Asset Allocation 31
    Patrizio Merciai

Dealing with Currencies 46
    Paul Duncombe

Are U.K. Investors Turning More Conservative? 59
    Martyn Hole, CFA

European Pension Funds: Turning More Aggressive? 72
    Daniel Witschi

Client Expectations and the Demand to Minimize Downside Risk 85
    Mark Tapley, CFA

Strategic Asset Allocation and Total Portfolio Returns 92
    D. Don Ezra

Tactical Asset Allocation 102
    William A.R. Goodsall

Uses of Futures and Index Funds 111
    James R.C. Woodlock

Rebalancing the Portfolio 117
    Stephen Lowe

Risk Allocation Instead of Asset Allocation 126
    Ronald G. Layard-Liesching

A Different Approach to Benchmarks 136
    John Morrell

Self-Evaluation Examination
    Questions 143
    Answers 145

Selected Publications 147

ICFA Board of Trustees, 1998–99

Philippe A. Sarasin, CFA, *Chair*
 Geneva, Switzerland

Dwight D. Churchill, CFA, *Vice Chair*
 Merrimack, New Hampshire

Frank K. Reilly, CFA, *AIMR Chair*
 Notre Dame, Indiana

R. Charles Tschampion, CFA, *AIMR Vice Chair*
 New York, New York

Thomas A. Bowman, CFA, *AIMR President and CEO*
 Charlottesville, Virginia

Abby Joseph Cohen, CFA
 New York, New York

Jon T. Ender, CFA
 Chicago, Illinois

Martin S. Fridson, CFA
 New York, New York

Khalid Ghayur, CFA
 London, United Kingdom

George W. Long, CFA
 Hong Kong

Deborah H. Miller, CFA*
 Boston, Massachusetts

Janet T. Miller, CFA
 Atlanta, Georgia

Fred H. Speece, Jr., CFA
 Minneapolis, Minnesota

ex officio

AIMR Education Committee, 1998–99

Fred H. Speece, Jr., CFA, *Chair*
 Minneapolis, Minnesota

Thomas A. Bowman, CFA
 Charlottesville, Virginia

Dwight D. Churchill, CFA
 Merrimack, New Hampshire

Robert R. Johnson, CFA
 Charlottesville, Virginia

Lee N. Price, CFA
 San Francisco, California

Katrina F. Sherrerd, CFA
 Charlottesville, Virginia

AIMR Senior Education Staff

Thomas A. Bowman, CFA
 President and CEO

Katrina F. Sherrerd, CFA
 Senior Vice President

Judith H. Brownrigg
 Vice President

Terence E. Burns, CFA
 Vice President

Julia S. Hammond, CFA
 Vice President

Robert R. Johnson, CFA
 Vice President

Robert M. Luck, Jr., CFA
 Vice President

Craig K. Ruff, CFA
 Vice President

Donald L. Tuttle, CFA
 Vice President

Barbara L. Higgins
 Director

Paul W. Turner
 Director

Foreword

Ever since investors have had a choice about where to invest their assets (whether dollars, drachmas, or doubloons), they have been making asset allocation decisions. And ever since the dawn of time, the world has been changing. Thus, allocating assets in a changing world is not a new phenomenon. What is new is how (and why) investors are making those asset allocation decisions.

Asset allocation naturally requires determining how much to invest in which assets. Strategies based on tactical asset allocation and strategic asset allocation can help with the allocation decisions, but effective asset allocation cannot stop there. Investors must determine when (and if) to rebalance the portfolio, which are the appropriate benchmarks to use, whether to use derivatives to control the asset mix, and how to handle currency issues.

Asset allocation also requires a great deal of forward-looking thinking. For example, investors must consider not only how formation of the European Monetary Union will affect diversification opportunities but also how it will affect the demand for equities. In addition, the global trend from defined-benefit to defined-contribution pension plans, changing demographic patterns, and the attempts by countries to move their social security systems from unfunded to funded systems might all alter an investor's long-term asset allocation decisions.

The authors in this proceedings delve into the aforementioned issues in an attempt to shed light on the age-old problem of how to allocate assets in a constantly changing world.

We would like to extend a special thanks to Jan R. Squires, CFA, Southwest Missouri State University. His help on this book was much needed and is much appreciated.

We are grateful to John C. Stannard, CFA, at Frank Russell Company, for serving as moderator for the conference. We also wish to thank all the authors for their assistance with producing this book: Paula Dawson, HSBC Asset Management; Paul Duncombe, State Street Global Advisors U.K.; D. Don Ezra, Frank Russell Company; Khalid Ghayur, CFA, HSBC Asset Management; William A.R. Goodsall, First Quadrant; Martyn Hole, J.P. Morgan Investment Management; Ronald G. Layard-Liesching, Pareto Partners; Stephen Lowe, UBS Brinson, London; Patrizio Merciai, Lombard Odier & Cie; John Morrell, John Morrell and Associates; Mark Tapley, CFA, WestLB Asset Management; Roger Urwin, Watson Wyatt Worldwide; Daniel Witschi, UBS Brinson; and James R.C. Woodlock, Barclays Global Investors.

Although no one can stop the world from changing (or accurately predict the direction of change), investors can try to make sure their portfolio compositions are changing with global changes, not against them, by being informed about the latest developments in the area of asset allocation.

Terence E. Burns, CFA
Vice President
Educational Products

Biographies

Paul Duncombe serves as investment director for State Street Global Advisors U.K. Limited and is responsible for currency management. Previously, he was a senior investment manager at PanAgora Asset Management, where he was responsible for developing the firm's currency overlay program. Prior to PanAgora, he worked as an investment manager for Posthorn Global Asset Management. Mr. Duncombe holds a degree in engineering from Cambridge University and an M.B.A. from London Business School.

D. Don Ezra is director of European Consulting at Frank Russell Company, where he serves on Russell's Operating Committee and leads Russell's Practice Groups. Prior to joining Russell, Mr. Ezra worked as a life insurance actuary. In addition to numerous articles and papers, he has authored several books, including *Understanding Pension Fund Finance and Investment* and *The Struggle for Pension Fund Wealth*. Mr. Ezra holds a B.S. in mathematics from Calcutta University and an M.A. in mathematics and economics from Cambridge University.

Khalid Ghayur, CFA, is director and global head of research at HSBC Asset Management Ltd., where he is responsible for supervising and coordinating the development and implementation of all quantitative research efforts. Prior to joining HSBC, Mr. Ghayur worked for Credit Lyonnais Asset Management as a senior quantitative analyst and for Union National Bank as a portfolio manager. He is a member of AIMR's Board of Governors and is founder and president of the London Society of Investment Professionals. Mr. Ghayur holds an M.B.A. in finance from Ecole Nationale des Ponts et Chaussees in Paris and an M.A. in economics from the University of Karachi.

William A.R. Goodsall is managing director for the London operations of First Quadrant, Limited. He is founder of Barbican Capital Management, which was later acquired by First Quadrant. Mr. Goodsall makes regular appearances on conference platforms and writes frequently for magazines. He is chair of the Institute for Quantitative Investment Research and an associate of the Institute of Investment Management and Research.

Martyn Hole, CFA, is managing director of the International Equity and Balanced Group at J.P. Morgan Investment Management. He also serves as a client portfolio manager for U.K. clients, is a member of the global equity strategy group, and is chair of the U.K. balanced strategy group. In a prior position with J.P. Morgan, he was Head of the Macro Research Group in London. Mr. Hole holds a degree in natural and engineering science from Cambridge University.

Ronald G. Layard-Liesching is a founding partner and director of research at Pareto Partners. Previously, he was the director of quantitative products for County NatWest Investment Management and served as managing director of Chase Investment Bank, where he was responsible for managing Chase Manhattan Bank's currency exposure. Mr. Layard-Liesching holds a B.A. in mathematics and economics from Lancaster University.

Stephen Lowe is Executive Director of Account Management and Business Development at UBS Brinson Limited, London. Previously, he served as principal of the Global Policy Group at Gartmore Investment Management, where he was responsible for strategic research and tactical asset allocation. Mr. Lowe also served Gartmore as Head of U.S. equity management. He holds an M.A. from Cambridge University.

Patrizio Merciai is chief economist and investment strategist at Lombard Odier & Cie, where he is responsible for worldwide asset management. He is also an associate professor of banking and investment at Geneva University. Previously, Mr. Merciai lectured in economics and served as a business consultant. He holds a doctorate from the Graduate Institute of International Studies.

John Morrell is chair and principal of John Morrell and Associates. Previously, he served as chair of Baring International and Henderson Baring and as managing director at Robert Fleming Company, Ltd. Mr. Morrell is a member of council of the U.K. Society of Investment Analysts. He is a frequent contributor to publications such as the *Financial Times*, *Global Investor*, and *Pensions & Investments*. Mr. Morrell holds a degree in philosophy, politics, and economics from Oxford University.

©Association for Investment Management and Research

John C. Stannard, CFA, is managing director, United Kingdom, at Frank Russell Company, where he is responsible for Russell's consulting and analytical services. Prior to joining Russell, he was an investment analyst and assistant portfolio manager at Barclays Bank and was also employed at Hallmark Associates, a computer software firm. Mr. Stannard is a member of the AIMR Performance Presentation Standards Implementation Committee and the Global Performance Presentation Standards Subcommittee, participates in the National Association of Pension Funds Limited performance monitoring group, and is vice president of the London Society of Investment Professionals. Mr. Stannard holds a B.S. in pure mathematics from Royal Holloway College, University of London.

Mark Tapley, CFA, is chief investment officer at WestLB Asset Management (formerly Quorum Capital Management, Ltd.) where he is responsible for managing global bond and equity portfolios for institutional clients. He was previously employed at Posthorn Global Asset Management, American Express Asset Management, and J.P. Morgan Investment Management. Mr. Tapley is a member of the New York Society of Security Analysts and the U.K. Society of Investment Analysts. He holds an M.A. in philosophy and psychology from Oxford University and an M.S. in business administration from the London Business School.

Roger Urwin serves as global director of investment consulting at Watson Wyatt Worldwide. Previously, he was responsible for business development and quantitative investment at Gartmore Investment Management and served as an investment consultant for Bacon Woodrow and Mercer Fraser. Mr. Urwin is a fellow of the Institute of Actuaries. He is a graduate of Oxford University.

Daniel Witschi works in the area of economic and market analysis at UBS Brinson (formerly SBC Brinson), where he is head of the strategic research group and a member of the global asset allocation and fixed-income committees. Previously, he served SBC Brinson as head of financial markets group and as deputy chief economist. Mr. Witschi holds an M.A. in economics and a Ph.D. in monetary economics from the University of Basle.

James R.C. Woodlock is managing director of the quantitative division of Barclays Global Investors. Previously, he was at Barclays Life Managed Pensions. Mr. Woodlock serves on the FTSE Actuaries Steering Committee and is an associate of the Chartered Institute of Bankers. He holds an agriculture degree from Leeds University.

Overview: Asset Allocation in a Changing World

The asset allocation decision for an individual portfolio or an entire pension plan is a critical part of the investment decision-making process. Even though asset allocation is a topic that is much discussed, it is often misunderstood. Asset allocation is known to be critical to the assessment of risk for both individual and institutional investors. The importance of asset allocation for any form of investment cannot be underestimated. Some studies indicate that more than 90 percent of the variation in total returns can be attributed to the asset allocation decision. Even though other studies conclude that the effect of the asset allocation decision is much lower than 90 percent, they still emphasize the benefits of effective asset allocation.

The first step in the investment decision-making process is to develop an investment policy statement based on the investor's or a pension plan's return objectives, risk tolerance, and constraints, including liquidity, time horizon, tax status, legal or regulatory factors, and unique needs and circumstances. That investment policy statement provides guidance to the portfolio manager and the plan sponsor in determining the appropriate asset allocation. Historically, investors in different countries have had large variations in objectives and constraints. For example, U.K. investors traditionally have had high equity allocations and continental European investors relatively low equity allocations. But this heterogeneity is changing. Given the rapid pace of change in world markets, the development of new financial instruments, and the globalization of financial markets, investors and plan sponsors must review the assumptions underlying their asset allocation decisions and make sure their asset allocations fit within this rapidly changing world.

The seminar from which this proceedings was developed was intended to give participants a broad understanding of four important areas of the asset allocation decision from a U.K. and continental European perspective: fundamentals, whether pension funds are turning more aggressive or more conservative, strategy, and benchmarks. The authors from this proceedings draw on their extensive experience to help readers understand the importance of the asset allocation decision and analyze many of the potential issues that ultimately influence that decision. The authors' insights help in understanding the importance of fundamentals, evaluating whether a pension fund's asset allocation is too conservative or too aggressive, determining an appropriate asset allocation strategy, and using benchmarks to evaluate the quality of investment management decisions.

Fundamentals

In developing an asset allocation strategy, portfolio managers need to make assumptions about risk premiums, the expected returns of various asset classes, the volatility of returns, and the correlations of risks and returns between asset classes. Many portfolio managers rely on historical data in making assumptions about the future, but the use of history to estimate the future is, of course, questionable. Volatilities may be rising; with increased globalization of the markets, correlations may be increasing. Given the recent crises in emerging market currencies, effectively managing currency risk remains an important issue.

Roger Urwin indicates that determining an appropriate asset allocation must start with forecasts of risk and return, which requires a good look at risk premiums and current yields. Using a global model helps with analyzing long-term trends in dividend yields, GDP growth, and inflation, but local historical data must be taken into account, especially in inefficient markets. Urwin explains that modeling equilibriums of consensus viewpoints is useful for most pension fund committees that seek to act prudently as a group, but he adds that cutting-edge pension funds use scenario-based analyses to examine how asset classes might perform under different economic conditions.

Global investors also need to understand how the correlations of returns between stocks and bonds have fluctuated over time and how that fluctuation can influence the asset allocation decision. Low correlations for country returns allow investors to diversify risk globally—to reduce risk while obtaining better, or similar, returns. Khalid Ghayur and Paula Dawson examine whether global market returns are converging by analyzing the behavior of cross-country equity and bond return correlations in various economic, market return, and return volatility scenarios. They find that global correlations, on average, have not increased significantly during the 1990s, that global correlations are unfortunately unstable across countries and are time-period specific, and even worse, that correlations increase just when investors need the benefits of international diversification the most—when volatility increases

©Association for Investment Management and Research

or when markets are declining. As a result, they suggest that the asset-class risk of investing in equities is increasing, which has significant implications for asset allocation.

Patrizio Merciai reexamines several golden rules of asset allocation and conventional wisdom in an international context and cautions investors that before making a global asset allocation decision, they must realize that conventional wisdom and theoretical findings may not hold in reality. For example, he finds that the base currency can have a significant impact on the risk–return relationship and the local currency efficient frontiers of global investors and that arguments in favor of universal hedging of currency risk do not hold true in the real world. He suggests that tactical asset allocation may offer opportunities for enhancing returns and reducing risks and that bonds and equities have different hedging solutions.

Dealing with currency risk is a very important issue for global investors, and the hedging decision is probably one of the most intensely debated investment management decisions. Paul Duncombe cautions global investors to watch out for the currency surprise and the holding-period effect. Although longer holding periods can cancel out adverse currency returns, Duncombe warns pension funds not to ignore the substantial risk of unfavorable short-term currency movements. Some funds cannot afford to wait long periods for currency movements to wash out. Duncombe demonstrates how asset allocation changes in a mean–variance optimization framework by using hedged versus unhedged returns. So, if investors decide to hedge, they need to adjust the return, volatility, and correlation assumptions to reflect hedged results and they need to take into account the costs of hedging. Currency overlay managers can help manage currency risk, but investors need to clearly define the risk they want to manage and be able to distinguish between overlay managers that use dynamic hedging and overlay managers that attempt to forecast the direction and/or magnitude of currency returns.

More Conservative or Aggressive

Significant debate is occurring about whether pension funds in the United Kingdom and continental Europe are turning more conservative or more aggressive in their asset allocations. Although this debate is ongoing, one needs to understand the issues that influence their asset allocations.

In 1997, domestic and international equities accounted for nearly 73 percent of all U.K. pension plan investments. Martyn Hole suggests that whether U.K. pension funds are becoming more conservative depends on how one defines conservative. Although that U.K. allocation to equities seems high compared with other countries, Hole discusses a number of factors that explain why U.K. pension funds allocate such a high percentage to equities. Financial, legal, accounting, actuarial, cultural, and historical factors influence the asset allocation decision for U.K. funds. Supply and demand, other uncontrollable factors, and deliberate choices also play a role in that decision. The introduction of the minimum funding requirement legislation, plans' funding statuses, return expectations, and abolition of the Advance Corporation Tax (ACT) credit in the United Kingdom also continue to influence the asset allocation of U.K. pension funds. Hole presents evidence that U.K. pension funds may actually be turning more aggressive in terms of international equity allocations—not more conservative—as a result of the abolition of the ACT credit. Although it is an open question whether or not U.K. funds are turning more conservative, Hole notes that more and more U.K. funds are turning away from consensus-driven asset allocation and moving toward customized benchmarks.

In contrast to the United Kingdom's pension fund history, the majority of pension assets in continental Europe have historically been invested conservatively—in bonds. Daniel Witschi explains that to assess whether continental European pension funds are moving toward higher equity exposures, one must analyze how current pension provisions, demographics, costs, and recent pension reforms will influence the asset allocation decision. Witschi explains how accounting standards, funding rules, portfolio regulations, the structure of fund management, high taxation, and higher historical absolute and real returns on bonds than on equities contribute to the small equity allocation relative to U.K. and U.S. counterparts. Cultural precedent and limited domestic equities in which to invest also contribute to the relatively small equity allocation. Now that many state-controlled pensions are being privatized, European funds may follow a more aggressive path. Finally, Witschi presents a simple theoretical asset allocation model that assumes a multiyear time horizon, changing risk premiums, and constant rebalancing to estimate a pension plan's capacity for equities.

In order to expand a global investment management business, European investment managers need to know more about U.K. investors and vice versa. Mark Tapley looks at the cultural and structural differences between U.K. and European investors to explain why U.K. investors have such high equity allocations and why continental European investors have such low equity allocations. Tapley also looks at how the pension surplus contributes to an important source of asset allocation differences between U.K. and continental European investors' experiences. Although U.K. pension plans have relatively mature pension liabilities, they have high equity allocations because U.K. pension plans may be trying to manage business risk at the expense of managing clients' financial risk, or they may just be benefiting from the recent equity bull market and enjoying healthy pension surpluses. On the other hand, the experience of investors in continental Europe indicates that clients seek both downside risk protection and upside return participation. Tapley analyzes whether managers can deliver nonlinear payoffs, identifies what can go wrong with such a strategy, and points out the importance of comparing the performance of that strategy with an appropriate customized benchmark.

Strategy

Any pool of assets has an implied risk, and that implied risk is probably best defined by the asset allocation. The individuals responsible for that pool of assets should determine where that risk should be, and asset allocation is the best tool for making that determination. Asset allocation is often presented as a mechanism for adding value (i.e., the asset allocation is not fixed but changes over time, and investors often want to change that asset allocation to exploit short-term differences in performance). Unfortunately, asset allocation is misunderstood for a number of reasons, often because of the terms that are used to describe it.

Strategic asset allocation is often considered to be the determinant of the long-term asset allocations of a fund. Don Ezra discusses how strategic asset allocation represents a conscious trade-off between opportunity and safety—ultimately the investor's risk policy—that each investor must make and explains how that trade-off is the most important decision that an investor or plan sponsor will make because wealth accumulation represents the lion's share of aggregate wealth over time. Ezra explains that asset allocation has its place in a series of decisions and tasks to be performed, starting with governance and determining investment objectives and concluding with performance measurement and evaluation. The asset allocation decision itself takes into consideration determining which systems to model, identifying the investors' goals and fears, modeling expected future performance, making decisions based on model output, and knowing what to do next, including periodically revisiting the asset allocation decision. Ezra reviews the characteristics of three alternative modeling approaches and concludes that multistage stochastic programming provides distinct advantages over mean–variance optimization and simulations—especially the ability to take real life problems into account. Finally, Ezra demonstrates that the asset allocation decision explains most of a portfolio's return pattern.

Tactical asset allocation (TAA) is often considered to be short-term deviations around the long-term strategic asset allocation. In TAA, the assumption is that the investor's objectives and constraints are steady. Thus, what drives changes in the asset mix is changes in capital market conditions—returns, volatilities, or correlation expectations. William Goodsall discusses how to manage asset allocation once a fund-specific benchmark for strategic asset allocation has been set. The choices include drifting (the do-nothing approach), using some form of mechanistic rebalancing (the passive approach), or using TAA (an active approach). Although TAA has its shortcomings, Goodsall explains that it can potentially add value over the other alternatives. But managers need to be cognizant of behavioral issues (such as cognitive bias and framing errors), important assumptions, the investment style, and the quantitative approach used.

Once the strategic, tactical, or global asset allocation decision is determined, the important issue is how best to implement the desired asset allocation. James Woodlock reviews the costs and complexity involved with using an underlying equity basket, futures, or index funds to implement global asset allocation. Obviously, buying the equity basket is straightforward; the only drawback for global asset allocation is dividend withholding taxes, which can be reclaimed. Futures quickly provide desired exposure and a return advantage over an equities basket but involve commission costs from rolling futures contracts, margin financing, and basis risk. Although index funds eliminate basis risk, reduce transactions costs, and are readily available, Woodlock explains that global index funds will probably not replace futures contracts as the global asset allocation tool of choice because creating a global index fund takes time.

When current allocations deviate from the long-term strategic allocations, the question then becomes how and when the plan rebalances the portfolio. On the one hand, avoiding the rebalancing decision assumes that the liability risk changes as the asset mix changes so as to keep assets matched with liabilities. But that assumption is flawed; the result can be drifting from the strategic asset allocation, an asset-liability mismatch, or shortfall risk. On the other hand, the decision to rebalance raises the issue of the method and frequency of rebalancing. Stephen Lowe discusses three approaches for rebalancing a portfolio—periodic, trigger, and specific rebalancing—that can reduce shortfall risk and enhance returns. Lowe explains how periodically rebalancing at certain intervals is primarily used to reduce risk but can also be used to enhance returns, especially when a pension fund wants to exploit the tendency of equities to perform better than bonds. Trigger rebalancing works better than the periodic approach when the fund wants to exploit pure asset volatility. Lowe demonstrates how specific rebalancing might be used to exploit the full volatility of one component of a portfolio while minimizing the amount of turnover in other components of the portfolio. Regardless of the reasons or frequency for rebalancing, managers must understand how practical considerations, such as administrative issues, performance measurement, return relationships, covariance matrix stability, and judgment, can influence the rebalancing decision. More importantly, managers must understand the ideal conditions for successfully rebalancing the portfolio.

The conventional approach for allocating pension fund assets to available asset classes and active managers is to use mean–variance analysis. Ronald Layard-Liesching points out that mean–variance optimization merely reflects the implications of model inputs and that it has its share of problems. The major problem is that the distribution of financial returns has fat tails that are not captured by the normal distribution. Layard-Liesching also points out that poor market timing, poor equity selection results, poor country allocation decisions, and the minimum funding requirement are leading to the widespread move away from balanced fund management toward specialist management. Layard-Liesching explains that forecasting returns and determining the asset allocation that will expose a portfolio to the highest-performing assets is extremely difficult in large efficient markets because of technology. But strong evidence indicates that risks can be forecasted. Given that performance attribution can decompose the separate components of return and risk, Layard-Liesching proposes a revolutionary portfolio management framework—risk allocation—in which pension funds can budget their use of risk. Thus, risk can be controlled or allocated simply by altering a portfolio's exposure to risky assets.

Benchmarks

Benchmarks are the measure used to judge the effectiveness of management decisions. For international asset classes, managers must build customized benchmarks by combining various country-specific benchmarks and selecting the proper weights. If a benchmark is properly designed, it can clearly distinguish between managers that are managing their business risk and managers that are managing their clients' risk. John Morrell points out that, although investment consultants have made important contributions to the investment management business, consultants have fallen short with respect to the art of investing—especially with regard to defining risk, the use of book value, and benchmarks. The result is that many managers have fallen into the consensus trap (i.e., using an index or peer universe as the benchmark). Morrell explains the origin of the consensus trap and proposes several remedies to avoid that trap. Finally, Morrell presents a value-based investment method that focuses on fundamentals to define a neutral benchmark, and he outlines suggestions for improving the investment management industry.

Conclusion

Asset allocation remains one of the most important decisions for investors and pension fund managers and has the largest impact on total portfolio returns. One needs to understand the historical, cultural, legal, and structural differences among countries to understand why investors and pension funds in different countries have such diverse asset allocations. Of course, once the long-term strategic asset allocation is determined, managers need to determine the best way to implement such a strategy and need to periodically review the strategy to make sure it fits within the ever-changing financial world.

The authors of these presentations help in understanding how to analyze the fundamentals that influence the outcome of the asset allocation decision, how to assess whether a fund is too conservative or too aggressive, how to determine an appropriate asset allocation or risk allocation framework, and how to design an effective benchmark (rather than rely on the consensus) to evaluate the success of that decision.

The Forecasting Pyramid

Roger Urwin
Global Director, Investment Consulting
Watson Wyatt Worldwide

> Determining a pension fund's strategic asset allocation should start with forecasts of risk and return. A look at risk premiums, current yields, and local history is helpful, but a global model is more useful, especially for modeling long-run forecasts of returns. In addition to history, perspective plays an important role in the forecasting process. One must consider how much history should influence future forecasts, whether a global or local perspective should be used, and how sensitive forecasts should be to current market conditions.

The key benefit from forecasting risk and return is determining the strategic asset allocation for a fund. From a position 10 years ago, when strategic asset allocation studies were in their infancy in the United Kingdom, U.K. pension funds have now come to regard them as part of their due diligence process. Funds perform asset allocation studies by looking at liabilities, thinking about policy alternatives, and having dialogues with their managers.

Looking at risk premiums is just the beginning of a long process that leads to a fund's asset allocation policy. Fund sponsors and trustees need to think about risk premiums and forecasting returns in some detail. The forecasting process is based on five steps: looking at the current yield structure, analyzing local history, considering global history, modeling projectable equilibriums, and modeling projectable scenarios.

As part of this five-step process, four rather philosophical issues must be considered. First is the balance between using historical data sensibly and using data to make judgments. The judgment side is more important than many people think because history is actually quite misleading in some areas. Second is the question of whether using a local perspective is sufficient. Many people model foreign equities as a separate category, but should they be thinking globally? The third question is how much influence should come from pure logic and how much from intuition? The answer is context driven. Being entirely logical and consensus based has its place, but so does using scenarios that are based on intuition. The final issue is how sensitive forecasts should be to today's market conditions. For long-term investors, current market conditions do not need to play a large part in a study, but these studies sometimes incorporate a tactical position in which current conditions can influence strategy.

Risk Premiums

At Watson Wyatt Worldwide, we are trying to decide "central" returns—middle of the road returns—for the future. The term "risk premium" is used to denote the differences in returns that are attributable to differences in risks. We think of risk premiums in stochastic terms, probability-based terms, and thus, volatilities and correlations are important.

Risk premiums require some benchmark against which to compare returns, usually the risk-free position. In the United States, cash and T-bills are commonly thought of as risk-free positions. But cash and T-bills as risk-free positions are not really applicable to a lot of liability situations—especially pension obligations. Treasury bonds can, therefore, be a better risk-free position. In many markets, indexed bonds (bonds indexed to changes in inflation) are now available. About six countries in the world have such bonds, but in no single country is the market mature. As a result, they are inadequate guides for the aggregate behavior of the marketplace. They may be quite reasonable to use when starting an analysis, but they are certainly not priced efficiently because the markets are rather thin. So, be careful with indexed bonds as a risk-free position.

Inflation itself is a good risk-free position. Investors cannot "buy" inflation, of course, but it is a good way to think about returns. For long bonds, the risk premium relative to cash is roughly 2 percent a year; for inflation index-linked bonds, which have a guarantee relative to inflation, the risk premium is a bit less, about 1.5 percent a year.

Current Yield

The initial step in forecasting returns is to look at the current yield structure. The current yield information for the United Kingdom is shown in **Table 1**. The dividend yield of equities is 2.8 percent, but that figure needs to be adjusted to allow for various items, such as inflation, real GDP growth, corporate sector growth, and share repurchases. Corporate sector growth is a short-term figure and perhaps the most controversial because the United Kingdom is at a high point in the cycle of corporate profits relative to GDP. Public limited companies (PLCs) in the United Kingdom have had good reason to distribute a major part of their cash flow and earnings through dividends because pension funds have been attracted to the tax-free income that has come from those distributions, but PLCs no longer have the incentive to do so. Therefore, we assert that share repurchases will be on the rise, which is one reason why the dividend yield is relatively low at the moment. Those adjustments add about 7 percent to the 2.8 percent dividend yield of equities, thus giving about a 9.8 percent total return for U.K. equities. The current long-bond yield is at 6.2 percent, so a 3.6 percent risk premium is implied in those terms at the moment, which explains why investors are not moving out of U.K. equities into U.K. bonds.

Table 1. Current U.K. Yield Structure

Asset	Return
Equities	
Dividend yield	2.8%
Dividend growth	
Inflation[a]	3.0
Real GDP growth[a]	2.5
Corporate sector versus GDP[a]	0.5
Share repurchase[a]	1.0
Subtotal	7.0%
Total	9.8%
Bonds	
Yield	6.2%

[a]Consensus estimates.

Figure 1 shows the long-bond yield, equity dividend yield, and inflation for a 20-year period. Inflation was very high in the early part of this period, but it has stabilized, as has the long-bond yield. The long-bond yield has come down over this period of time, reflecting low inflation expectations, and the same has happened to equities. These yield data provide a reasonable amount of information about the future, but more information is needed to predict total returns.

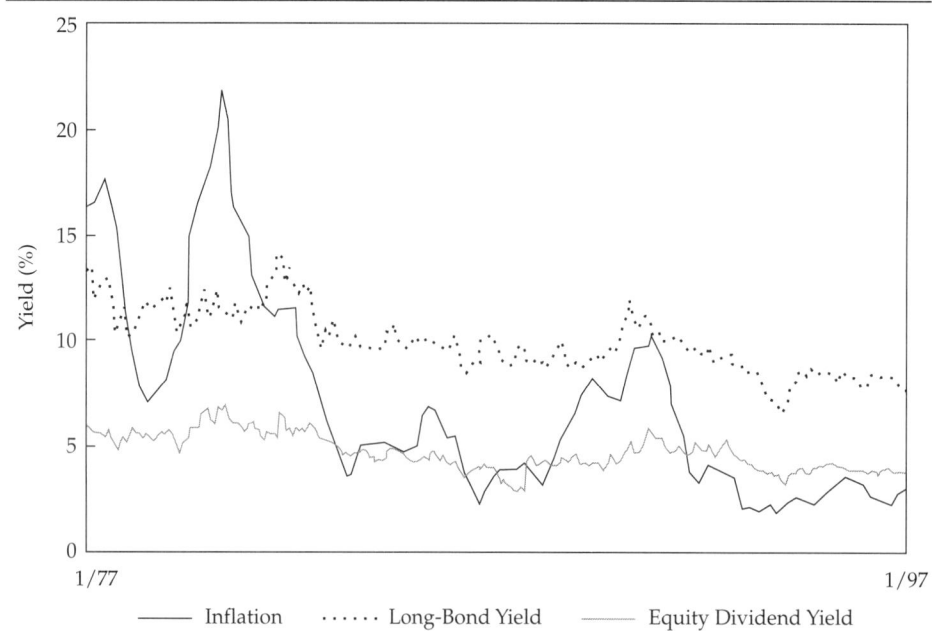

Figure 1. U.K. Equity and Bond Yield History, 1977–97

Local History

Once the yield data have been examined, the local historical data must be taken into account. **Table 2** shows compound annual returns for a 20-year and a 10-year period. An equity–bond risk premium of 6.1 percent for the 20-year period represents a high U.K. equity return in the first 10 years of that period. In the second period, the equity–bond risk premium drops to 3 percent. The 3 percent equity risk premium is plausible for the future; the 6.1 percent is not. The difference in equity risk premiums between the two periods can be explained by a strong start-period bias for the 20-year period. That finding comes as a surprise to many people, because they think that over the long term, 20 years, any bias or trend would have vanished. But one of the ways to examine that point about trending is to use the actuarial technique of smoothing out returns by looking at the two components of return: average yield and dividend growth. This approach shows a detrended return of about 9.2 percent, 2.5 percentage points a year lower than the 11.7 percent figure in Table 2. That detrending analysis is quite effective. It does not have much impact on the 10-year figures, but it has a big impact on the 20-year figures. The risk premium relative to bonds, using the detrended numbers, is 3.6 percent for the 20-year period and 2.2 percent for the 10-year period. Those risk premiums are plausible for the future. Notice that GDP growth has not changed much over the entire period, but inflation has come down quite a bit.

Table 2. Domestic Historical Annual Real Returns

Measure	1977–96	1987–96
U.K. equities	11.7%	9.6%
U.K. bonds	5.6	6.6
Equity–bond risk premium	6.1%	3.0%
U.K. equities yield	4.9	4.5
Dividend growth	4.2	4.2
U.K. equities detrended return	9.2	8.8
GDP growth	2.1	2.0
Inflation	6.7	4.5

That 20-year period turned out to be an unusual period; the data are significantly skewed in statistical terms. The U.K. equity return from that period has a confidence interval at the one standard deviation level of about ±4 percentage points. So, the interesting point is that one can infer nothing reasonable at all from the 20-year result. Most investment professionals think 20 years is long enough to draw a definite conclusion, but it is certainly not long enough to use on its own. Detrending helps with the analysis.

It more than doubles the accuracy of the forecasting by looking at yield and dividend growth separately. Nevertheless, the historical data alone do not produce a good forecast. Judgment needs to come into play.

Global History

Investors need to think of the world as a global market, which requires some soft interpretation of hard data. Using only domestic data to forecast future returns can yield disappointing results. By looking at data from other countries, investors can get better information about what is a realistic long-run forecast. Investors can build a better model if they build a global model. In addition, using a global model is helpful because investors have more data to explain results in the context of such variables as GDP or inflation. Using a global model is vital, but local variations have to be considered because the world is not a perfectly efficient market for stocks.

Table 3 shows real equity returns, in local currency terms, for various countries over a 20-year period. The crucial point is the existence of outliers—14.2 percent for the Netherlands and 6.5 percent for Japan—which are not sustainable in the long run. Thus, the average value, which is about 9 percent, may provide some reasonable information about what might be sustainable in the future. **Table 4** shows the domestic equity risk premiums for the same 20-year period as in Table 3. Notice that the numbers are particularly large. The global average is about 4.5 percent. Because the data in Table 3 and Table 4 have not been detrended, one has to wonder if those numbers are sustainable.

Trend Analysis. To better understand the data, investors need to examine the trends during that 20-year period. **Table 5** shows the average dividend

Table 3. Real Returns on Domestic Equities, 1977–96

Country	Return[a]
Netherlands	14.2%
Ireland	13.0
Hong Kong	12.5
United Kingdom	11.7
France	10.3
Australia	9.0
United States	8.7
Switzerland	8.5
Germany	7.5
Canada	7.3
Japan	6.5

[a]Percent per annum.

Asset Allocation in a Changing World

Table 4. Performance Margin: Domestic Equities over Domestic Bonds, 1977–96

Country	Margin[a]
Netherlands	8.8%
Switzerland	6.5
United Kingdom	6.1
France	4.9
United States	4.4
Germany	2.7
Canada	1.8
Japan	0.6

[a]Percent per annum.

Table 5. Average Dividend Yields on Equities, 1977–96

Country	Yield
Netherlands	5.2%
United Kingdom	4.9
Australia	4.4
Hong Kong	4.1
United States	4.0
France	3.6
Canada	3.5
Germany	2.6
Switzerland	2.5
Japan	1.2

yield for each country listed. The average dividend yield, taking a naive average, over the entire period for all those countries is roughly 3.6 percent. **Table 6** shows the real growth in dividends. The average for all countries is about 2.25 percent over that 20-year period. The detrended results, shown in **Table 7**, yield a global average real return on equities of about 6 percent, which is a typical long-run projected real return for equities. So, the trend approach has helped in the analysis.

GDP Growth. The next question is, what drives those figures? Real GDP growth is one answer. In other words, superior growth in a market produces

Table 6. Real Growth in Dividends, 1977–96

Country	Dividend Growth[a]
Hong Kong	7.2%
United Kingdom	4.2
Netherlands	4.1
Australia	3.0
Switzerland	2.7
United States	1.4
Germany	0.6
France	0.0
Japan	–0.2
Canada	–0.3

[a]Percent per annum.

Table 7. Detrended Real Returns on Equities, 1977–96

Country	Return[a]
Hong Kong	11.4%
Netherlands	9.5
United Kingdom	9.2
Australia	7.4
United States	5.4
Switzerland	5.2
France	3.6
Germany	3.3
Canada	3.1
Japan	1.0

[a]Percent per annum.

high real equity returns. Unfortunately, the data do not support that assertion, as shown in **Figure 2**. The line of best fit (if one can be drawn) points a bit downward, which is a rather disappointing result. A cluster of emerging markets shows some evidence that conforms to the pattern of high GDP growth and high returns, but the data are sketchy. So, the data show half-useful, half-disappointing results.

Figure 2. Real GDP Growth versus Real Domestic Equity Returns, 1977–96

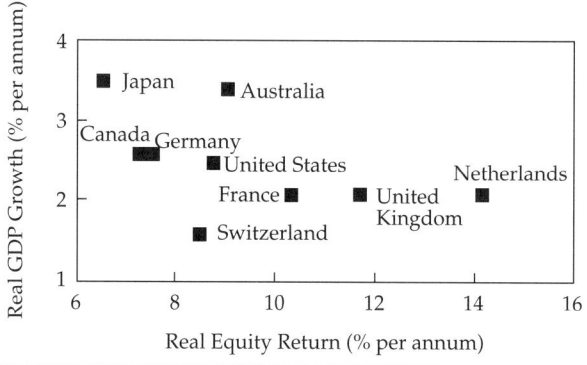

Inflation Analysis. An alternative way of looking at the drivers of the detrended data is to focus on inflation. **Figure 3** shows the correlations between real returns on domestic equities and inflation growth for the 20-year period under investigation. Researchers have shown that a little inflation is good for equity markets but that a lot of inflation is bad. Thus, one might have expected Figure 3 to have a downward-sloping regression line. The data clearly show, however, that the line of best fit does not point downwards at all. It points upwards, which is strange. Why did that extra inflation make such a difference to real returns?

Figure 3. Inflation versus Real Returns on Domestic Equities, 1977–96

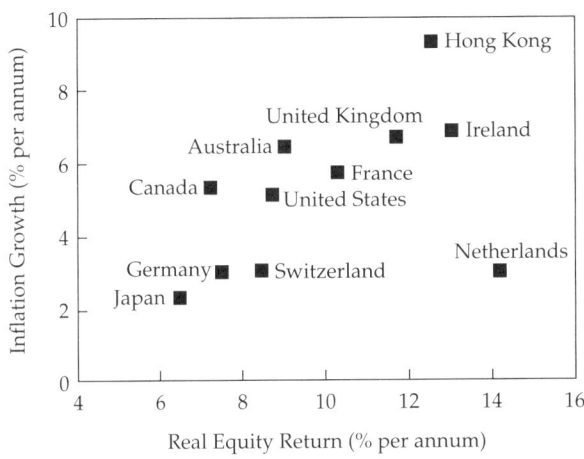

The answer lies in inflation improvement, shown in **Figure 4**. The 1977–96 period started with high inflation and then had secular improvement in inflation in a number of markets, which has been very good for those equity markets. This pattern captures what happens in the majority of those countries, with Hong Kong and the Netherlands as outliers—Hong Kong for growth reasons and the Netherlands because of the concentration of the market in a narrow set of global stocks. So, inflation improvement has had a big influence on good real returns. Therefore, using historical data without an adjustment in forecasts would actually imply that one expects to have similar levels of future inflation improvement, which is implausible. The next step is to turn that knowledge of history, with the appropriate adjustments, into a forecast of central premiums.

Figure 4. Real Equity Return versus Inflation Improvement, 1977–96

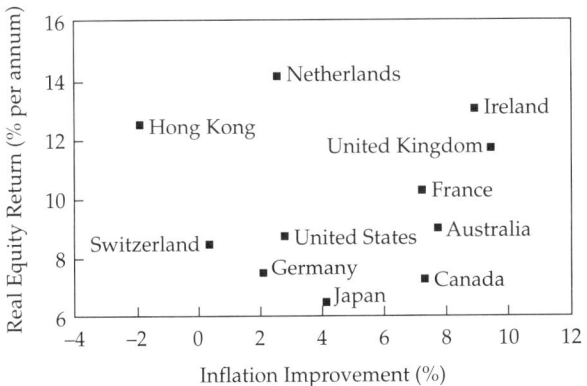

Modeling Equilibriums

Equilibrium points in market returns are based on logical analysis. Projecting certain equilibriums between markets essentially aligns one's forecasts so that they are consistent with the risks and, to an extent, the tax positions of investors. Therefore, the modeler is postulating a perfect capital market line, in which a line can be drawn from the low risk/low return end to the high risk/high return end. The assumption is that all markets lie thereabouts on the capital market line. The key point is to take into account what I call consensus positions, because the nature of this analysis is to be logical and plausible. Individual scenarios should not be used at this point because these are equilibrium positions.

Risk can be defined in a number of ways, but the most commonly used measure is volatility. **Table 8** shows the return volatility for various equity markets. Twenty years of data show a high level of volatility attached to high growth countries, which often implies unstable politics. One particular outlier is Hong Kong. The liquid markets that have tight disclosure, good regulations, and low transaction costs have low volatility. The leading markets show a gradation in volatility, and I think these volatilities may well be of a similar order in the future.

Table 8. Equity Real Return Volatility in Local Currency, 1977–96

Country	Volatility[a]
Hong Kong	33.0%
France	21.7
Australia	20.6
Japan	20.6
Germany	19.4
Switzerland	18.3
United Kingdom	16.7
Canada	15.7
Netherlands	15.5
United States	14.4

[a]Standard deviation percent per annum.

Bond market volatility data, illustrated in **Table 9**, show the opposite from equity markets. But this example is one in which statistics are not in a perfect form, or rather, capital markets are not necessarily in a perfect form. Canada, the United States, and the United Kingdom have genuine long-bond markets (i.e., long duration assets with high volatility), whereas the other markets on the list have bonds that are much shorter duration, hence less volatility. I think the same sort of conclusion applies to bond volatility as to equity volatility: These markets may well have

Table 9. Bond Real Return Volatility in Local Currency, 1977–96

Country	Volatility[a]
Canada	12.1%
United States	11.1
United Kingdom	10.8
Japan	7.8
France	7.0
Germany	6.4
Netherlands	5.8
Switzerland	5.3

[a]Standard deviation percent per annum.

similar levels of volatility across the board. I have not addressed the extent to which I expect these volatilities to change. That is a discussion in its own right. Martyn Hole, however, asserts that the increased homogeneity of the European markets actually might have an influence on portfolio allocations, which might lead to a lower level of volatility in a composite European Monetary Union (EMU) basket.[1]

Modeling Scenarios

Up until this point in the forecasting process (looking at current yield, analyzing local and global historical data, and modeling projectable equilibriums), everything has been quite logical. A consensus conviction has gone into those assumptions such that if any of those assumptions are challenged, the forecaster could answer, "The assumptions are in the middle of most people's convictions, and therefore, I think they are reasonable." This framework is perfect for dealing with fiduciaries who look after other people's money. For example, most pension funds are managed by a group of people, fiduciaries, who have the responsibility to be prudent and to act as a group. They would do best to work their forecasts around the logical, consensus stance.

Scenario models are, in a sense, the opposite of equilibrium positions; they are based on intuition and individual convictions. Scenario-based analysis does not work well in a committee setting. Because committees are groups of individuals, they find it difficult to buy into a particular conviction or scenario as a group. A small number of cutting-edge pension funds might use scenario analysis, but the vast majority of pension funds will likely stop at the logical position, the consensus view.

Constructing a Scenario. The following discussion shows how one might think through a scenario of the U.K. equity market. Some firm evidence of portfolio disinvestment from the domestic stock market exists on two fronts. First, given the maturity of U.K. pension funds, many such funds have an increasing appetite for bonds rather than equities. Second, as U.K. pension funds start to move toward becoming eurozone investors, they will offload some of their domestic stock in search of eurozone equities. The sell-off of domestic equities by U.K. pension funds will not be counterbalanced by the rest of the European pension fund industry buying U.K. stocks in large numbers, because the European pension fund industry is too small to counterbalance that effect. So, the result is a bearish position for fund flows into U.K. equities.

On the other hand, new equity will be in limited supply because U.K. PLCs will be more inclined to pay cash out in capital terms (repurchase shares) than in income terms (pay dividends). Also, a declining supply of equity could come about because treasurers might see the corporate debt market as a more attractive way than the equity market to develop their balance sheets, and the leverage in U.K. companies, which has been at quite a low level, is likely to increase. So, an issue of limited supply exists, which is a bullish point for the U.K. equity market.

Thus, the sell-off of U.K. equities by U.K. pension funds and a declining supply of U.K. equities are the two big factors in the bear versus bull market predictions. No one knows exactly how those two factors will weigh against each other, but they clearly can form the basis on which one can make a proposition that is bullish or bearish for U.K. equities.

A number of economists are making assertions that are bearish for inflation in a post-EMU world, and a number are making disinflationary projections as well. The modeler has to decide where he or she stands on that scale.

With the so-called new paradigms of personal investment, one can perhaps see a market in which a natural equity culture is emerging from the growth in mutual funds and defined-contribution investing or, indeed, a market that is fueled by a change in the balance of the cost of capital; these consequences might affect the risk premium. All of those points are clearly relevant, and individuals can take their own views. In a stochastic model, the researcher can take account of an individual's views by attaching higher probabilities to certain outcomes and, therefore, having more of the stochastic simulations falling below or above the equilibrium forecast.

Useful Scenarios. Three particular scenarios concerning inflation and an improved corporate sector have proven quite useful during the past 20 years or so:
- secular improvement over a long cycle,
- secular improvement followed by cyclical regression, and

---

[1]See Mr. Hole's presentation in this proceedings.

- secular improvement followed by secular regression.

Four countries—the United States, the United Kingdom, the Netherlands, and Switzerland—have had a long cycle of secular improvement through reduced inflation and an improved environment for the corporate sector, which has resulted in higher values for return on equity and other measures of financial performance. In terms of a risk premium between equities and bonds, such as shown in **Figure 5** for the United States, these four countries have shown a consistent outperformance of equities relative to bonds, with very limited intervening periods of bond market relative strength. So, the scenario is interesting but not very plausible for the next 20 years.

Four countries —Australia, Canada, France, and Germany—have shown secular improvement in inflation and the corporate sector in the early part of the 20-year period followed by more cyclicality. That is, they have shown secular improvement for the first 10 years of this period and then gone back to a more normal level of volatility, with bond market returns being above equity market returns at certain periods in the cycle, as shown in **Figure 6** for Germany.

Japan, by contrast and in isolation, has shown secular improvement followed by decline. The equity risk premium for the past 20 years is shown in **Figure 7**.

Conclusion

The forecasting pyramid first consists of looking at the current yield structure. Then, the local history has to be analyzed, but it is subject to a great deal of sampling error. So, the global history has to be considered. Doing so unfortunately increases the degrees of freedom in the estimate. History, however, is limited. Consequently, equilibriums need to be introduced for thinking about the way that the market should behave in the next 10 or 20 years. Finally, depending on the context, the forecaster might form a view about different scenarios with different probabilities from those implied in an equilibrium model.

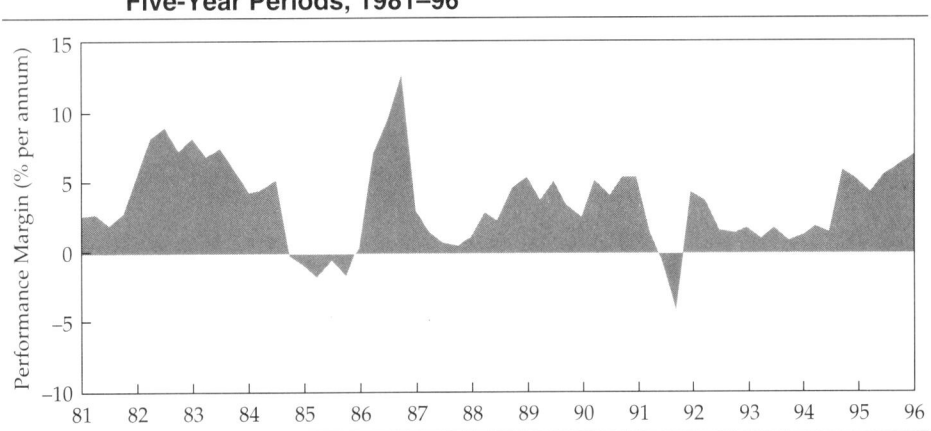

Figure 5. Relative Performance of U.S. Equities versus U.S. Bonds: Rolling Five-Year Periods, 1981–96

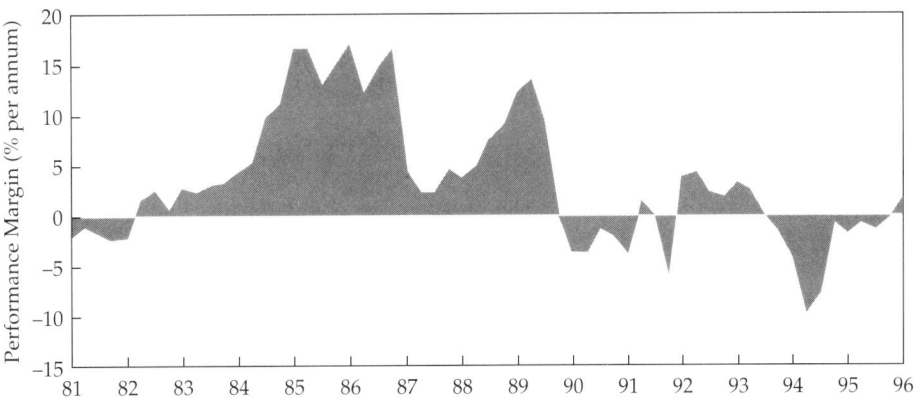

Figure 6. Relative Performance of German Equities versus German Bonds: Rolling Five-Year Periods, 1981–96

Figure 7. Relative Performance of Japanese Equities versus Japanese Bonds: Rolling Five-Year Periods, 1981–96

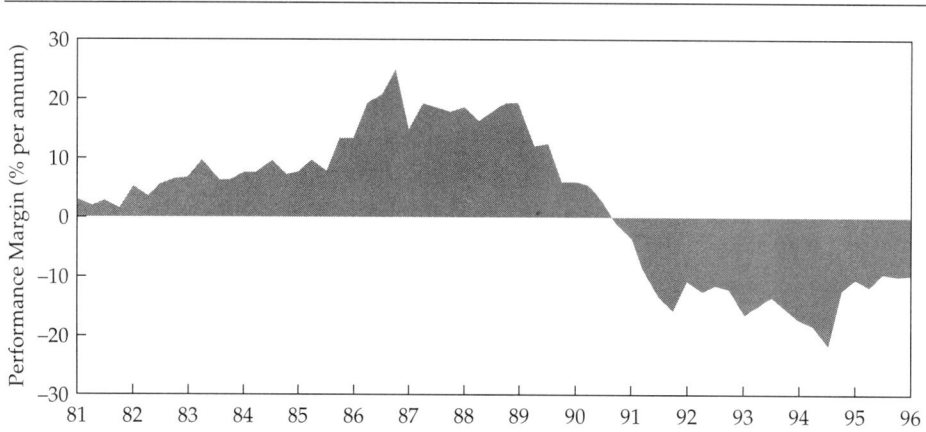

As for my philosophy of long-run forecasting, I think judgment should take precedence over history. History provides a great deal of guidance, but personal judgment should have the strongest influence on the forecast. If I had to use numerical terms, I would say the emphasis should be 40 percent history/60 percent judgment. Local analysis is important, but one would lose out if one did not think of the world globally and use the advantage of global thinking in the forecasting process. The forecaster must, in any situation, distinguish between an equilibrium model, which is distilled wisdom that groups of people (such as trustee boards) can share, and a scenario model, which is about one or two people having a vision of the way the world will be and applying that vision in their own funds. Finally, current market terms are a vital part of the whole process.

Question and Answer Session

Roger Urwin

Question: Is drawing conclusions from average risk premiums meaningful when the range of deviation around the mean is so high?

Urwin: Any conclusions drawn from historical data are based on only a sample of stock market conditions. The conclusions, therefore, are subject to a skew related to those conditions, so the level of meaningfulness is low. The answer is to go behind the data, understand the data, and adjust the results, if you will, to reflect a more normal situation for the next 20 years or the particular scenario that you expect for the next 20 years. The ultimate answer is that no period of past history is a reliable indicator of the future.

Question: How, if at all, would you vary your key points of philosophy for a defined-contribution versus a defined-benefit audience?

Urwin: The methodology is the same as for defined-benefit plans, but it has a different spin and different dialogue. The advantage of a defined-benefit pension fund, in modeling terms, is that it has a very specific goal to meet certain liabilities. A defined-contribution plan is not hugely different, although instead of well-defined liabilities the plan has ill-defined expectations and goals. So, part of the plan sponsor's challenge is to formulate the ambitions of those investors and then create a model for optimizing the investment policy relative to those defined goals and expectations. The investment world has a great deal of work to do to articulate those goals and expectations in a way that personal investors can identify with.

Question: As you've walked pension fund trustees through this process, have you found that they are able to embrace it?

Urwin: For the most part, no. They do not find this work easy and so do not embrace it. At Watson Wyatt, we feel very strongly that we're asking too much of trustee boards to have them depart heroically from the conventional wisdom of the time. We always consider the peer-group position in our work. So, in a sense, there tends to be a constraint on how far we can move a pension fund away from peer-group average positions. But then we have a dialogue with the client saying that we know the average pension fund distribution is not built on efficient lines, so we have valid reasons to challenge the distilled wisdom in the peer-group position. We'll gradually suggest a limited variation, perhaps linked to liability issues, from the peer-group position. It could be into a particular mix of bonds, or it could be into a particular mix of U.K. and overseas equities in which modeling asserts that the average pension fund distribution is not trading risk and reward efficiently.

I think the confidence level of the pension fund community in these methods has certainly improved, but it still remains rather fragile. Part of the problem is that there are no standards in the modeling area; there are no consistencies of asset-liability modeling. In the same way that performance presentation has been a major issue to get right in terms of standards, I assert that asset-liability modeling should be next in line. The methodology for establishing these standards, however, is quite challenging. It is probably a 10-year process to get these sorts of standards in place, but at the end of 10 years, I hope that the trustee community knows more clearly what they're getting out of asset-liability modeling.

Question: How much does survivorship bias affect the validity of historical equity indexes?

Urwin: All historical data, such as historical equity indexes, have the problem of being samples from history. Because the sample (equity indexes) has survivorship bias in it, one can attach finite probabilities to the mortality of certain stock markets. By putting history and judgment together, we can start to build in overrides to what the historical data indicate.

Question: Can you comment on asset allocation in the context of the balanced manager approach?

Urwin: Balanced management has failed in some areas for two major reasons. First is that the tactical asset allocation of balanced managers has become quite timid because it has been largely unsuccessful. Second is that balanced management has been concentrated too much in the hands of too few managers. But this issue is more about the implementation of policy than the policy itself.

We see our job as developing a strategic asset allocation policy in partnership with our clients. When we look at how to implement strategic asset allocation, we can do it in one of two fundamentally different ways. The client can use balanced (multiasset) managers or specialist managers.

©Association for Investment Management and Research

Are Global Market Returns Converging?

Khalid Ghayur, CFA
Director, Global Head of Research
HSBC Asset Management Limited

Paula Dawson[1]
Quantitative Analyst
HSBC Asset Management Limited

> The analysis of whether global market returns are converging indicates both good news and bad news. If the good news is that average correlations at the global level have not increased significantly during the 1990s, the bad news is that international correlations are not constant through time and across countries and that correlations tend to increase when volatility increases and when markets are declining. These results suggest that average, or unconditional, correlations may overstate diversification benefits, especially in the short run, and that the asset-class risk for global equities is increasing.

In this presentation, we analyze international return volatility and cross-country return correlations at a global and European level and explore whether the returns of global markets are converging. We have conducted the analysis from the perspective of five different investors: a U.S. dollar investor, a German mark investor, a Japanese yen investor, a U.K. pound investor, and a fully hedged investor (i.e., the perspective of local currencies). This presentation includes the results for only the U.S. dollar returns and local currency returns at the global level and German mark returns and local currency returns at the European level.[2] Finally, we consider both equities and bonds in our analysis.

The presentation is divided into three main parts. First, we look at the evolution of international market correlations and return volatilities. This section essentially concentrates on average correlations, which are sometimes called unconditional correlations. Second, we present some fresh evidence that seems to suggest a link between correlations and market return phases and return volatility phases. That particular section focuses on conditional correlations—those that are conditional on market returns and on market volatility phases. Third, we summarize the main findings of our research and discuss some of the implications for portfolio management.

Correlations and Volatilities

A review of the long-term and the more recent behavior of international market volatilities and correlations helps show whether combining equities and bonds from volatile markets in different countries can provide diversification benefits and reduce overall portfolio risk.

Long-Term Horizon. To look at a long-term horizon for the evolution of correlations and volatilities, we examined data from January 1970 to January 1998 for equities and from January 1985 to January 1998 for bonds. The evidence on average correlations between sample country and U.S. returns and volatilities for both equities and bonds is shown in **Table 1**. At the global level for equities, we used data from nine countries: Australia, Canada, France, Germany, Hong Kong, Italy, Japan, the United Kingdom, and the United States. For bonds, we used data from eight countries: Australia, Canada, France, Germany, Italy, Japan, the United Kingdom, and the United States.

---

[1] Paula Dawson contributed greatly to the original research and the writing of this presentation. This material was presented at the conference solely by Khalid Ghayur, CFA.

[2] To see the results for other currencies, please contact the authors at HSBC Asset Management, 6 Bevis Marks, London EC3A 7QP, United Kingdom.

Are Global Market Returns Converging?

Table 1. Monthly Correlations and Volatilities in U.S. Dollar and Local Currency Terms

Countries	Correlation versus United States		Volatility	
	U.S. Dollars	Local Currency	U.S. Dollars	Local Currency
Equities				
Australia	46.0%	50.7%	25.5%	22.1%
Canada	70.0	72.5	18.5	16.8
France	42.9	47.4	23.3	20.8
Germany	24.8	40.1	20.3	18.0
Hong Kong	31.1	32.7	39.4	37.5
Italy	22.7	25.5	26.4	24.9
Japan	25.0	31.9	22.9	18.8
United Kingdom	49.7	55.2	24.6	22.1
United States	—	—	15.1	15.1
Average	40.3%	44.5%	24.0%	21.8%
Bonds				
Australia	16.4%	36.9%	15.6%	9.3%
Canada	67.4	77.8	11.5	9.5
France	42.7	54.2	13.4	8.1
Germany	31.2	53.6	13.4	4.8
Italy	17.9	32.3	17.6	8.5
Japan	24.1	43.6	15.6	6.6
United Kingdom	32.9	45.5	16.1	9.0
United States	—	—	9.8	9.8
Average	33.3%	49.7%	14.1%	8.2%

Note: Data for equities are from January 1970 to January 1998. Data for bonds are from January 1985 to January 1998. Data for Italy's bond market start in January 1991.

Source: Based on data from MSCI indexes.

All of these countries combined cover 90–95 percent of the world market capitalization in their respective asset classes (equities or bonds).

■ *Equities.* For this sample period, with returns expressed in U.S. dollars, the correlation of U.K. equities with U.S. equities was 49.7 percent. When returns were expressed in local currencies, the correlation was slightly higher at 55.2 percent. The average correlation between the United States and all of these countries was 40.3 percent with returns expressed in U.S. dollars and 44.5 percent when returns were expressed in local currencies.

The volatilities of these different markets are shown on the right-hand side of Table 1. For example, when returns were expressed in U.S. dollars, the volatility (i.e., the standard deviation of returns) for the United Kingdom was 24.6 percent; the volatility was 22.1 percent when returns were expressed in local currency terms (i.e., U.K. pounds). The average volatility for all the markets was 24.0 percent in U.S. dollar terms and 21.8 percent in local currencies.

Note that the average correlations in local currency terms are higher than the average correlations in U.S. dollar terms. On the other hand, the market volatilities computed using local currency returns are lower than the market volatilities based on U.S. dollar returns. These differences are caused by currency fluctuations, which have the net effect of lowering the common currency return correlation between the domestic and foreign market and increasing the volatility of the foreign market's return.

The average correlations—40.3 percent U.S. dollar terms and 44.5 percent local currency terms—are relatively low. These low correlations imply that from the perspective of a U.S. dollar investor or a fully hedged investor, international investing for the 1970–98 period would have brought about significant diversification benefits. To put these numbers into perspective, note that for the 1985–98 period, the correlation between the U.S. equity and U.S. bond markets was 37.5 percent, which was only slightly lower than the average cross-country return correlations across global equity markets.

■ *Bonds.* When returns for bonds were expressed in U.S. dollar terms, the average correlation was even lower than for equities—33.3 percent. In local currency terms, however, the correlation was higher—almost 50 percent. Similarly, the average volatility for U.S. dollar returns across all markets was 14.1 percent, considerably higher than the average volatility of 8.2 percent for local currency returns. Bonds exhibit a big difference in correlation coefficients and return volatilities when expressed in local currency and U.S. dollar terms, unlike for equities. The reason for that difference is that foreign currency returns are not a major part of total returns for equities. On average, foreign currency returns are 10–15 percent of total equity returns. In the case of bonds, however, foreign currency contributions to total returns could be as high as 60–70 percent. Therefore, in the case of bonds, whether one is using local currency returns, U.S. dollar returns, or some other base currency returns makes a big difference.

■ *European correlations.* The general conclusion that can be drawn from Table 1 is that during the period under study, average correlation coefficients remained low at the global level. We did the same analysis within Europe and found that the average correlation of 12 European equity markets with Germany when expressed in German marks was 46 percent and when expressed in local currencies was 48 percent. The correlation in the case of bonds was 52 percent within Europe in German marks and 68 percent in local currencies. So, the average correlation coefficients within Europe, for equities at least, have remained low. The average correlation coefficient for bonds was much higher—almost 70 percent—when expressed in local currency terms.

Recent Past. The important question is not what average correlations and volatilities have been over a long period (roughly 30 years) but whether a discernible trend appears in the recent past.

■ *Volatility.* For global equity markets, **Table 2** shows the average volatility of the nine markets in our study in U.S. dollars and in local currencies. For the

Table 2. Average Volatility and Average Correlation: Global and European Markets

Currency	1970–98	1970–79	1980–89	1985–89	1985–98	1990–98
Average volatility						
Global markets[a]						
Equity						
U.S. dollars	24.0%	25.5%	25.2%	—	—	19.4%
Local currency	21.8	23.1	22.2	—	—	18.4
Bond						
U.S. dollars	—	—	—	16.2%	13.6%	11.7
Local currency	—	—	—	8.6	8.1	7.8
European markets						
Equity						
German marks	20.4	18.4	21.5	—	—	20.1
Local currency	19.5	17.3	20.7	—	—	19.2
Bond						
German marks	—	—	—	7.7	7.9	8.0
Local currency	—	—	—	6.0	6.6	6.9
Average correlation[b]						
Global markets[a]						
Equity						
U.S. dollars	40.3	38.8	41.5	—	—	43.7
Local currency	44.5	40.5	47.5	—	—	49.4
Bond						
U.S. dollars	—	—	—	33.1	35.8	40.4
Local currency	—	—	—	48.8	51.9	57.2
European markets						
Equity						
German marks	52.2	33.7	40.6	—	—	68.2
Local currency	53.8	35.9	43.0	—	—	69.6
Bond						
German marks	—	—	—	51.9	57.4	60.8
Local currency	—	—	—	60.8	68.7	73.1

Note: Data for equities are from January 1970 to January 1998. Finland and Ireland are excluded from European equity markets. Data for bonds are from January 1985 to January 1998. Italy is excluded from global bond markets. Denmark, Italy, and Spain are excluded from European bond markets.
[a]Monthly returns.
[b]Global correlations are versus the United States; European correlations are versus Germany.
Sources: MSCI and Salomon Brothers indexes.

entire period (1970–1998), the average volatility at the global level was 24.0 percent in U.S. dollar terms and 21.8 percent in local currency terms, as already shown in Table 1. By looking at three subperiods (1970–1979, 1980–1989, and 1990–1998), one can see a clear trend, at least in the recent past, of declining volatility. Table 2 shows average numbers for simplicity, but when one looks at individual countries, the decline in volatility can be shown to be statistically significant for many markets. That finding also holds true for equity markets within Europe. In general, one can say that volatilities in the recent past for many individual markets have actually declined. The bond markets show a similar trend; volatilities have not significantly increased in the recent past, no matter which base currency is considered.

Correlation. Table 2 also shows average correlations in the global and European markets. For the entire period, at the global level, the average correlation expressed in U.S. dollars of the nine equity markets with the United States was 40.3 percent; expressed in local currencies, it was 44.5 percent. During the 1970s, that correlation in U.S. dollars was 38.8 percent; it increased to 41.5 percent in the 1980s; and it currently averages 43.7 percent for the 1990s. Average correlations for global equity markets have increased over time, but the increases are not statistically significant. In Europe, however, correlations have actually doubled relative to their values in the 1970s. This finding is true whether returns are expressed in German marks or local currencies. In the 1970s, the average correlation of equity returns in German marks was 33.7 percent, compared with 68.2 percent in the 1990s; in local currencies, it was 35.9 percent in the 1970s compared with almost 70 percent in the 1990s. Those increases are statistically significant. The bond markets tell the same story. At a global level, the increases are not statistically significant, but at the European level, they are. In addition, the absolute levels of cross-country equity and bond return correlations within Europe are now very high.

Rolling five-year data. In actual portfolio construction, investors tend to use rolling five-year volatilities and rolling five-year correlations in an optimization exercise. **Table 3** shows the same kind of trends as in Table 2 but using rolling five-year volatilities and rolling five-year correlations. In other words, Table 3 shows a decrease in volatilities for global markets (but not for European markets) and a significant increase in correlations for European markets (but not for global markets). The fact that correlations have not increased significantly at the global level comes somewhat as a surprise. Clearly, the popular press would seem to suggest that correlations and volatilities have increased significantly

Table 3. Average Five-Year Rolling Volatilities and Correlations: Global and European Markets

Currency	1975–79	1980–89	1990–98
Average volatility			
Global markets[a]			
Equity			
U.S. dollars	28.0%	24.2%	21.5%
Local currency	25.4	21.0	19.8
Bond			
U.S. dollars	—	—	13.6
Local currency	—	—	8.1
European markets			
Equity			
German marks	19.9	19.7	21.1
Local currency	19.0	18.6	20.3
Bond			
German marks	—	—	7.9
Local currency	—	—	6.6
Average correlation[b]			
Global markets[a]			
Equity			
U.S. dollars	44.7	36.1	43.4
Local currency	45.0	40.3	49.1
Bond			
U.S. dollars	—	—	35.8
Local currency	—	—	51.9
European markets			
Equity			
German marks	36.9	28.2	59.1
Local currency	39.6	31.5	60.6
Bond			
German marks	—	—	57.4
Local currency	—	—	68.7

Note: Data for equities are from January 1970 to January 1998. Finland and Ireland are excluded from European equity markets. Data for bonds are from January 1985 to January 1998. Italy is excluded from global bond markets. Denmark, Italy, and Spain are excluded from European bond markets.
[a]Monthly returns.
[b]Global correlations are versus the United States; European correlations are versus Germany.
Sources: MSCI and Salomon Brothers indexes.

across all markets, but the data do not support that claim. So, why have correlations at the global level not increased significantly despite growing globalization and integration (i.e., fewer restrictions on the free movement of capital flows across markets)? We believe that the answer has to do with unsynchronized business cycles.

Business cycles. The year-over-year growth rate in real GDP is a reliable indicator of business cycles. **Figure 1** shows these growth rates for four major countries: the United States, Germany, Japan, and the United Kingdom. Excluding the 1991–92 period, which was clearly an unusual period for Ger-

Figure 1. Year-over-Year Change in Real GDP: Global Countries, 1990–98

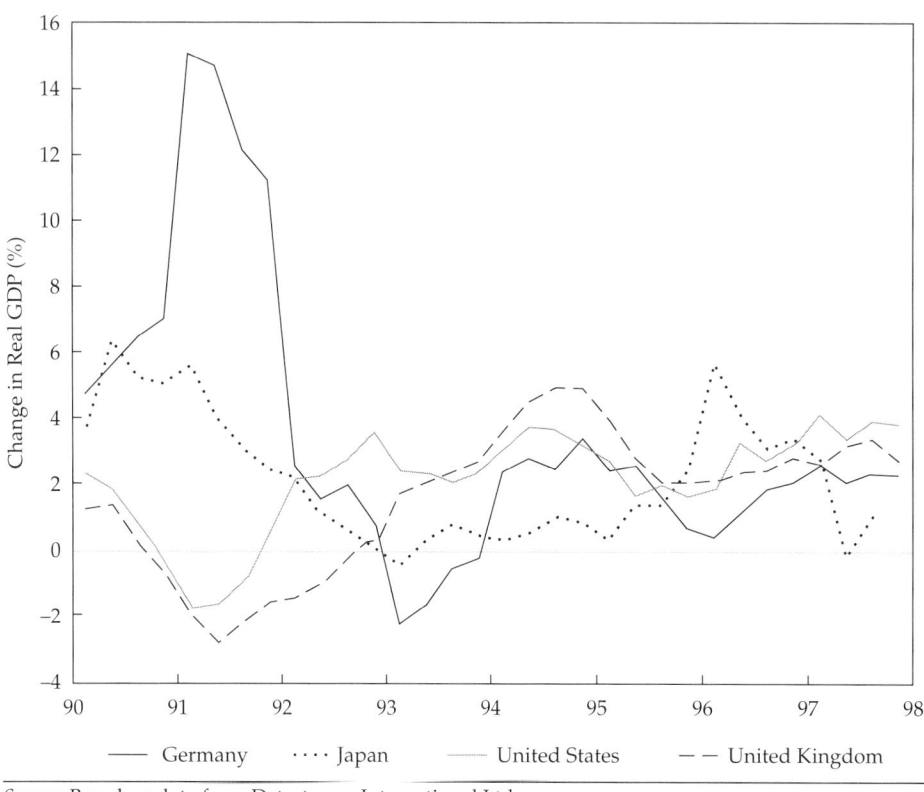

Source: Based on data from Datastream International Ltd.

many, Figure 1 shows that during the 1990s (i.e., the most recent cycle), business cycles in different countries have been out of sync. The United States was the first country to go into recession and the first to come out of recession in 1991. The United Kingdom came out of recession in 1992, Germany in 1993, and Japan is still struggling. In our opinion, the reason why average correlations have not picked up significantly at a global level, despite growing globalization and integration of financial markets, is because the business cycles have been out of sync. Integration/globalization and synchronization are two very different concepts. Indeed, increased capital market integration (i.e., freedom of money flows between markets) does not necessarily lead to better economic synchronization or higher market return correlation. **Figure 2** shows year-over-year change in real GDP in four European countries. Again, excluding this unusual period in 1991, one can clearly see the existence of economic integration. In this sense, Figure 2 is very different from Figure 1 and shows to some extent why correlations have increased in European markets. In essence, for correlations to be significantly high, a high degree of economic and financial integration is needed.

Summary. First, by looking at average volatilities, we found that return volatility has actually declined during the 1990s. For many countries, this decline in return volatility has also been found to be statistically significant. Second, at a global level, average correlations (i.e., unconditional correlations) have not increased significantly during the 1990s, and perhaps more importantly, the absolute value of average correlation coefficients remains relatively low. Within Europe, however, average correlations have increased quite significantly during the 1990s. Additionally, these average correlations now stand at the very high level of around 70 percent for both equity and bond markets.

New Perspective

From a global perspective, the fact that average correlations have remained low is certainly good news because it suggests that in the recent past, international investing would have provided some diversification benefits to global investors. Unfortunately, the bad news is that international correlations are not constant but are very unstable through time and across countries.

Figure 3 highlights the instability of five-year rolling correlations of various equity markets with the U.S. market. Not only are these correlations unstable across time, but they are also quite unstable across countries.

Figure 2. Year-over-Year Change in Real GDP, 1990–98: European Countries

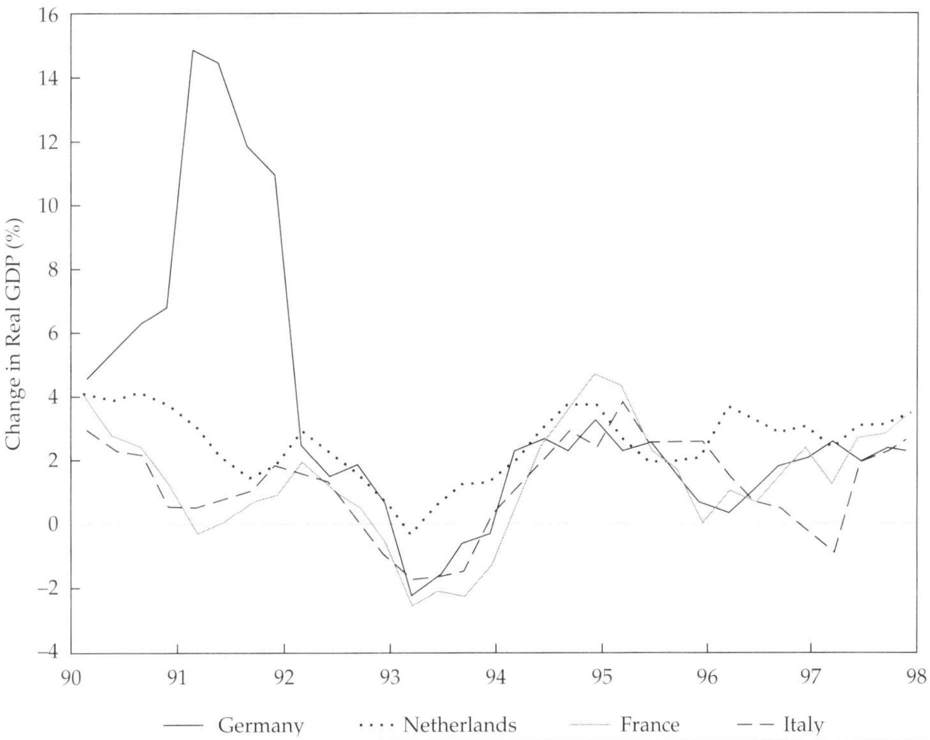

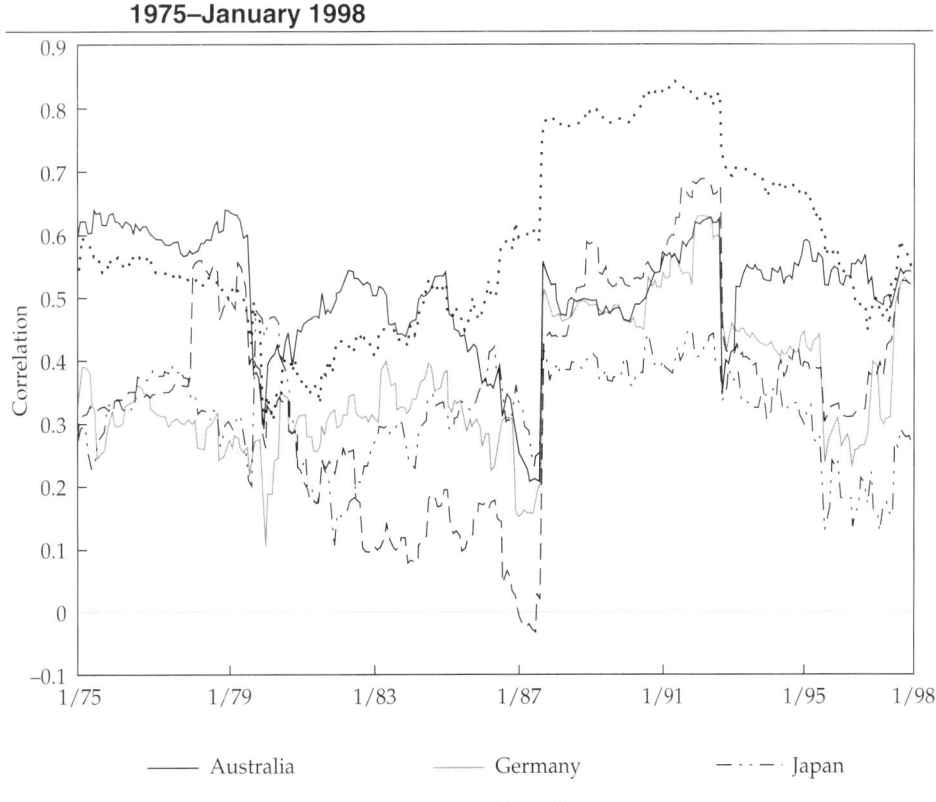

Source: Based on data from Datastream International Ltd.

Figure 3. Five-Year Rolling Correlations with the United States, January 1975–January 1998

Note: Data are in local currency terms.

Approach. Another way of looking at the instability of correlation coefficients would be to look at average five-year rolling correlation coefficients between the United States and other markets and their minimum and maximum values. **Table 4** shows these correlations between January 1970 and January 1998. For example, the average five-year rolling equity return correlation between the U.K. and the U.S. markets was 58 percent, but it had a minimum value of 27 percent and a high of 84 percent. This finding shows considerable variation in the correlation coefficient with the maximum value being more than three times greater than the minimum value. Equity return correlation coefficients show the same kind of variability both at the global and European level.

The bond market return correlation coefficients also depict some variability at the global level, although the range is narrower than for equities. Within Europe, however, a very different picture emerges. European bond return correlation coefficients show very little variation around their average values. They appear to behave like one asset.

Link with Market Phases. According to some recent analysis, cross-country equity correlations appear to be linked with market phases. In essence, researchers have discovered that cross-country equity return correlations seem to increase when markets are falling—just when the benefits of international diversification are needed most. For example, the average correlation of the United States with the United Kingdom for the 1970–98 period was about 50 percent. But the correlation between the two countries jumped to almost 58 percent when both markets were declining, as Panel A in **Figure 4** shows. When both markets were rising, it dropped to 36 percent. Thus, the correlation on the down side, when both markets were falling, was substantially higher than the correlation on the upside, when both markets were rising. These differences, needless to say, are statistically significant.

By looking at some of the other countries in Figure 4, one can clearly see that correlations were much higher when markets were declining. In some cases, the differences are truly enormous. For example, for Hong Kong when both markets were declining, the correlation was 50 percent. When both markets were rising, it was about 6 percent, which is almost zero correlation. Most investors, however, seem to have the impression that the Hong Kong market is highly correlated with the U.S. market, but the Hong Kong market appears to be highly correlated with the U.S. market only to the extent that it is correlated on the downside.

Similar evidence is found for European correlations, as Panel B in Figure 4 shows. For example, when both the U.K. and German markets were declining, the correlation was 48.5 percent. When both markets were rising, the correlation coefficient dropped to 16.0 percent. Downside correlations were three times as high as upside correlations. Again, the same general trend emerges as with global correlations: Correlations on the downside are much higher than correlations on the upside.

Table 4. Average Five-Year Rolling Correlations for Global and European Markets

Countries	Average	Minimum	Maximum
Global markets[a]			
Equity			
Australia	50.9%	20.4%	64.0%
Canada	72.1	50.2	86.1
France	47.2	28.7	66.2
Germany	36.4	10.9	62.9
Hong Kong	34.9	–3.2	68.8
Italy	23.6	–4.8	48.1
Japan	31.8	10.3	48.1
United Kingdom	58.2	27.3	84.1
Bond			
Australia	41.8	–2.8	72.9
Canada	72.9	63.0	85.9
France	53.9	43.8	61.8
Germany	51.6	40.8	63.0
Italy	33.2	25.1	44.6
Japan	42.1	26.4	57.8
United Kingdom	45.4	34.9	62.1
European markets[b]			
Equity			
Austria	38.2	–18.0	78.2
Belgium	49.7	7.5	73.2
Denmark	31.9	–2.0	68.3
Finland	47.0	36.8	57.2
France	51.0	15.1	81.1
Netherlands	60.5	38.0	84.7
Ireland	57.5	44.6	63.5
Italy	33.0	–2.5	71.8
Spain	32.1	–16.7	73.3
Sweden	33.6	3.3	63.2
Switzerland	60.5	39.2	81.1
United Kingdom	43.7	10.6	63.2
Bond			
Denmark	71.2	66.3	77.8
France	79.5	60.6	87.9
Netherlands	54.2	51.3	57.9
Italy	82.1	70.2	95.3
Spain	58.8	55.1	66.4
Switzerland	56.5	43.8	67.6
United Kingdom	61.0	48.6	79.6

Note: Correlations in local currency terms. Data for equities are from January 1970 to January 1998; data for Finland and Ireland start from 1988. Data for bonds are from January 1985 to January 1998; data for Denmark start in January 1989; data for Italy and Spain start in January 1991.
[a]Correlation versus United States.
[b]Correlation versus Germany.
Sources: MSCI and Salomon Brothers indexes.

Are Global Market Returns Converging?

Figure 4. Correlations between Domestic Equity Markets (U.S. or German) and Foreign Equity Markets for Different Market Phases: Both Markets Rising or Falling, January 1970–January 1998

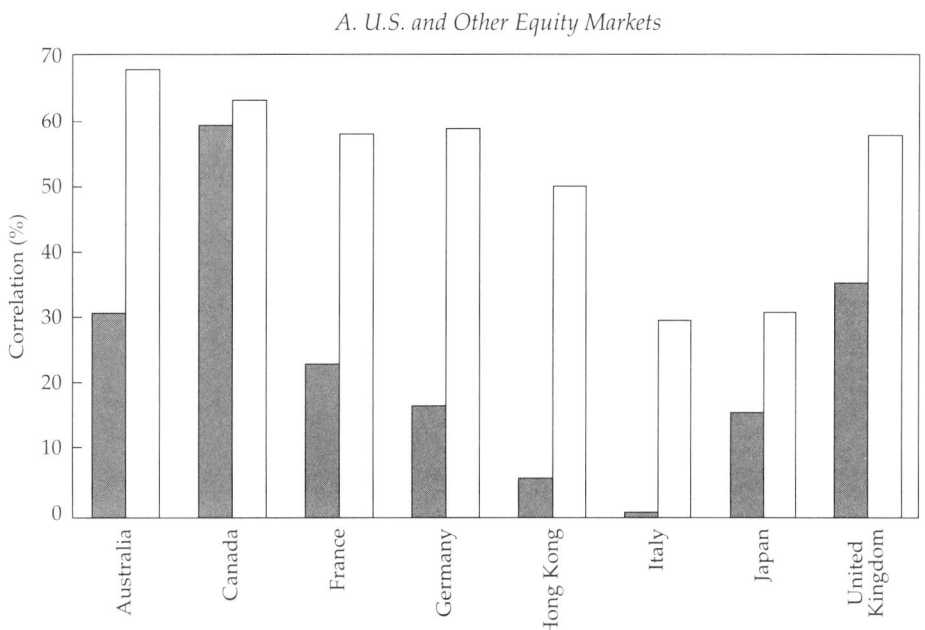

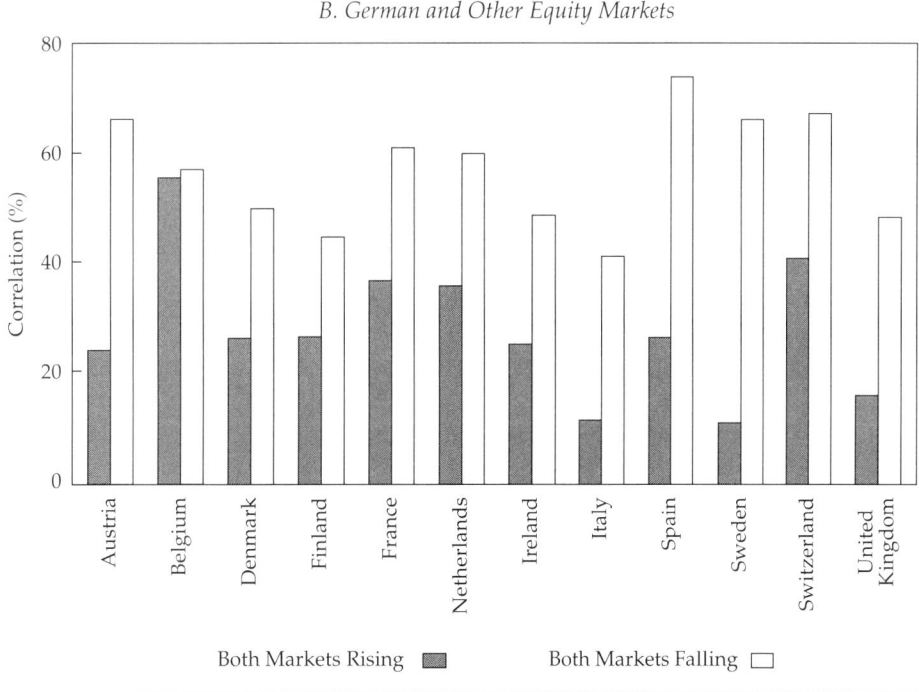

Both Markets Rising ■   Both Markets Falling ☐

Note: Returns are in local currency terms.
Source: Based on data from MSCI monthly market indexes.

From a portfolio management perspective, the important point is not whether both markets are declining or both markets are rising; what is important is what happens to the correlation between domestic and international markets when the investor's domestic market is declining. After all, investors want to diversify because they want to reduce the risk of being in a declining market. So, a U.S. dollar investor is concerned about what is happening to correlations when the U.S. equities and bond markets are declining and when they are rising.

Links between Domestic and Rising and Falling Markets. Unfortunately, we found the same general pattern as in Figure 4 when we investigated markets in relation to a rising or falling domestic market, with the United States and Germany serving as the two domestic markets under analysis. As Panel A of **Figure 5** shows, when the U.S. equity market was

Figure 5. Correlations between Domestic Equity Markets (U.S. or German) and Foreign Equity Markets for Different Market Phases: Domestic Market Rising or Falling, January 1970–January 1998

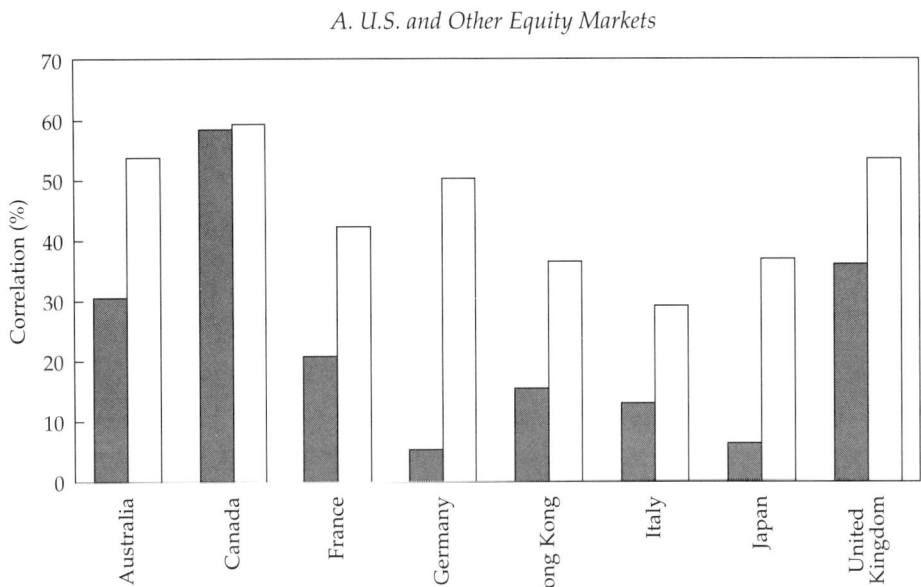

A. U.S. and Other Equity Markets

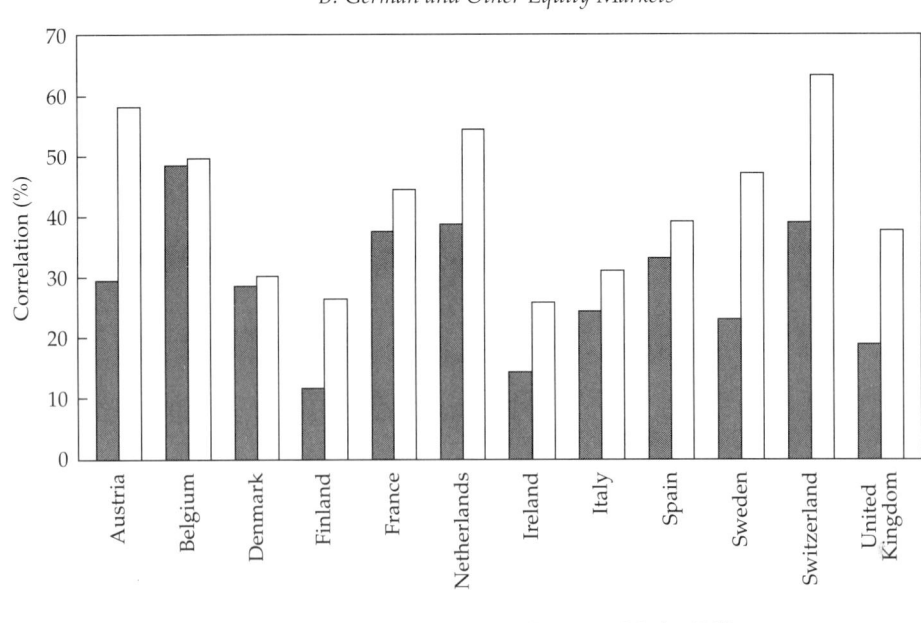

B. German and Other Equity Markets

Note: Returns are in local currency terms.
Source: Based on data from MSCI monthly market indexes.

falling, the correlation between the U.K. market and the U.S. market was 54 percent. When the U.S. equity market was rising, the correlation dropped to 36 percent. Again, in many of these cases, the differences are statistically significant. The same story is found within Europe, as shown in Panel B of Figure 5. When the German equity market was falling, the correlation with the United Kingdom was high, at about 38 percent; when the German equity market was rising, the correlation was only about 19 percent.

No significant links between correlations and market phases were discovered in the analysis of bonds. Indeed, we found no evidence to suggest that bond market correlations increase when bond market returns are falling (i.e., when yields are rising), but quite different results were obtained when we looked at hedged versus unhedged returns. Clearly, the contribution of currency returns, which is a significant factor, distorts the results. (Essentially, in the case of bonds, we found no evidence of general patterns of correlations being linked to market return phases.)

Links between Correlations and Volatilities. While investigating the relationship between correlations and volatilities, we found more bad news: Increases in volatility are positively linked to increases in correlations. Thus, when capital markets become more volatile, they also become more correlated. Some regression results are shown in **Table 5**

for global equity markets. We regressed monthly changes in three-year rolling correlations of the home market with the United States against monthly changes in the three-year rolling volatility of the home market and the three-year rolling volatility of the U.S. market. For example, we regressed the monthly change in the three-year rolling correlation between the United States and United Kingdom against the monthly change in the volatility of the U.K. market and the monthly change in the volatility of the U.S. market. These regressions show that changes in correlations are directly related to changes in volatilities. The coefficients have positive signs, and they are statistically significant, meaning that when equity market volatility increases, the correlation of global equity market returns also increases. Notice the R^2 values are high for monthly change variables, which means that changes in the home country volatility and U.S. volatility explain a high percentage of the change in the correlation of global equity market returns.

Table 6 shows exactly the same analysis for the European equity markets but substitutes Germany for the United States. In this case, for example, we regressed the monthly change in the three-year rolling correlation of the United Kingdom and Germany against the monthly change in the three-year rolling volatility of the U.K. stock market and the monthly change in the three-year rolling volatility of the Ger-

Table 5. Global Equity Markets: Regression of Monthly Changes in Three-Year Rolling Correlations against Monthly Changes in Three-Year Rolling Home Volatilities and U.S. Volatilities, January 1970–January 1998

	Local Currency				U.S. Dollars			
Country	Alpha	Home Volatility Beta	U.S. Volatility Beta	R^2	Alpha	Home Volatility Beta	U.S. Volatility Beta	R^2
Australia	0.00 (0.65)	3.11 **(14.12)**	0.60 (1.36)	62.1%	0.00 (0.36)	2.43 **(10.44)**	1.41 **(3.06)**	49.9%
Canada	0.00 (0.19)	1.62 **(6.62)**	0.50 **(1.90)**	31.5	0.00 (0.26)	1.36 **(5.71)**	0.73 **(2.67)**	27.2
France	0.00 (0.75)	1.17 **(3.69)**	2.63 **(7.12)**	26.8	0.00 (0.44)	0.94 **(3.59)**	2.83 **(7.87)**	26.1
Germany	0.00 (0.26)	1.96 **(4.29)**	1.85 **(4.25)**	18.6	0.00 (0.22)	1.88 **(4.54)**	2.28 **(5.28)**	19.4
Hong Kong	0.00 (0.63)	–0.14 (–0.95)	3.83 **(8.43)**	20.4	0.00 (0.57)	–0.42 **(–3.45)**	4.06 **(8.82)**	20.8
Italy	0.00 (0.60)	–0.66 **(–2.44)**	2.45 **(6.77)**	14.0	0.00 (0.35)	–0.52 **(–1.88)**	2.24 **(5.82)**	10.7
Japan	0.00 (0.08)	1.35 **(3.16)**	0.84 **(1.97)**	5.3	0.00 (–0.09)	0.82 **(2.14)**	0.41 (0.93)	2.0
United Kingdom	0.00 (0.44)	1.00 **(6.68)**	1.46 **(4.39)**	27.7	0.00 (0.23)	1.07 **(6.87)**	1.97 **(5.74)**	30.6

Note: *t*-Statistics shown in parentheses. *t*-Statistics that are significant at the 90 percent level are shown in bold.
Source: Based on data from MSCI indexes.

Asset Allocation in a Changing World

Table 6. European Equity Markets: Regression of Monthly Changes in Three-Year Rolling Correlations against Monthly Changes in Three-Year Rolling Home Volatilities and German Volatilities, January 1970–January 1998

	Local Currency				German Marks			
Country	Alpha	Home Volatility Beta	German Volatility Beta	R^2	Alpha	Home Volatility Beta	German Volatility Beta	R^2
Austria	0.00 (0.74)	−0.36 (−1.31)	2.74 (**6.90**)	14.0%	0.00 (0.71)	−0.31 (−1.13)	2.69 (**6.72**)	13.4%
Belgium	0.00 (−0.05)	0.27 (0.77)	2.41 (**5.72**)	15.1	0.00 (−0.07)	0.53 (1.47)	2.28 (**5.36**)	16.1
Denmark	0.00 (1.08)	−0.40 (−0.95)	2.22 (**5.74**)	10.1	0.00 (1.10)	−0.39 (−1.03)	2.24 (**5.93**)	10.6
Finland	0.00 (1.07)	−0.51 (−1.27)	2.09 (**3.88**)	15.6	0.00 (1.32)	−1.04 (**−2.83**)	2.06 (**3.64**)	18.0
France	0.00 (0.11)	1.24 (**4.63**)	1.24 (**3.78**)	18.8	0.00 (0.06)	1.19 (**4.65**)	1.24 (**3.77**)	18.6
Ireland	0.00 (1.31)	0.41 (0.82)	1.55 (**2.93**)	10.8	0.01 (1.43)	0.33 (0.66)	1.28 (**2.42**)	7.7
Italy	0.00 (0.53)	−0.42 (**−1.65**)	1.69 (**4.70**)	7.1	0.00 (0.57)	−0.26 (−1.23)	1.67 (**4.97**)	7.7
Netherlands	0.00 (0.66)	1.60 (**7.25**)	1.17 (**4.46**)	33.3	0.00 (0.69)	1.60 (**7.13**)	1.19 (**4.47**)	32.9
Spain	0.00 (−0.02)	1.98 (**6.29**)	1.00 (**2.62**)	19.6	0.00 (0.11)	1.04 (**4.13**)	1.35 (**3.75**)	12.7
Sweden	0.00 (0.30)	0.19 (**0.69**)	3.01 (**7.63**)	19.5	0.00 (0.27)	1.56 (**4.33**)	2.09 (**4.98**)	22.5
Switzerland	0.00 (0.21)	1.45 (**4.94**)	1.15 (**3.38**)	22.3	0.00 (−0.01)	1.67 (**5.14**)	1.16 (**3.32**)	22.2
United Kingdom	0.00 (0.34)	1.19 (**7.32**)	1.90 (**5.00**)	28.4	0.00 (0.64)	1.06 (**6.89**)	1.78 (**5.10**)	26.4

Note: *t*-Statistics shown in parentheses. *t*-Statistics that are significant at the 90 percent level are shown in bold.
Source: Based on data from MSCI indexes.

man stock market. Once again, the data clearly show that an increase in the volatility of the German stock market leads to an increase in the correlation of European equity market returns.

When we conducted the same analysis for bonds, we found evidence that correlations across global bond markets also tend to increase when global bond market volatility increases, as shown in **Table 7**. Once again, the *t*-statistics are highly significant and are positive. The same result is obtained within European bond markets, as shown in **Table 8**.

Portfolio Management Implications

Three major conclusions can be drawn from these data: International equity and bond market return correlations are unstable over time and across countries, global equity market return correlations increase when markets are declining, and international equity and bond market return correlations tend to increase when volatility increases. These conclusions have important implications for investment management. For example, they suggest that the asset-class risk of investing in equities is increasing. Thus, if you are a U.S. dollar investor who wants to invest outside the United States to hedge against an expected fall in U.S. equities, then unfortunately, you will not be able to substantially reduce the risk of your portfolio experiencing a decline in value during a U.S. equity market downturn by investing in international equities. Our data show that if the U.S. market falls, sharply and precipitously, all other markets are likely to fall as well, and some of the foreign markets that are more volatile than the U.S. market are likely to decline even more than the U.S. market. So, the portfolio is subject to asset-class risk—the risk of being in equities.

Diversifying asset-class risk mainly involves investing in another asset class. As such, the only way to diversify the downside risk of being in equities, if one expects a significant fall in U.S. or German equity markets, for example, is to invest in another asset class, such as bonds or cash. This finding raises several interesting questions: What if a direct relationship exists between equity correla-

Table 7. Global Bond Markets: Regression of Monthly Changes in Three-Year Rolling Correlations against Monthly Changes in Three-Year Rolling Home Volatilities and U.S. Volatilities, January 1985–January 1998

		Local Currency				U.S. Dollars		
Country	Alpha	Home Volatility Beta	U.S. Volatility Beta	R^2	Alpha	Home Volatility Beta	U.S. Volatility Beta	R^2
Australia	0.01 (**2.12**)	1.07 (0.85)	4.36 (**3.35**)	11.9%	0.01 (1.49)	1.26 (**1.90**)	2.40 (**1.84**)	6.2%
Canada	0.00 (0.50)	3.45 (**5.31**)	0.76 (1.23)	31.7	0.00 (0.45)	1.09 (1.62)	2.44 (**2.86**)	13.6
France	0.00 (0.85)	1.93 (**1.68**)	4.89 (**6.22**)	32.2	0.00 (−0.05)	2.92 (**3.85**)	2.14 (**1.99**)	15.2
Germany	0.00 (0.83)	3.16 (**2.08**)	4.89 (**5.30**)	26.3	0.00 (−0.38)	2.25 (**2.28**)	0.60 (0.45)	4.6
Italy	−0.01 (−1.11)	0.68 (0.33)	2.06 (1.01)	3.2	0.00 (−0.42)	0.55 (0.73)	3.33 (1.49)	5.4
Japan	0.00 (0.02)	−0.57 (−0.36)	4.44 (**3.75**)	11.3	0.00 (−0.52)	−0.53 (−0.81)	2.07 (**1.69**)	2.8
United Kingdom	0.00 (1.53)	5.10 (**4.47**)	2.90 (**2.38**)	26.9	0.00 (1.04)	1.97 (**2.38**)	3.81 (**3.04**)	12.7

Note: *t*-Statistics shown in parentheses. *t*-Statistics that are significant at the 90 percent level are shown in bold. Data for Italy are from January 1991.
Source: Based on data from Salomon Brothers indexes.

Table 8. European Bond Markets: Regression of Monthly Changes in Three-Year Rolling Correlations against Monthly Changes in Three-Year Rolling Home Volatilities and German Volatilities, January 1985–January 1998

		Local Currency				German Marks		
Country	Alpha	Home Volatility Beta	German Volatility Beta	R^2	Alpha	Home Volatility Beta	German Volatility Beta	R^2
Denmark	0.00 (1.64)	1.44 (1.34)	9.21 (**6.33**)	51.0%	0.00 (1.55)	−1.98 (**−4.84**)	6.60 (**4.24**)	37.7%
France	0.00 (**1.79**)	2.76 (**3.55**)	−2.14 (**−2.43**)	10.3	0.00 (1.55)	2.93 (**3.49**)	−1.48 (−1.47)	9.4
Italy	0.00 (0.20)	2.37 (1.47)	9.08 (**2.94**)	28.5	0.01 (1.03)	0.12 (0.20)	9.07 (**2.66**)	13.5
Netherlands	0.00 (1.11)	1.20 (1.00)	4.77 (**4.36**)	25.4	0.00 (1.10)	2.00 (**1.81**)	4.27 (**4.18**)	27.2
Spain	0.00 (1.04)	4.95 (0.86)	34.18 (**3.52**)	34.1	0.00 (−0.11)	−2.60 (**−1.67**)	10.55 (**2.89**)	15.6
Switzerland	0.00 (−0.48)	4.34 (**3.32**)	−0.65 (−0.42)	8.6	0.00 (−0.73)	1.66 (1.34)	−1.30 (−0.73)	1.9
United Kingdom	0.01 (**1.83**)	2.31 (**1.78**)	10.48 (**4.01**)	49.8	0.01 (1.58)	1.64 (0.90)	15.84 (**3.31**)	32.6

Note: *t*-Statistics shown in parentheses. *t*-Statistics that are significant at the 90 percent level are shown in bold. Data for Denmark are from January 1989; data for Italy and Spain are from January 1991.
Source: Based on data from Salomon Brothers indexes.

tions and bond correlations? What if equity correlations are rising when bond correlations are also rising? What if equity market volatilities, which are directly related to equity market correlations, are rising when bond market volatilities are also rising? If these links between equity and bond markets do exist, investors may find diversifying across asset classes difficult, thus causing a serious problem at the portfolio level.

Fortunately, no significant relationship appears to exist between changes in global equity market correlations and changes in global bond market correlations, as **Table 9** shows. Regressing monthly changes in three-year rolling equity market correlations between domestic and U.S. markets against changes in three-year rolling bond market correla-

Asset Allocation in a Changing World

Table 9. Global Markets: Regression of Changes in Domestic and U.S. Markets of Three-Year Rolling Equity Correlations against Changes in Three-Year Rolling Bond Correlations, January 1985–January 1998

Country	Local Currency Alpha	Local Currency Beta	Local Currency R^2	U.S. Dollars Alpha	U.S. Dollars Beta	U.S. Dollars R^2
Australia	0.00 (0.39)	–0.35 (**–3.74**)	10.5%	0.00 (–0.06)	–0.07 (–0.60)	0.3%
Canada	0.00 (–0.41)	0.23 (**2.21**)	3.9	0.00 (–0.17)	0.39 (**4.69**)	15.6
France	0.00 (–0.12)	0.25 (**2.26**)	4.1	0.00 (–0.15)	0.29 (**3.43**)	9.0
Germany	0.00 (0.17)	0.07 (0.64)	0.3	0.00 (0.17)	0.10 (1.23)	1.3
Italy	0.01 (**1.92**)	–0.22 (–1.22)	3.3	0.01 (1.13)	0.34 (**2.40**)	10.9
Japan	0.00 (–0.09)	0.15 (–1.52)	1.9	0.00 (0.39)	0.22 (**2.17**)	3.8
United Kingdom	0.00 (–1.23)	0.13 (**2.34**)	4.4	0.00 (–0.87)	0.24 (**3.83**)	11.0

Note: *t*-Statistics shown in parentheses. *t*-Statistics that are significant at the 90 percent level are shown in bold. Data for Italy begin in January 1991.
Sources: Based on data from MSCI and Salomon Brothers indexes.

Table 10. European Markets: Regression of Changes in Domestic and German Markets of Three-Year Rolling Equity Correlations against Changes in Three-Year Rolling Bond Correlations, January 1985–January 1998

Country	Local Currency Alpha	Local Currency Beta	Local Currency R^2	German Marks Alpha	German Marks Beta	German Marks R^2
Denmark	0.00 (0.86)	0.13 (0.94)	1.3%	0.00 (0.67)	0.10 (0.75)	0.8%
France	0.00 (0.20)	0.20 (1.47)	1.8	0.00 (0.17)	0.07 (0.54)	0.2
Italy	0.00 (0.34)	0.53 (**3.11**)	18.4	0.00 (0.48)	0.07 (0.56)	0.7
Netherlands	0.00 (0.67)	0.14 (1.28)	1.4	0.00 (0.64)	0.18 (**1.72**)	2.4
Spain	0.00 (–0.76)	0.13 (0.65)	0.9	0.00 (–0.67)	0.16 (1.10)	2.5
Switzerland	0.00 (–0.48)	0.13 (1.50)	1.8	0.00 (–0.46)	–0.01 (–0.06)	0.0
United Kingdom	0.00 (–0.09)	0.31 (**3.05**)	7.2	0.00 (0.65)	0.18 (**2.92**)	6.7

Note: *t*-Statistics shown in parentheses. *t*-Statistics that are significant at the 90 percent level are shown in bold. Data for Denmark's bond markets start in January 1989; data for Italy's and Spain's bond markets start in January 1991.
Sources: Based on data from MSCI and Salomon Brothers indexes.

tions between domestic and U.S. markets results in low beta coefficients and low R^2 values for each country studied. **Table 10** shows the same story within Europe: No serious relationship exists between European equity market correlations and European bond market correlations.

To be sure that investors can diversify the risk of being in equities by investing in another asset class, such as bonds, one more issue needs to be checked—the relationship between equity market correlations and bond market volatilities, shown in **Table 11** for global markets. In other words, what if equity markets become more correlated when bond markets are becoming more volatile? We know a relationship exists between higher volatilities and higher correlations in the bond markets. Again, the results suggest no direct relationship between monthly changes in correlations across equity markets and monthly changes in volatilities of bond markets. **Table 12** shows the same results for European markets.

Are Global Market Returns Converging?

Table 11. Regression of Changes in Three-Year Rolling Equity Correlations against Changes in Three-Year Rolling Bond Volatilities for Global Markets, January 1985–January 1998

	Local Currency				U.S. Dollars			
Country	Alpha	Change in Domestic Bond Volatility	Change in U.S. Bond Volatility	R^2	Alpha	Change in Domestic Bond Volatility	Change in U.S. Bond Volatility	R^2
Australia	0.0 (0.1)	6.0 (**4.5**)	−1.3 (−1.0)	14.9%	0.0 (0.6)	2.6 (**3.3**)	0.3 (0.2)	8.8%
Canada	0.0 (−0.4)	2.6 (**3.0**)	−0.8 (−1.0)	7.7	0.0 (−0.1)	0.5 (0.8)	0.0 (0.0)	0.6
France	0.0 (0.1)	−0.4 (−0.2)	1.7 (1.5)	1.9	0.0 (0.0)	0.1 (0.1)	3.0 (**2.8**)	6.2
Germany	0.0 (0.4)	2.1 (1.0)	1.5 (1.1)	2.5	0.0 (0.3)	−1.0 (−1.1)	3.5 (**3.0**)	7.5
Italy	0.0 (**2.2**)	−0.7 (**−1.6**)	−2.7 (−1.2)	12.7	0.0 (1.4)	0.7 (0.9)	−3.5 (−1.5)	6.6
Japan	0.0 (0.2)	1.6 (0.9)	1.3 (0.9)	2.1	0.0 (0.5)	0.1 (0.1)	2.2 (1.6)	2.2
United Kingdom	0.0 (−0.9)	0.4 (0.5)	0.4 (0.4)	0.7	0.0 (−0.4)	0.0 (0.1)	2.2 (**2.3**)	4.6

Note: *t*-Statistics shown in parentheses. *t*-Statistics that are significant at the 90 percent level are shown in bold. Data for Italy begin in January 1991.
Sources: Based on data from MSCI and Salomon Brothers indexes.

Table 12. Regression of Changes in Three-Year Rolling Equity Correlations against Changes in Three-Year Rolling Bond Volatilities for European Markets, January 1985–January 1998

	Local Currency				German Marks			
Country	Alpha	Change in Domestic Bond Volatility	Change in U.S. Bond Volatility	R^2	Alpha	Change in Domestic Bond Volatility	Change in U.S. Bond Volatility	R^2
Denmark	0.0 (1.0)	0.0 (0.0)	1.6 (0.8)	0.9%	0.0 (1.0)	0.2 (0.4)	1.5 (0.7)	1.1%
France	0.0 (0.5)	3.5 (**2.9**)	−1.6 (−1.2)	6.8	0.0 (0.2)	2.3 (**2.0**)	−1.1 (−0.8)	3.3
Italy	0.0 (0.7)	4.8 (**2.2**)	2.3 (0.6)	14.8	0.0 (0.7)	0.4 (0.4)	6.8 (**1.8**)	9.3
Netherlands	0.0 (0.7)	1.6 (1.0)	−0.2 (−0.2)	1.1	0.0 (0.7)	1.2 (0.8)	0.0 (0.0)	0.7
Spain	0.0 (−0.7)	0.2 (0.5)	2.3 (0.6)	1.4	0.0 (−0.7)	−0.8 (−0.4)	2.9 (0.7)	1.2
Switzerland	0.0 (0.4)	−3.2 (−1.3)	−1.8 (−0.5)	4.1	0.0 (0.5)	−2.9 (−1.1)	−1.4 (−0.3)	2.7
United Kingdom	0.0 (0.2)	0.5 (0.5)	3.9 (**2.0**)	4.6	0.0 (0.9)	−0.3 (−0.5)	5.2 (**3.3**)	8.6

Note: *t*-Statistics shown in parentheses. *t*-Statistics that are significant at the 90 percent level are shown in bold. Data for Denmark's bond markets start in January 1989; data for Italy's and Spain's bond markets start in January 1991.
Sources: Based on data from MSCI and Salomon Brothers indexes.

Conclusion

The financial press reports that markets are becoming more volatile and more highly correlated. The evidence, however, suggests no upward trend in market return volatility or correlations. In fact, our analysis shows that in many countries, volatility has declined substantially, and the decline has been statistically significant for the recent past. At the international or the global level, again, we found no evidence that correlations have increased significantly. Within Europe, however, we did find evidence of a substantial increase in market correlations. Average correlations remain relatively low at the global level but have recently become very high within Europe. But a worrying aspect of equity market correlations, globally and within Europe, is that cross-country return correlations appear to rise significantly when markets are declining. With respect to both equity and bond markets, a significant relationship seems to exist between increases in correlations and increases in volatility. That is, correlations increase when volatility increases. Finally, equity market correlations do not seem to be linked to either bond market correlations or bond market volatilities.

In our opinion, the average level of correlation across international markets has been low because economic cycles in different countries have been out of sync. To the extent that business cycles continue to be out of sync, the absolute level of average correlation coefficients is likely to remain relatively low at the global level.

Average, or unconditional, correlations may overstate the benefits that can be achieved through international diversification, especially in the short term. Although average correlations computed over long periods of time remain low, correlations jump significantly during shorter periods when markets are declining or are becoming more volatile. This finding implies that optimization exercises, which generally use average or unconditional correlations, may indicate an exposure to global equities that may prove to be too high in declining markets or rising market volatility environments. This conclusion may be particularly troublesome for investors with short-term investment horizons but should not be a major concern for strategic, long-term investors.

The significant difference between conditional and unconditional correlations also raises questions about the validity and usefulness of typical mean–variance optimization and portfolio-construction techniques.

Finally, growing economic and financial integration within Europe has led to a substantial increase in market correlations in the recent past. As Europe moves closer to the start of the European Monetary Union and the adoption of a single monetary policy, market correlations are set to rise further. This result implies that going forward, the potential to add value through country selection is likely to be limited within Europe.

Question and Answer Session

Khalid Ghayur, CFA

Question: Your data show no decrease in European equity volatility in the 1970s, 1980s, and 1990s. What explains the significant decrease in the volatility of equity market returns?

Ghayur: The most significant decrease in volatility has occurred in the case of the United States. The return volatility of the U.S. market has shrunk considerably. We have conducted some analysis to see why. We believe that the risk inherent in the U.S. economy has been reduced considerably.

A lot of people compare the 1990s with the 1960s. In my view, that comparison is not appropriate for the simple reason that, although the United States seems to be growing at a relatively healthy pace with no inflation (as it did in the 1960s), one fundamental difference exists between the 1990s and the 1960s. The U.S. economy today is much less risky than it was in the 1960s. The standard deviation of growth rates in real GDP—the volatility of GDP growth rates—is almost half of what it used to be in the 1960s. Similarly, the volatility of inflation today is close to zero in the United States. I think similar changes have happened in many capital markets, including Europe. For various reasons, the volatility of major economic drivers, such as inflation and real GDP growth, has declined considerably, which may partly explain the decline in the volatility of equity market returns.

Question: Above what level of correlation does diversification become not worthwhile?

Ghayur: Diversification benefits in a portfolio context are driven not only by correlations but also by volatilities and returns. So, it is a little difficult to answer that question only in terms of correlations, but as a rough guide, keep in mind that the average correlation between two stocks within a country tends to be almost 60–70 percent. And it still pays to diversify across many stocks in different industries.

Question: When investigating international diversification effects, isn't it more useful to analyze the risk premium (i.e., stock or bond returns minus the risk-free rate) rather than total returns so that different levels of inflation in the different countries will be considered?

Ghayur: Yes, it is more useful to analyze risk premiums, simply because the returns that nondomestic investors can capture are not the local currency returns. They are basically hedged returns (i.e., risk premiums). But with respect to correlations and volatilities, an analysis based on local currency returns provides identical results to an analysis based on hedged returns.

Question: Do you expect the decline in return volatility during the 1990s to continue?

Ghayur: To the extent that the risk coming in from the macroeconomic drivers remains low, the equity market return volatility should also remain low. But if the markets were to go through a significant valuation correction, volatility could pick up.

Question: Are the dependent and independent variables in the regressions shown in Tables 5 through 8 related by definition because they have common inputs?

Ghayur: This question of relatedness or serial correlation in variables is the focus of a big debate. Erb, Harvey, and Viskanta wrote a famous article on forecasting international returns; they did not regress the changes in correlations but rather absolute correlation levels against other variables.[1] They were using 60-month rolling correlations. So, the regression results were obviously subject to a serious serial correlation problem. Solnik, Boucrelle, and Le Fur subsequently suggested the methodology that we used, which is to look at changes in rolling correlations and volatilities.[2]

It can be shown that subsequent monthly changes in correlations, even rolling correlations, are independent and, similarly, that subsequent monthly changes in volatilities are also independent. So, the two time series are somewhat independent. If a structural problem existed with the regressions, then we would get a systematically high R^2 in each and every regression that we ran because if it is a problem of common inputs, then it is common input for each and every country. But you see in the tables that for some countries, the R^2 values are very low relative to those of other countries.

---

[1] Claude B. Erb, Campbell R. Harvey, and Tadas E. Viskanta, "Forecasting International Equity Correlations," *Financial Analysts Journal* (November/December 1994):32–45.

[2] Bruno Solnik, Cyril Boucrelle, and Yann Le Fur, "International Market Correlation and Volatility," *Financial Analysts Journal* (September/October 1996):17–34.

Question: Do you think the average correlation data for equities that you presented explains the home country bias in asset allocation?

Ghayur: No. Average correlations, which remain low, suggest that investors should hold more outside their home country and that the domestic bias is an anomaly that remains unexplained in this context. In other words, investors are holding a lot more in the domestic market than they really should, based on the average correlation coefficient. But it may simply be that investors are actually looking at the downside correlations and, therefore, saying: "Diversification works, but in the short term, there might be some problems, and hence, I will cut down on the exposure that average correlation coefficients would seem to suggest." Maybe investors view risk in much broader terms than traditionally defined in finance theory.

Global Asset Allocation

Patrizio Merciai
Chief Economist and Investment Strategist
Lombard Odier & Cie

> International asset returns, currency risk, and correlation patterns have a profound effect on the "investment kaleidoscope"—the dizzying array of asset allocation combinations—for global investors in different base currencies. Investors must realize that the golden rules of asset allocation and some conventional wisdom may not hold in the real world of global investing. The world is not yet a "global village," and tactical asset allocation may offer significant opportunities for enhancing returns and avoiding harmful exposures.

For those implementing global investment strategies for the first time, taking advantage of others' experiences in international diversification for different clients or in different base currencies can be helpful. Experience helps distinguish between academic principles and conventional wisdom that hold true in global financial markets and those that do not. Changing base currencies forces investors to view the world from a different perspective, and the resulting portfolios often end up with different asset allocations.

This presentation highlights some of the theories and conventional wisdom about international diversification—such as return patterns, volatilities, risk reduction, market timing versus policy asset allocations, stock and industry picking, and the role of currency hedging—that do not always hold in the real world. The discussion covers the effects and causes of differences between global reality and theory and suggests a common approach for dealing with varying investor situations and currencies.

Conventional Wisdom and Reality

A number of important theoretical findings based on specific assumptions have over time become conventional wisdom and continue to be considered valid even when the initial assumptions are relaxed or no longer hold. In the complex financial world, reality often challenges such conventional wisdom. Some golden rules of investing that must be reexamined in an international context are as follows:

- Bond returns are consistently less volatile than equity returns. Thus, to reduce risk, portfolios should be allocated to bonds rather than equities.
- The longer one's time horizon, the greater one's tolerance for volatility. Thus, investors with long-term horizons should prefer stocks to bonds.
- International diversification is a necessity in any portfolio because it significantly reduces risk.
- Getting the long-term asset allocation correct is more important than market timing.
- Asset allocation is everything; industry or stock selection is nothing.
- A sizable part of foreign assets, if not all, should be hedged against currency losses.

These golden rules seem straightforward. The question is: Do they apply to international diversification in the real world?

Return and Risk. The conventional wisdom regarding the relative returns and risks of bonds and equities tends to hold true in the global market as well as the U.S. market for long horizons. **Table 1**, for example, shows similar return and risk patterns for long-term bond and equity assets denominated in two different base currencies—the U.S. dollar and the Swiss franc. Stock and bond volatilities in U.S. markets and at the world level depend on the time period studied, however, and for short time periods, volatilities show no clear relative patterns.

International Diversification. A portfolio's return is simply the weighted average of the returns of each asset in the portfolio, but its volatility will be lower than the average of the individual volatilities if the covariance of each pair of assets is low. Thus, conventional wisdom asserts that international diversification, whether the return on foreign assets is or is not greater than the return on domestic assets,

Table 1. Return and Risk Patterns: U.S. Dollar Assets and Swiss Franc Assets

Asset	Mean Annual Return	Volatility
U.S. assets (115 years)		
Risk-free assets	4.9%	3.1%
Long bonds	5.3	7.1
Equities	8.6	19.1
Swiss assets (70 years)		
Risk-term free assets	na	na
Long-term bonds	4.6	3.8
Equities	9.7	20.3

na = not applicable.
Source: Charles P. Jones and J.W. Wilson, "Stocks, Bonds, Paper, and Inflation: 1870–1985," *Journal of Portfolio Management* (Fall 1987):20–24.

significantly reduces risk by adding assets that have low correlations with domestic assets. As **Table 2** shows, the incentive is all the greater if one considers world market capitalizations. The scope for diversification for any domestic investor is enormous. But international diversification raises new issues.

First, although international diversification should reduce total risk, it introduces currency risk—more so for bonds than equities. Currency risk significantly increases bond volatility, as **Figure 1** shows. In local-currency terms, a yen bond for a Japanese investor and a German mark bond for a German investor have roughly the same return pattern and level of volatility for these time periods. The volatility of Japanese bonds and German bonds, however, is more than double for a U.S. dollar-based investor, regardless of the time period.

In the case of equities, the added volatility for the U.S. dollar-based investor is much less. Indeed, during recent time periods, as **Figure 2** shows, the volatility of German stock returns in U.S. dollars has actually been less than the volatility in German marks. Most of the large-capitalization stocks in developed countries such as Germany are those of huge multinationals that generate earnings throughout the world. Thus, when their earnings are expressed in a world reference currency, such as the dollar, the volatility of the earnings is less than when those foreign earnings and the valuation of foreign earnings are translated into German marks.

The conventional wisdom that bonds are much less volatile than equities may not be true globally when returns are measured in dollars for a U.S.-based investor. As the comparison in **Figure 3** suggests, the volatility of non-U.S. stock and non-U.S. bond returns generally shows the conventional pattern of less volatility for bonds than equities, but the volatility of non-U.S. bonds for a U.S.-based investor rises to approximately 12–14 percent annual standard deviation.

■ *Correlations.* Gaining the benefits of international diversification rests on the assumption that correlations between markets are low. In fact, U.S. and foreign markets do react differently to the same events. As **Figure 4** shows, the major world financial markets provide a U.S. bond investor more diversification than a U.S. equity investor. After taking the currency effect into account, U.S. bond returns have a very low correlation with foreign bonds. The U.S. equity market has a relatively high correlation, however, with the world index, the European index, and countries such as the United Kingdom, Canada, and the Netherlands. The correlation of U.S. equities with the Morgan Stanley Capital International EAFE (Europe/Australasia/Far East) Index is lower. The correlation of U.S. securities with Japanese securities has been low in the 1988–97 period because of currency issues and local market movements.

Although financial theory suggests that the world financial markets are becoming more integrated, correlation data do not clearly indicate such a trend. Emerging markets have become closely integrated into the mainstream of the world investment universe, but correlations among industrialized countries are not increasing. As **Figure 5** shows, correlations exhibit no clear pattern over time and

Table 2. Percentage of World Market Capitalizations by Country

Country/Currency	Share
Stock market, total capitalization = US$18.2 trillion[a]	
United States	47.2%
Europe ex-United Kingdom	15.5
Japan	12.5
United Kingdom	11.5
Switzerland	3.2
Canada	3.0
Other Asian countries	2.9
Hong Kong	1.9
Sweden	1.4
Denmark	0.5
Norway	0.4
Bond market, total capitalization = US$21.6 trillion[b]	
U.S. dollar	44.5
Euro	28.1
Japanese yen	17.0
U.K. pound	3.1
Other European currencies	3.0
Canadian dollar	2.1
Other currencies	1.2
Swiss franc	1.1

[a]Data as of December 31, 1997.
[b]Data as of mid-1997.

Global Asset Allocation

Figure 1. Annual Bond Return Volatility: U.S. Dollar, Japanese Yen, and German Mark Bonds

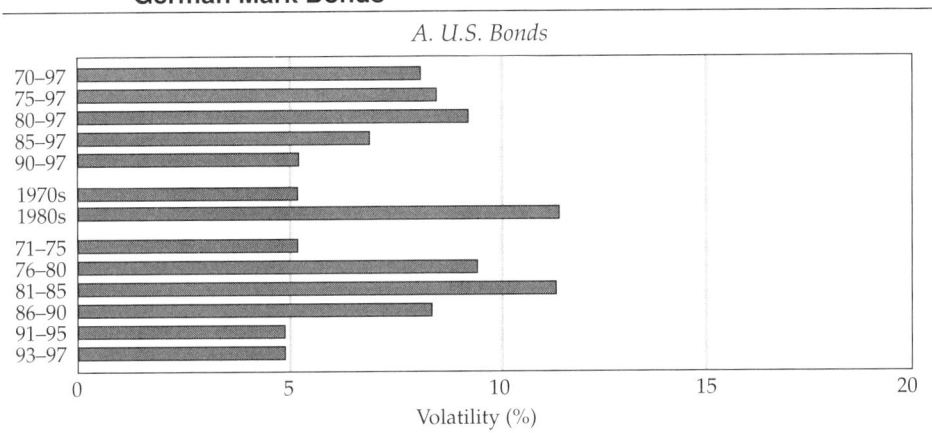

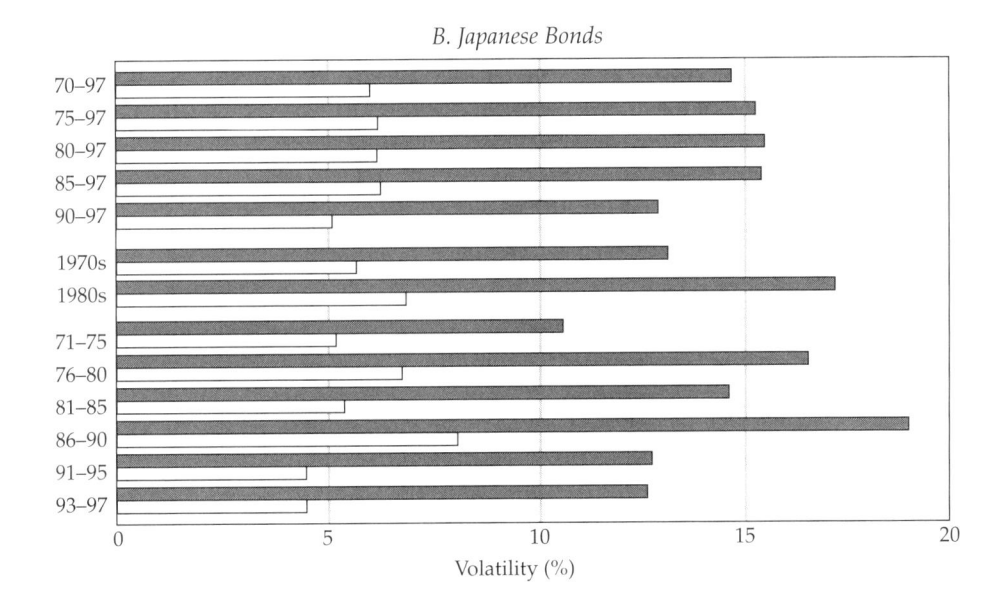

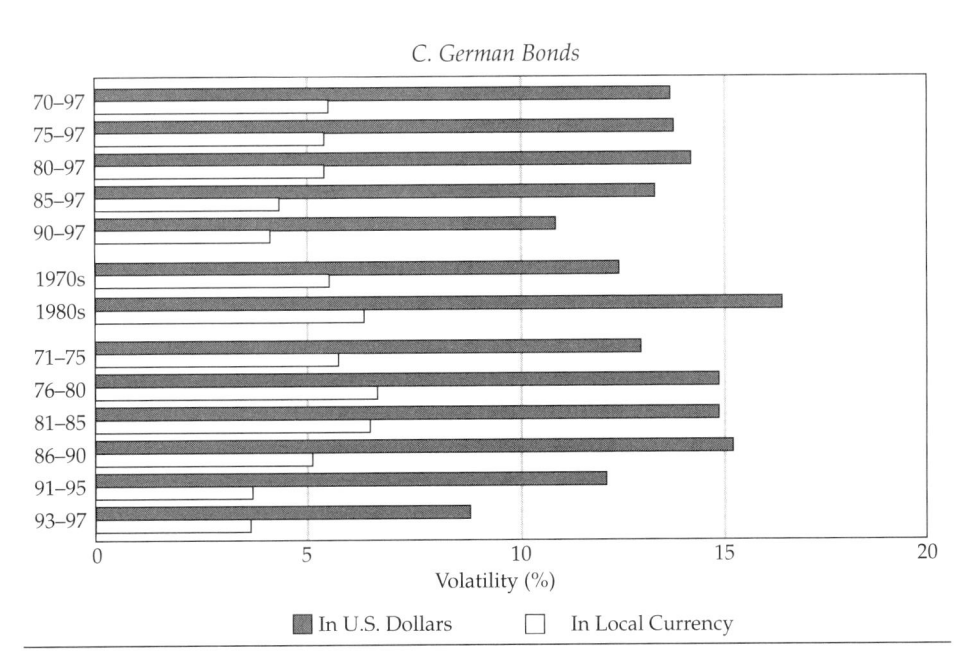

A. U.S. Bonds

B. Japanese Bonds

C. German Bonds

■ In U.S. Dollars   □ In Local Currency

Asset Allocation in a Changing World

Figure 2. Annual Stock Return Volatility: U.S., Japanese, and German Stocks

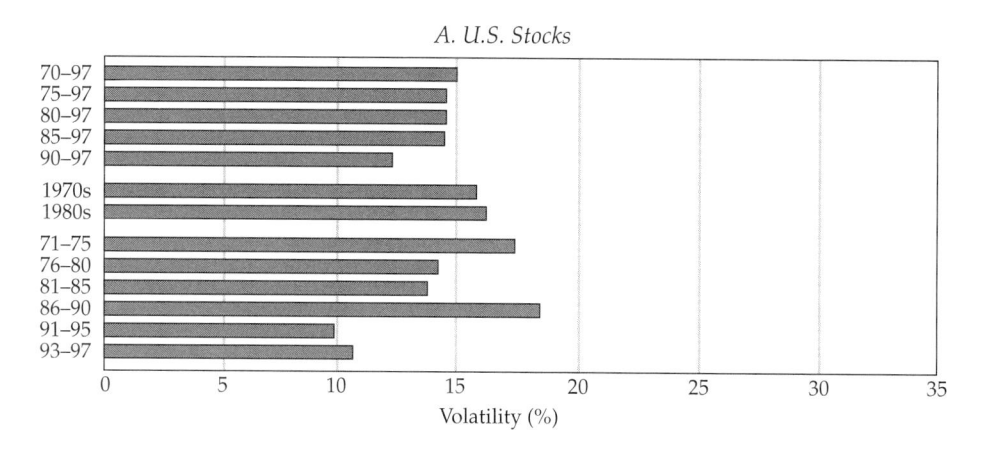

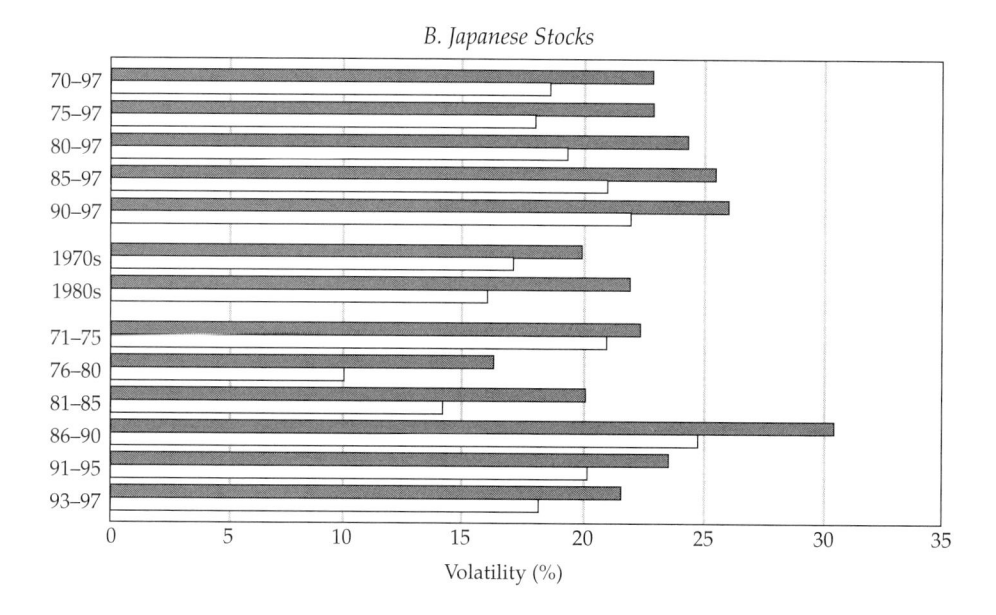

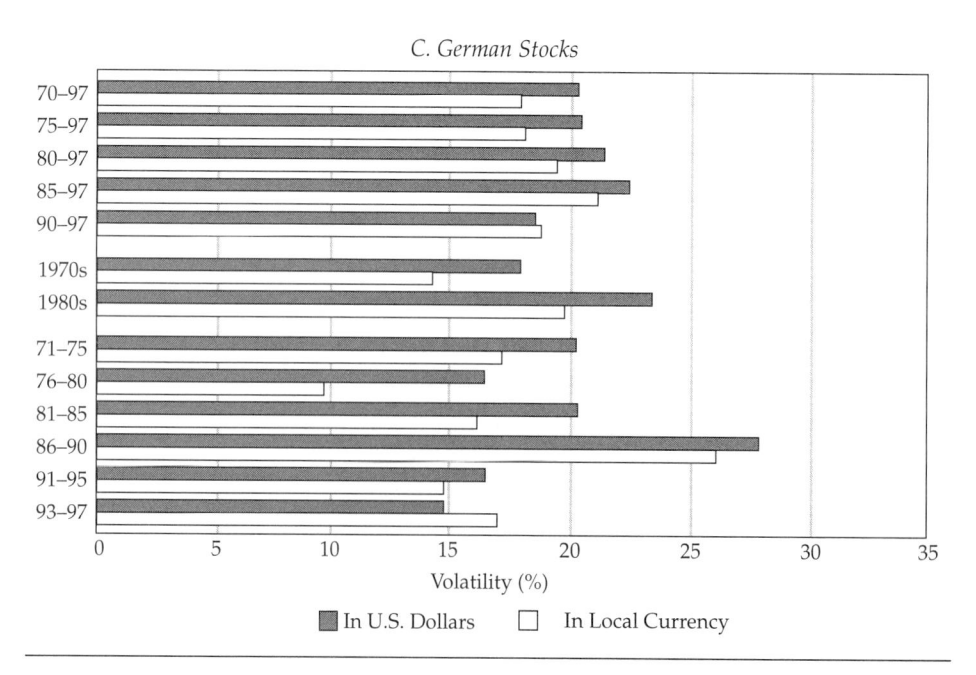

A. U.S. Stocks

B. Japanese Stocks

C. German Stocks

■ In U.S. Dollars   □ In Local Currency

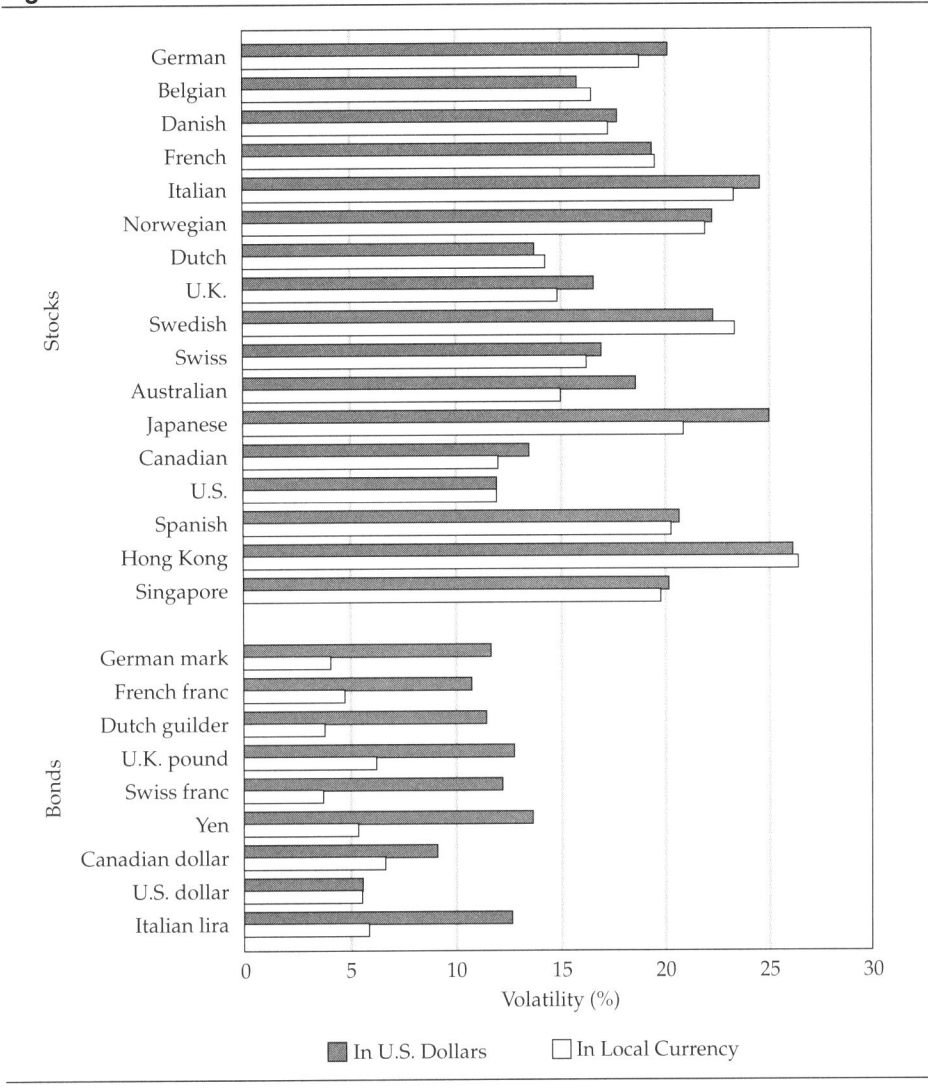

Figure 3. Annual Volatilities in Local Currencies and in U.S. Dollars, 1988–97

[Bar chart showing annual volatilities (%) in U.S. Dollars and Local Currency for stocks and bonds across various countries/currencies. Stocks listed: German, Belgian, Danish, French, Italian, Norwegian, Dutch, U.K., Swedish, Swiss, Australian, Japanese, Canadian, U.S., Spanish, Hong Kong, Singapore. Bonds listed: German mark, French franc, Dutch guilder, U.K. pound, Swiss franc, Yen, Canadian dollar, U.S. dollar, Italian lira.]

depend on the time period measured. For example, during a number of short time periods, such as 1971 through 1975, the correlation between U.S. and Japanese equities was relatively high, but for long time periods, such as 1970 through 1997, the correlation has been relatively low. In short, although investment professionals may sense that the world is becoming a global village, many notable exceptions to increasing correlation exist in the data.

■ *International asset allocation.* The theoretical benefits of international diversification for a U.S.-based investor are clearly demonstrated in **Figure 6** by the changes that occur in the efficient frontier as non-U.S. assets are added to a portfolio's investment universe. These benefits are not so easily seen, however, from another home country's perspective. This outcome is a bit disturbing because the results and investment rules should be the same in any base currency or from any national perspective. Furthermore, different time periods will produce different results.

■ *The effect of currency gains and losses.* From a theoretical standpoint, currency gains and losses balance out over the long term, but in the real world, currency depreciation or currency appreciation can extend throughout short periods. Thus, currency gains and losses are a significant part of total returns. **Figure 7** demonstrates the significant impact currency has on total returns. For example, the yen, even though it is currently a weak currency, has nevertheless appreciated by 30–40 percent against the U.K. pound since 1985. The U.S. dollar, however, depreciated by 30 percent over the same period. For investors based in a traditionally strong currency such as the Swiss franc, long-term currency losses are implied by holding hedge investments (i.e., foreign assets as viewed from Switzerland, such as the U.S. equity and bond markets).

Currency moves interact with specific market features to result in wide differences in the relative

Figure 4. Correlation of U.S. Stock and Bond Returns with World, Regional, and Selected Countries' Returns, 1988–97

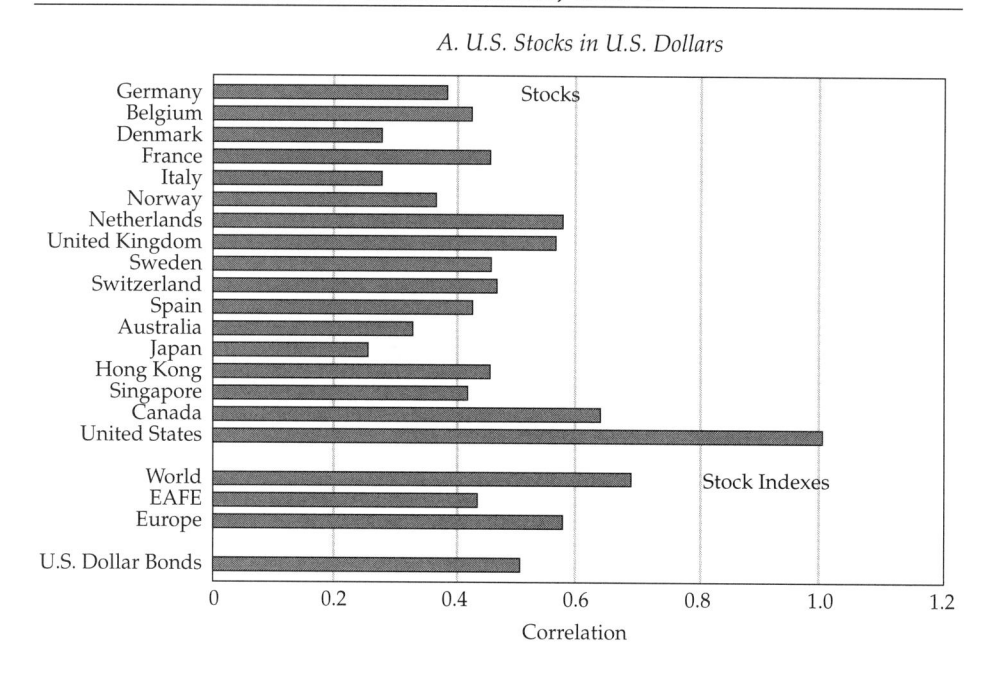

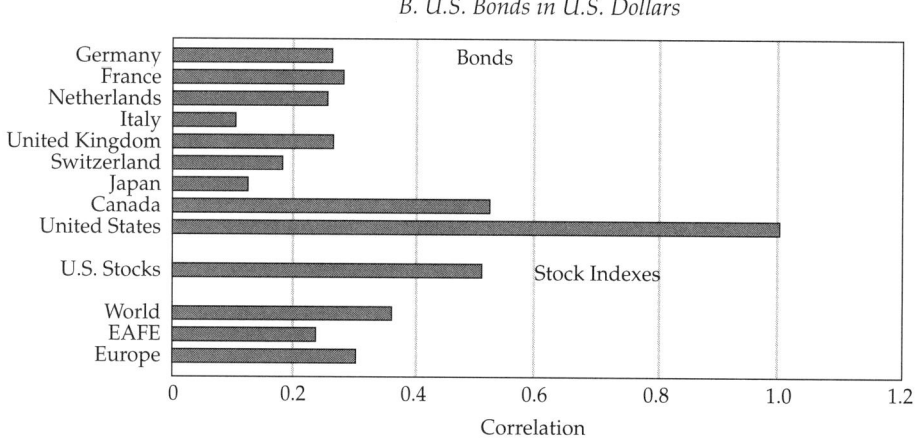

A. U.S. Stocks in U.S. Dollars

[Bar chart showing correlations of U.S. stocks with stocks of: Germany, Belgium, Denmark, France, Italy, Norway, Netherlands, United Kingdom, Sweden, Switzerland, Spain, Australia, Japan, Hong Kong, Singapore, Canada, United States; and with Stock Indexes: World, EAFE, Europe; and U.S. Dollar Bonds. X-axis: Correlation, 0 to 1.2.]

B. U.S. Bonds in U.S. Dollars

[Bar chart showing correlations of U.S. bonds with bonds of: Germany, France, Netherlands, Italy, United Kingdom, Switzerland, Japan, Canada, United States; and with Stock Indexes: U.S. Stocks, World, EAFE, Europe. X-axis: Correlation, 0 to 1.2.]

volatility of bonds and equities. Specific equity or bond markets may be more or less sensitive to interest rates, which produce various risk–return patterns and correlations. For example, for a pound-based investor, such major foreign equities as U.S. stocks do not carry much more risk than domestic equities. The risk levels are roughly plus or minus one percentage point in volatility. For a Japanese investor, Japanese equities are very volatile and U.S. and similar foreign stocks are slightly less volatile than domestic stocks.

Viewed from small volatile markets, such as Italy (which has about 25 percent annual volatility), investing in major foreign equities is a defensive strategy. The U.S. equity market is much less volatile than the Italian market for an Italian investor, even after the effects of currency risk. On the other hand, U.S. bonds are three times more volatile for a Swiss investor than domestic Swiss bonds. That is not to say that Swiss investors should not invest in U.S. bonds, only that these instruments are very risky for Swiss franc-based (or German mark-based) investors.

■ *The investment kaleidoscope.* Asset returns, currency risks, and correlation patterns make for a dizzying array of asset allocation combinations when the vantage point shifts from one country to another.

Investors from different countries will have different perspectives on the ideal country and asset allocation. The Swiss equity market, for example, has a relatively high correlation with Wall Street and the world indexes because it is dominated by a few big

Figure 5. Correlation of U.S. Stock Returns with EAFE, European, and Japanese Stock Returns

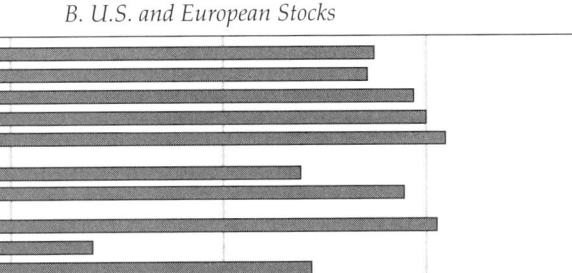

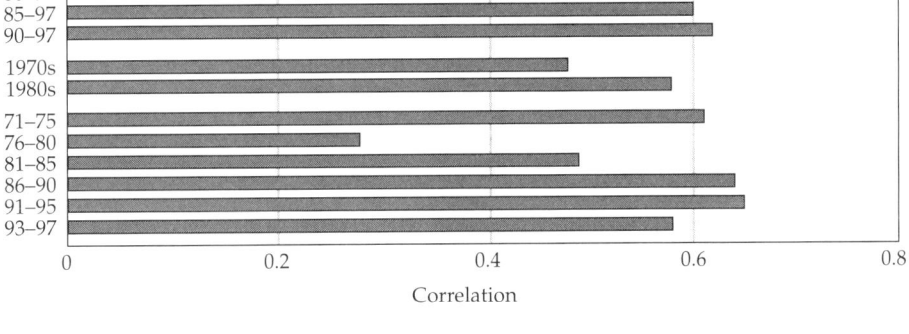

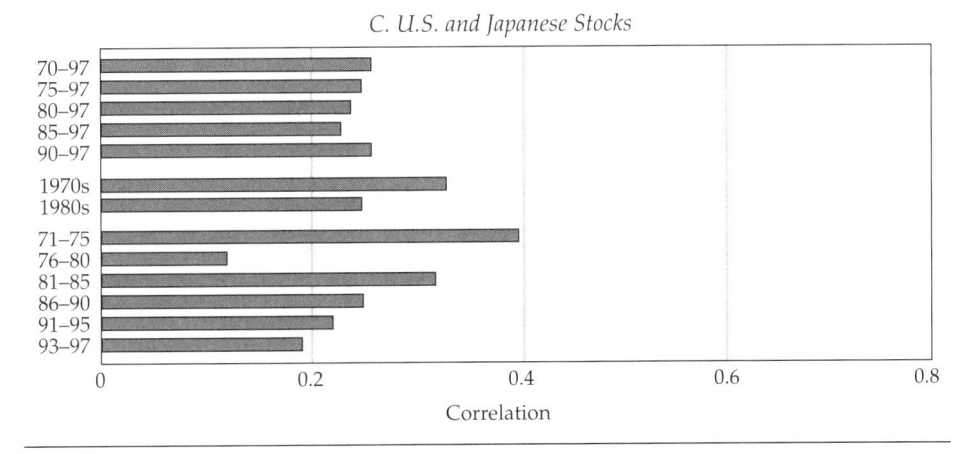

A. U.S. and EAFE Stocks

B. U.S. and European Stocks

C. U.S. and Japanese Stocks

multinationals that tend to react to major world news and financial events as other multinationals react. Switzerland has a correlation of approximately 60 percent with most major markets, and correlations with other major markets for Dutch equity investors exhibit an even stronger pattern. Thus, counter to financial theory, because of relatively high correlations between markets, investing in other markets is often not as good a diversification technique for many global investors as it is for a U.S. or Japanese investor.

■ *Local-currency efficient frontiers.* When everything is put together, global investors have as many solutions, or as many answers to the diversification question, as they have possible combinations of assets and base currencies. The base currency has a significant impact on risk–return relationships and efficient frontiers. **Figure 8** depicts the effect of various global diversification strategies on investors based in a number of currencies for the 1987–96 period. As Panel A of Figure 8 shows, currency

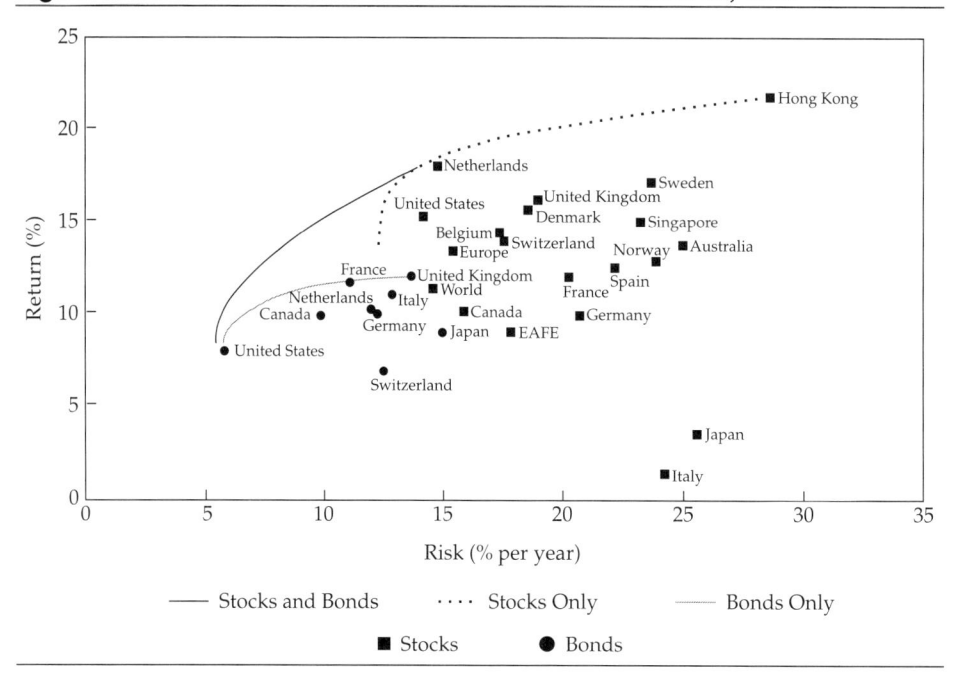

Figure 6. Efficient Frontiers for U.S. Dollar-Based Returns, 1987–96

volatility, reducing the reward-to-variability ratio, flattens the efficient frontier for U.K. investors, although pound-based investors can still achieve either more return or less risk by international diversification. Even though U.K. markets have a relatively high correlation with the U.S. markets, the pound sterling is a smaller currency and tends to have a life of its own, with currency volatility reducing pound-based stock and bond returns. Thus, bonds for pound-based investors are more volatile than they are for U.S. dollar-based investors; U.K. investors can achieve the best risk–return trade-off by low-risk investing.

The efficient frontiers shown for the yen-based investor in Panel B provide a prime example of the benefits of global diversification—zero return for 23 percent annual volatility for yen-based investors in Japanese equity alone versus more than 15 percent return with global equity investing for the same level of risk.

During the same time period, the picture in the Netherlands argues a reverse proposition for Dutch investors. International investing for a guilder-based investor in this period offered lower stock and bond returns for the same level of risk than domestic investing. Venturing outside the Netherlands was not worth the trouble.

These results are obviously specific to this data set and time period, but the results nevertheless cast doubt on the conventional wisdom on international asset allocation.

Market Timing versus Buy and Hold. Two of conventional wisdom's golden rules of investing are (1) long-term asset allocation is much more important than trying to time the market and (2) market timing is counterproductive and does not add value. As to the first point, asset allocation is certainly important in efficient markets; research shows that asset allocation accounts for as much as 95 percent of the variance in returns.[1]

Market timing is counterproductive if the market is efficient. Investors must stay in the market because they cannot predict the good periods. According to Shilling, compound returns of U.S. stocks in the DJIA in the 1946–91 period averaged 11.2 percent annually—a 116-times increase during the period.[2] Excluding the returns of the best 50 months during the same period would have reduced annual compound returns to 3.7 percent. No wonder conventional wisdom implies that investors should stay in the market in order not to miss the good periods.

Market timing, however, does have some appeal. In Shilling's research, if investors could have gotten out of the market during the 50 worst months,

---

[1] See Gary P. Brinson, L. Randolph Hood, and Gilbert L. Beebower, "Determinants of Portfolio Performance: An Update," *Financial Analysts Journal* (January/February 1995):133–38, and Burton Malkiel, *A Random Walk Down Wall Street* (New York: W.W. Norton, 1973).

[2] See A. Gary Shilling, "Market Timing: Better than a Buy-and-Hold Strategy," *Financial Analysts Journal* (March/April 1992):46–50.

Figure 7. Changes of Three Currencies against the U.K. Pound and the Swiss Franc, January 4, 1985, through March 27, 1998

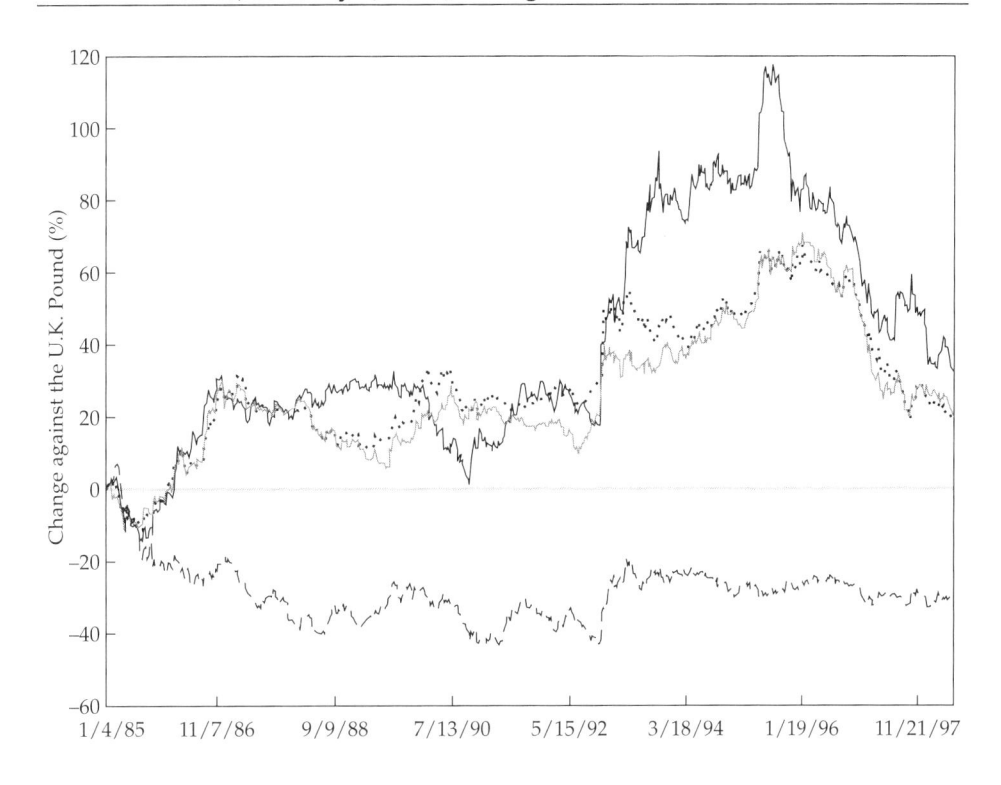

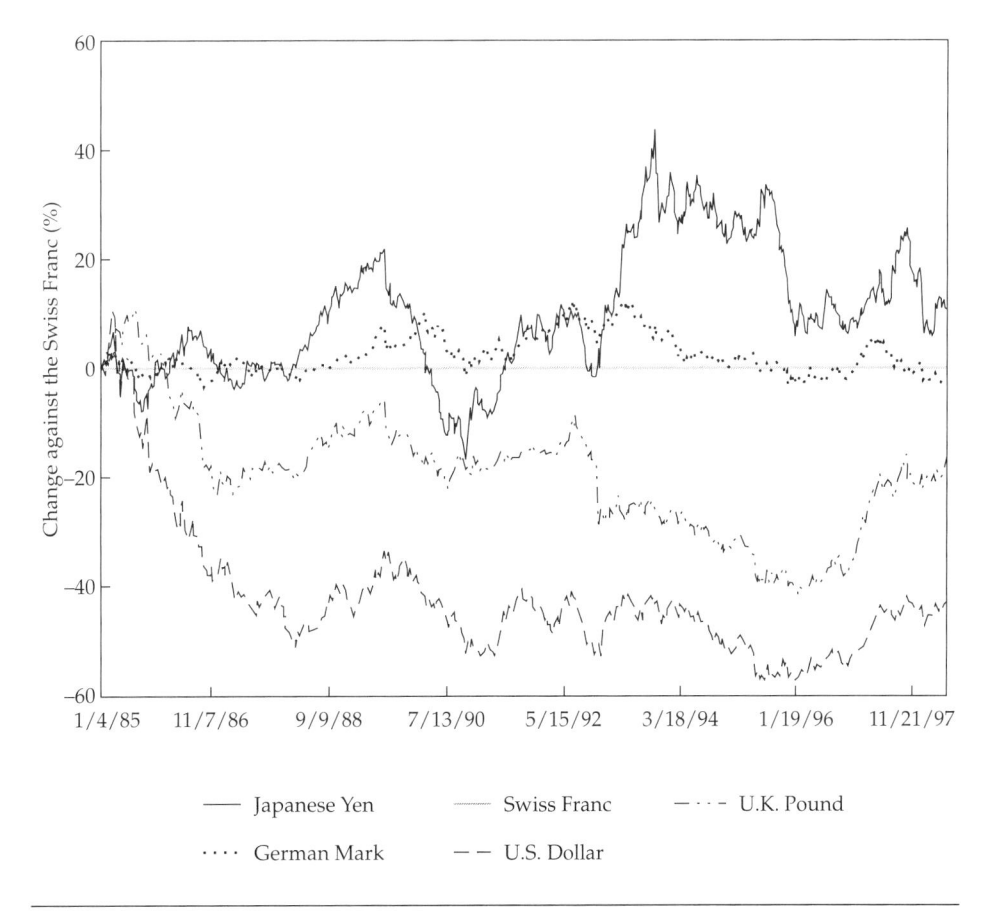

Asset Allocation in a Changing World

Figure 8. Efficient Frontiers for Three Portfolio Types in Three Base Currencies, 1987–96

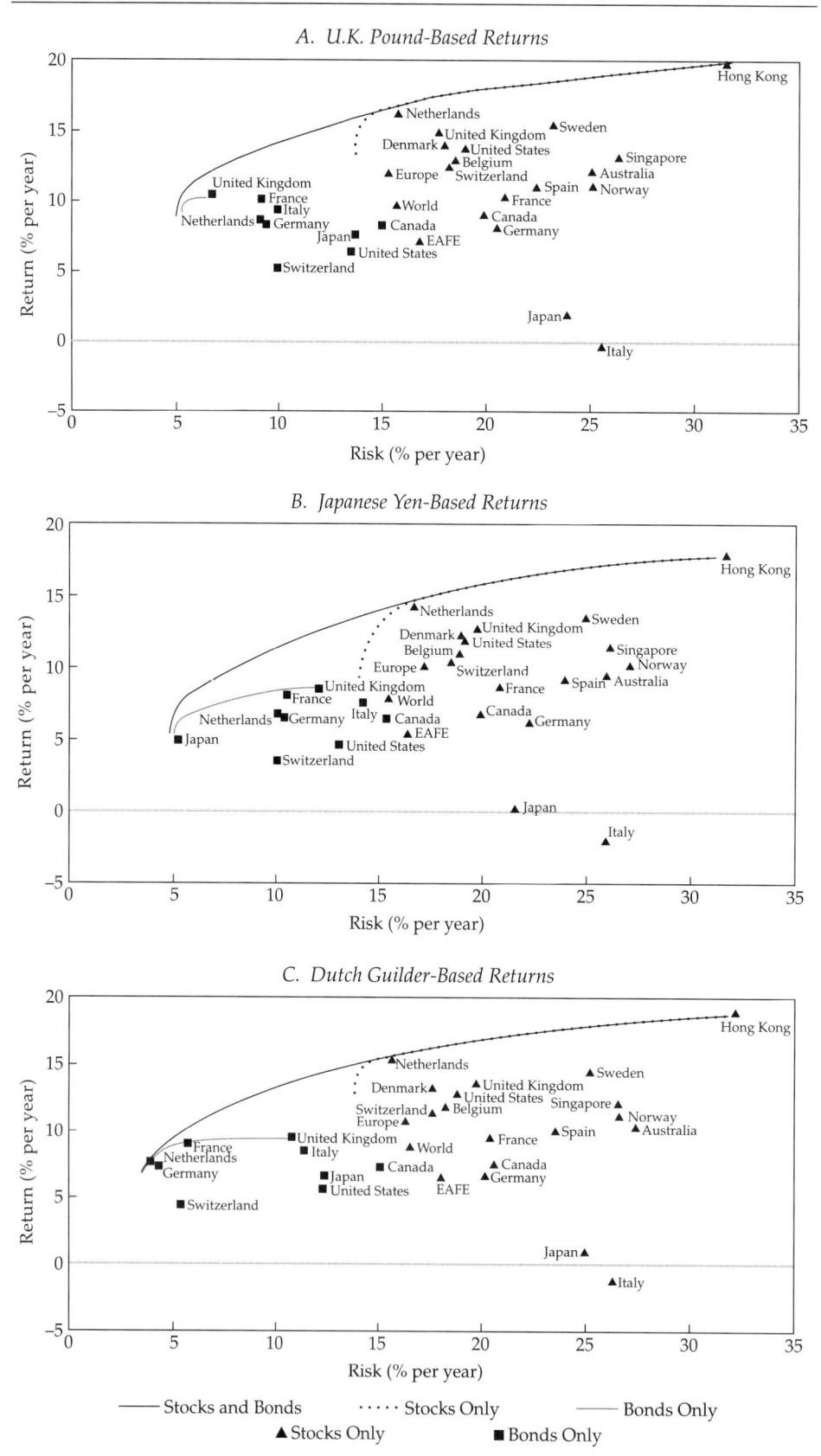

A. U.K. Pound-Based Returns

B. Japanese Yen-Based Returns

C. Dutch Guilder-Based Returns

— Stocks and Bonds ····· Stocks Only — Bonds Only
▲ Stocks Only ■ Bonds Only

their compound annual returns would have jumped to 19.0 percent—a 2,541-times increase over the period. Thus, although it is good to remain invested to avoid missing rising markets, it is even better to avoid falling markets.

At the world level, market timing is even more important than at the domestic level because major financial markets experience distinctive periods of over- and underperformance. It is better for a portfolio to be less than optimally diversified than to penalize returns. History provides plenty of examples to demonstrate this point, such as the spectacular outperformance of U.S. stocks in 1995 and 1996 and the underperformance of Japanese stocks in the 1990s. As **Figure 9** shows, after a stellar performance in the last part of the 1980s, when it completely ignored the 1987 crash, the Japanese stock market went into a nearly seven-year period of underperformance in terms of local-currency returns. Portfolios with passive asset allocations in Japan experienced significantly reduced portfolio returns, so investors saw the wisdom of maintaining flexibility or following a strategy of bailing out of the Japanese market at such times. The result was increased popularity of ex-Japan world and regional equity indexes. The Japanese market share of the world stock index diminished sharply. In summary, even if theoretical support exists for long-term asset allocation, from a global perspective, distinct opportunities remain for getting in or out of certain markets.

Asset Allocation versus Industry/Stock Picking. Given the importance of asset allocation, conventional wisdom says that investors should forget industry and stock selection. In global markets, however, certain industries or segments react differently to world events, such as changes in interest rates and currency movements, than the rest of the world market. For example, although the broad Tokyo Stock Price Index (TOPIX) underperformed during the 1995 to early 1998 period with a –20 percent return, investors could nevertheless have achieved positive returns in certain sectors. As **Figure 10** shows, the TOPIX exporters subindex, with an albeit modest 6 percent return, outperformed the broad TOPIX while the TOPIX banking subindex, at –44 percent, vastly underperformed the broad Japa-

Figure 9. Comparative Performance of European Stock Index, World Stock Index ex-Japan, and Japanese Stock Index, January 31, 1986, through March 31, 1998

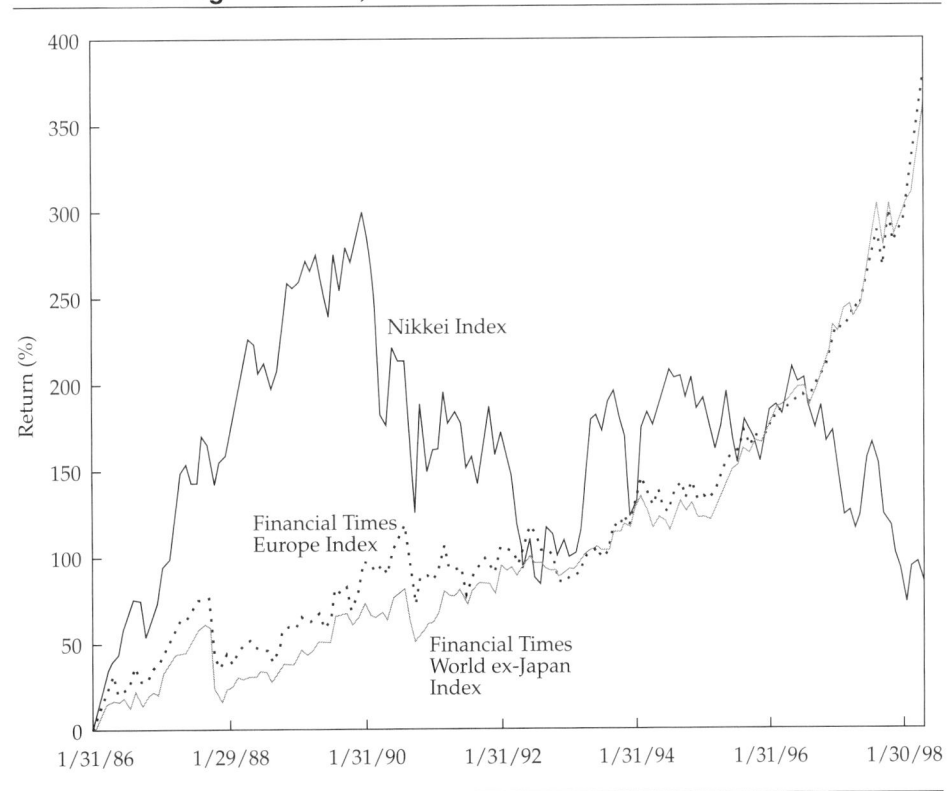

Asset Allocation in a Changing World

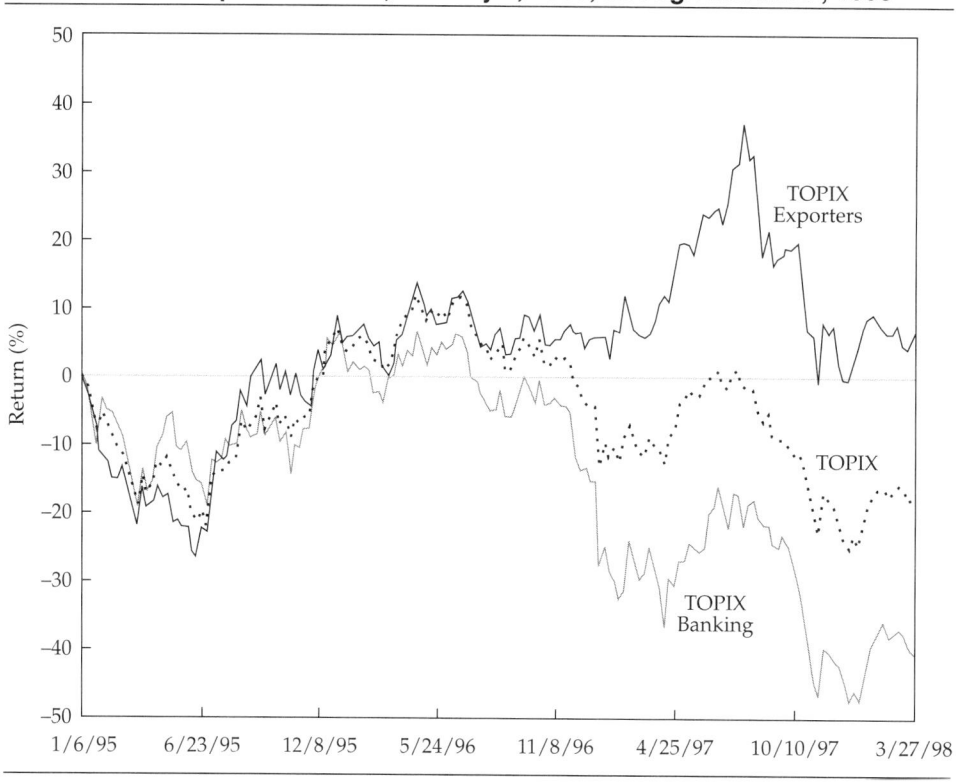

Figure 10. Comparative Performance of Japanese Stock Market, Bank Stocks, and Exporter Stocks, January 6, 1995, through March 27, 1998

nese market. The challenge in the Japanese market is to find sectors, such as the big electronic sector that includes Sony Electronics Inc. and Canon Inc., that avoid the underperformance of the broad Japanese market. The only risk to that sector is that it tends to react to events in the same way that European or U.S. stocks react.

The Hedging Issue. Exchange rate changes frequently exceed the forward interest rate spread, which adds to total volatility. Extensive research supports the argument for full and systematic hedging of currency risk, which is supposed to sharply reduce volatility while continuing to allow diversification among assets with low correlations. According to this approach, all investors, regardless of base currency, should assume only a small amount of currency risk and hedge the majority of their foreign holdings. Thus, everyone should have roughly the same exposure to foreign markets.

Although theoretical support exists for universal hedging, the supporting arguments do not hold true in the real world. Conventionally, a currency's contribution to total return is often assumed to be unsystematic, but long-term appreciation or depreciation trends in recent history have occurred for fundamental reasons. For example, the Swiss franc has been a strong currency because Switzerland has a structural current-account surplus as a result of large amounts of Swiss-controlled overseas investments. In short, certain currencies tend to be strong and to appreciate over the long run. Because the countries have consistently lower interest rates, hedging will be much more costly for investors based in the strong currencies—for example, a Swiss franc-based investor, a yen-based investor, or even a German mark-based investor—than for a U.S. dollar- or U.K. pound-based investor. The dilemma is that, although hedging is costly, investors based in the strong currencies are most likely to incur foreign exchange losses on their international portfolios.

This dilemma can be solved, but solutions for bonds and equities differ. Because of the strong covariance between exchange rates and interest rates, currency risk is a major component of the total risk for bonds but not so major for equities. Bond holdings are highly sensitive to currency risk because currency rates are influenced by interest rates, so common factors explain the behavior of bonds and currency risk. Currency risk adds little extra volatility to equities and, in some cases, even decreases volatility. Thus, as several researchers have concluded, hedging is more appropriate for bond holdings than for equity holdings.[3] At the same time, the net total return on hedged foreign bonds may be unattractive when hedging costs are exceptionally high, so one might challenge the wisdom of investing in international bonds altogether—precisely what investors tend to do in practical terms.

Equity investors should be unhedged and broadly diversified, whereas bond investors should be invested in domestic bonds or in bonds closely correlated with the home currency. Hedging should be more frequent for bond investors, but because hedging severely affects returns, bond investing should be more tactical. For example, European investors could be more opportunistic by investing in Japanese or U.S. bonds, whereas on other occasions, U.S. investors could invest in European bonds.

A Common Approach

Defining a common investment approach for investors with different investment goals, time horizons, risk constraints, and base currencies is a complicated and challenging task. Kahn, Roulet, and Tajbakhsh have pointed out that global asset allocation lies at the heart of global investing.[4] They explain that global asset allocation involves a three-step process: first, forecasting expected returns by asset classes—the "art" in global investing—second, building optimal mean–variance portfolios, which requires defining an appropriate benchmark for global asset allocation, and finally, conducting out-of-sample performance analyses of optimal portfolios using Sharpe ratios, information ratios, and cumulative return plots.

At each of the three steps, investors and portfolio managers encounter real-world problems. First, many investors have little familiarity with forecasting expected absolute returns, and forecasting expected excess returns is even less intuitive, especially in remote markets. Second, forecasting international asset returns in a single currency means forecasting the foreign exchange market—the most unpredictable of all markets. In addition, mean–variance optimization models are challenging. They are very sensitive to changes in return, correlation, and volatility. Even small changes in these variables can have a significant impact on the optimal allocation. A 10 basis point difference in expected returns may direct the model to, for example, recommend selling all the Dutch holdings and buying into Japanese holdings. Furthermore, the choice of benchmark is extremely important. Finally, out-of-sample testing may be inadequate because reliable historical data are lacking. Nevertheless, the challenge remains: how to forecast returns with some precision without producing misleading model results.

Tactical Asset Allocation. If applicable globally, TAA models could provide valuable help in fine-tuning return forecasts. TAA models are based on the assumption that asset valuations are linked and self-correlate to the average or long-term equilibrium. The models are good tools for defining expected return, especially excess return over cash, at any given period. Whether such models use a single factor, such as risk premiums, or several factors, they define the current point in the divergence and convergence cycle, which requires analytical methods that can be applied from one asset to another and that remain constant over time.

TAA models may work in a domestic universe but not in a global universe. Models based on risk premiums may not be adequate or appropriate for international assets because international markets have differing historical return patterns and behavior. For example, some European markets have had consistently negative risk premiums for bonds versus equities, whereas other markets have had positive risk premiums. The return patterns of equities versus bonds in the former high-interest-rate markets of Europe are no longer relevant because interest rates have dropped to levels comparable to those of major markets. Several researchers have shown that differences in growth rates, inflation, and political risks from one country to another affect not only exchange rates but also asset valuations.[5] Thus, one cannot use a TAA model that works in the United States to make comparisons in international markets.

As the search for an international TAA model continues, portfolio managers might consider a multifactor TAA model. At Lombard, Odier & Cie, we put the results in terms of information coefficients, as shown in **Table 3**. These information coefficients give the predictability of a sophisticated, multifactor model for forecasting bond and equity returns. The results are encouraging but inconsistent. For example, the model is good for forecasting German bond returns but ineffective for forecasting French and Japanese equity returns. The question of why this model works well on some assets and not on others merits its own debate. The conclusion is that using even fairly sophisticated techniques for forecasting mar-

---

[3] See Fischer Black and Robert Litterman, "Global Portfolio Optimization," *Financial Analysts Journal* (September/October 1992): 28–43, and Bruno Solnik, *International Investments* (Reading, PA: Addison-Wesley, 1988).

[4] Ronald N. Kahn, Jacques Roulet, and Shahram Tajbakhsh, "Three Steps to Global Asset Allocation," *Journal of Portfolio Management* (Fall 1996):23–31.

[5] Robert D. Arnott and Roy D. Henriksson, "A Disciplined Approach to Global Asset Allocation," in *Active Asset Allocation*, edited by Robert D. Arnott and Frank J. Fabozzi (Chicago, IL: Probus, 1992).

Table 3. Information Coefficients for Selected Asset Classes in a Proprietary TAA Model

Country	Bonds	Equities
France	35.4%	13.5%
Germany	34.7	17.7
Hong Kong	—	17.0
Italy	17.7	26.4
Japan	12.2	4.2
Singapore	—	–1.2
Spain	–14.2	39.7
Sweden	12.8	6.2
Switzerland	12.8	18.0
United Kingdom	13.0	25.8
United States	18.5	17.5

Note: Based on 60 monthly periods to August 1997.

kets produces unreliable results if the main goal is to have a broad universe for diversification purposes.

Strategic Asset Allocation. Theory contrasts "strategic asset allocation," or "policy asset mix," to tactical, dynamic asset allocation. The strategic approach traditionally confines review and rebalancing of the equity–bond allocations to once a year, whereas the tactical review is seldom done less than monthly. The strategic approach was originally designed for U.S. institutional investors, who operate over the long term and primarily in a single currency. Because some firms' strategic allocations make frequent adjustments, what those firms call strategic allocation may look like tactical allocation to others.

For a manager whose clients are diversified in terms of time horizon and investment universe, the traditional approach of setting the policy asset mix and changing it only infrequently cannot work. For global portfolios, the strategic approach is to review asset and currency allocations on a monthly, or at least a quarterly, basis. Whether the approach is still worthwhile will depend on the manager's clients. **Exhibit 1** shows the appropriate approach for various types of clients. Note that global institutional clients tend to have their own predefined policy asset mixes and long-term strategic allocations, which differ from one client to another because requirements differ in each country. Because these institutions are fully aware of the risk and return opportunities associated with international diversification, they increasingly demand global balanced benchmarks, an appropriate asset mix, and a good indication of the expected performance of the asset mix that takes into account all the effects of local-currency and common-currency returns. Wide price or exchange rate swings may initiate tactical adjustments. Thus, portfolio managers may find that they need to be more-active managers in terms of changing the asset allocation than would be the case for a domestic client base.

Because no single solution exists for each base currency and each type of client, portfolio managers must, first of all, clearly define the investment universe for each client and understand how that universe helps define the client's long-term investment policy. Before allocation adjustments can even be considered, the manager must determine what today's allocation would be under that investment policy.

Conclusion

Viewing the world from a global perspective should prompt investors and managers to challenge conventional wisdom in order to implement an effective global investment strategy. Experience as well as research teach the following lessons:

- Most investors need international diversification; it is a good tool for reducing risk.
- The currency issue, however, has a critical influence on both risk and return and must be addressed.
- Systematic adjustments of allocations within a strategy bandwidth must allow for some market-timing decisions. Portfolio managers with an international client base will tend to be more active in terms of asset allocation than they would be if they had only domestic institutional clients.
- Over the long term, investing in equities is the only way to achieve sustainable, long-term returns and protect the real value of capital.
- With proper diversification, the volatility of equity returns is tolerable for the long-term investor. Diversification in foreign bonds is more dependent on currency and interest rate developments.

Exhibit 1. Allocation Approaches by Client Type

Decision	Domestic Institutions	Worldwide Institutions	Private Clients
Policy asset mix	Predefined by the institution	Predefined but will differ from one client to another	Must be determined with the client
Asset allocation	Relative to a widely accepted benchmark	Increasing demand for "global balanced" benchmarks	Benchmark may include policy constraints
Tactical adjustments	Seldom cost-effective	May be required by wide price or exchange rate swings	

- For some base currencies, currency-hedged bond investments provide a better risk–return profile than do unhedged investments. Active management of bond portfolios—investing or divesting in bonds depending on the economic cycle and the currency outlook—is an effective way to add value.

In terms of practical issues, allocating assets for a wide range of clients is a complex task. Three steps are helpful in achieving global asset allocation: forecasting returns, optimization, and backtesting. Forecasting is obviously a difficult part of the process. To improve forecasts, managers can check judgmental, top-down, worldwide forecasts against bottom-up views and tactical models. Optimal asset allocation will depend on different constraints in terms of the risk–return expectations of different clients, will vary greatly from one country to another, and will reflect the use of different benchmarks. Strategic asset allocation in a global context requires at least monthly allocation reviews.

Dealing with Currencies

Paul Duncombe
Investment Director and Head of Currency
State Street Global Advisors U.K. Limited

> How to manage currency risk is a hotly debated topic. Some take the "why bother" approach; others believe in systematic full hedging. The best currency management approach involves analyzing the performance attribution of global investment returns and watching out for the currency surprise. Selecting a currency overlay manager can be a difficult decision, but understanding the overlay management approach and defining risk can help plan sponsors evaluate the managers under consideration—all of whom have seemingly plausible currency management styles.

The currency-hedging decision is often the most difficult decision for plan sponsors to make. Portfolio managers find actually managing the currency risk in global portfolios equally difficult. Unfortunately, financial research provides conflicting results about whether to hedge, and trustees have little experience selecting a currency overlay manager.

This presentation examines the impact of currency exposure on international portfolios by (1) reviewing various analytical methods used to analyze and measure currency returns, (2) analyzing how the underlying tactical asset allocation decision can be affected by the use of hedged and unhedged data, and (3) providing some insight on currency overlay management.

Analytical Methods

Money managers have a tendency to measure currency returns on a spot-to-spot basis, which can be quite misleading. Given the international nature of investors today, I constructed two portfolios (one for a U.S. investor and one for a U.K. investor) of four foreign currencies: the Japanese yen, U.S. dollar, German mark, and U.K. pound. Each portfolio consisted of a simple basket of the other three major foreign currencies with weightings typical of median funds in the United States and the United Kingdom.

For the U.K.-based investor, the distribution of rolling five-year returns from spot currency moves for the 1974–97 period shows that unhedged foreign currency exposure was profitable more than 90 percent of the time, as shown in **Figure 1**. Similar results for the U.S.-based investor, as shown in **Figure 2**, indicate that U.S. investors had positive returns about 80 percent of the time. So, on the surface, one might conclude that staying unhedged was a great strategy. Before making a firm conclusion, however, one should look at an attribution of the returns from an international investment.

The total return for an unhedged international asset is the product of the local market return and the currency return:

$$(1 + U) = (1 + L) \times (1 + C)$$
$$U = L + C + LC,$$

where
  U = unhedged return
  L = local return
  C = currency return

By ignoring the cross product return (LC), I can focus on the currency component and solve for $U = L + C$. The following relationship has been calculated by working out the percentage change between the initial spot rate and the final spot rate:

$$U = L + C$$
$$= L + \frac{(S_2 - S_1)}{S_1},$$

where
  S_1 = initial spot rate
  S_2 = final spot rate

The return can be broken down into two parts by incorporating the starting forward rate. I first calculate the difference between the initial spot rate and the starting forward rate and, second, the difference between the starting forward rate and the final spot rate. Thus,

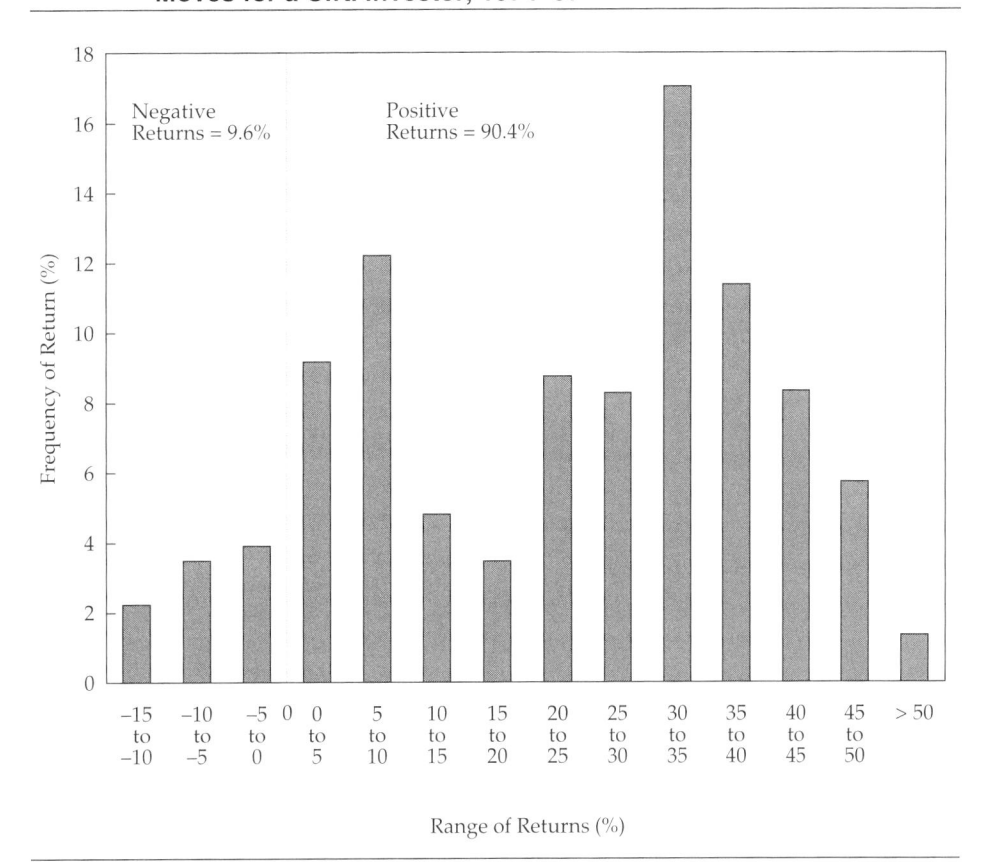

Figure 1. Distribution of Rolling Five-Year Returns from Spot Currency Moves for a U.K. Investor, 1974–97

Negative Returns = 9.6%
Positive Returns = 90.4%

Range of Returns (%)

$$U = L + \frac{(F_1 - S_1)}{S_1} + \frac{(S_2 - F_1)}{S_1},$$

where F_1 equals the starting forward rate.

Because the starting forward rate and the initial spot rate are known at the start of the measurement period, that part of the return is fixed and is effectively the forward premium, or discount. I have called the last element the "currency surprise" because that part of the return is unknown at the start of the measurement period. Thus, unhedged returns are equal to the following:

$U = L +$ Forward premium + Currency surprise.

In the absence of arbitrage opportunities, the forward premium between two currencies is approximately the same as the interest rate differential between the two countries. So, the equation can be rewritten as

$U = L - I_F + I_B +$ Currency surprise,

where

I_F = interest rate of the foreign currency
I_B = interest rate of the base currency

Therefore, the attribution of the unhedged return can be broken down into the hedged asset return and the currency surprise return:

$U =$ Hedged asset return + Currency surprise.

This result is entirely logical, because if an investor buys a foreign asset, the investor can never achieve the local return. If an investor wants to avoid the currency exposure, then he or she must hedge and earn the hedged return.

So, currency management ability should be measured for a period by comparing the final spot rate with the starting forward rate, not the starting spot rate. Thus, when a manager hedges into a high interest rate currency from a low interest rate one, attributing the profit from the forward points to skillful currency management is wrong and misleading.[1]

Hedged versus Unhedged Returns

The returns from international investments can vary

---

[1] For further reading on performance attribution, see Denis S. Karnosky and Brian D. Singer, CFA, *Global Asset Management and Performance Attribution* (Charlottesville, VA: Research Foundation of the Institute of Chartered Financial Analysts, 1994).

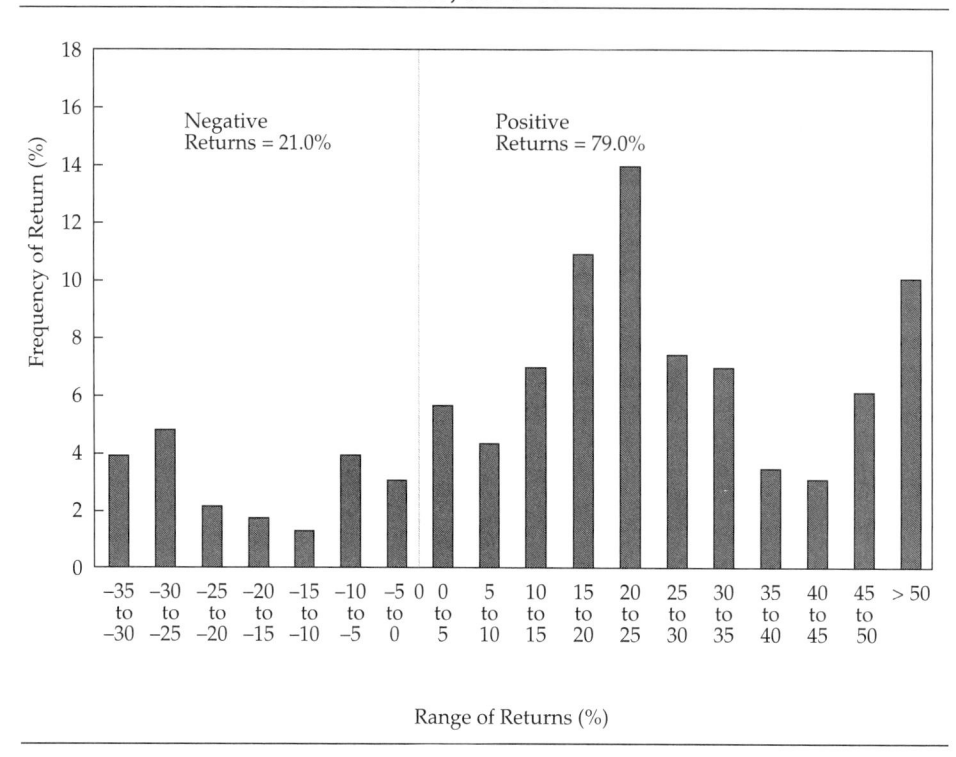

Figure 2. Distribution of Rolling Five-Year Returns from Spot Currency Moves for a U.S. Investor, 1974–97

depending on whether the currency risk has been hedged. Some examples of hedged and unhedged returns for investors in different base currencies at the single-country level demonstrate the impact that hedging can have on returns and volatility. Changing the holding period and historical data also influence returns.

Examples. One can clearly see the impact that hedging can have on returns by analyzing the returns from the perspective of a U.K. investor and from the perspective of a U.S. investor. In each of the following six examples, I have assumed that the underlying assets are invested in short-term cash deposits.

■ *U.K. investor perspective.* The first example looks at the performance of German assets during the December 1973 to December 1997 period, as shown in **Table 1**. Measuring the currency return on a spot-to-spot basis appears to show that owning German mark currency exposure earned 3.2 percent a year for the past 14 years. The hedged return, however, was considerably higher at 7.6 percent, giving a currency surprise return of –4.4 percent. Because the currency surprise is negative, the best currency decision would have been to be fully hedged during the period. The performance of the hedged strategy looks even more attractive when measured on a risk-adjusted basis,

Table 1. Hedged and Unhedged Returns and Volatility for a U.K. Investor, December 1973–December 1997

Country	Unhedged	Hedged	Currency Surprise
Germany			
Return	3.2%	7.6%	–4.4%
Risk	9.4	0.8	
Japan			
Return	5.0	5.2	–0.2
Risk	19.5	0.7	
United States			
Return	1.5	3.1	–4.6
Risk	11.5	0.8	

given that the volatility of the hedged return was 0.8 percent compared with 9.4 percent for the unhedged.

The story is similar when looking at the return on Japanese assets. Although the hedged return was only marginally higher than the unhedged return (5.2 percent versus 5.0 percent, respectively), the risk was substantially lower at 0.7 percent compared with 19.5 percent.

U.S. dollar assets looked very attractive on a hedged basis. Hedged returns were 3.1 percent a year compared with 1.5 percent for the unhedged returns.

In all three cases, the currency surprise was negative for the 14-year period. So, the best currency decision for the past 14 years would have been to avoid it. The return from the hedged assets was clearly higher.

■ *U.S. investor perspective.* For the U.S. investor, the story for hedged assets is not as compelling as it was for the U.K. investor. Turning to German assets in **Table 2**, one can see that unhedged and hedged German assets yielded roughly the same return, although the hedged assets obviously had a lower volatility and thus look more attractive on a risk-adjusted basis.

For Japanese assets, hedged assets underperformed unhedged assets, and so the currency surprise in this case is positive. Hedged assets still look quite attractive on a risk-adjusted basis.

As Table 2 indicates, the story is the same for U.K. assets. The currency surprise is also positive, but both hedged and unhedged assets show a negative return for the period.

Holding-Period Effect. Using 5-year or 10-year rolling returns can produce significantly different results from spot returns. Using data from 1974 to 1997, **Figure 3** shows the distribution of five-year rolling currency surprise returns for a U.K. investor. Compared with the spot returns, shown in Figure 1, the data show a more equal distribution of returns, both positive and negative, meaning that passively holding unhedged foreign currency exposure is not the superior strategy that many have claimed.

In addition, the *magnitude* of the cumulative return is greater than ±5 percent more than 82 percent of the time and greater than ±15 percent nearly 50 percent of the time. So, one can conclude that during five-year periods, the probability that currency returns will wash out is quite low.

By looking at an even longer holding period of 10 years, shown in **Figure 4**, one can see that only a 50 percent chance exists of the cumulative currency return being less than 10 percent in magnitude, or 1 percent a year.

Even though the majority of U.K. plans currently satisfy the minimum funding requirement (MFR) of the Pensions Act 1995, the question is, can U.K. plans afford to ignore risks of this magnitude in the years to come? The numbers show that very long holding periods are required for currency returns to have even a reasonable probability of washing out. In any case, the MFR rules will not permit plans to stay underfunded for 5-year or 10-year periods while they wait and hope that adverse currency returns will work out on their own. The choice is stark: Either reduce international asset holdings significantly, or understand, measure, and manage the currency risks associated with owning these international investments.

The statistics on currency surprise returns for U.S. investors are just as interesting as those for U.K. investors, as **Figure 5** shows. Again, using data from 1974 to 1997 and starting with the rolling five-year returns, one can see that the range of returns has been even wider than for the U.K. investor. In this case, the magnitude of the cumulative returns is greater than ±5 percent nearly 95 percent of the time and greater than ±15 percent more than 75 percent of the time.

Table 2. Hedged and Unhedged Returns and Volatility for a U.S. Investor, 1974–97

Country	Unhedged	Hedged	Currency Surprise
Germany			
Return	1.7%	1.6%	+0.1%
Risk	11.5	0.9	
Japan			
Return	3.2	2.0	+1.2
Risk	12.1	0.9	
United Kingdom			
Return	−1.4	−3.0	+1.6
Risk	11.4	0.8	

Asset Allocation in a Changing World

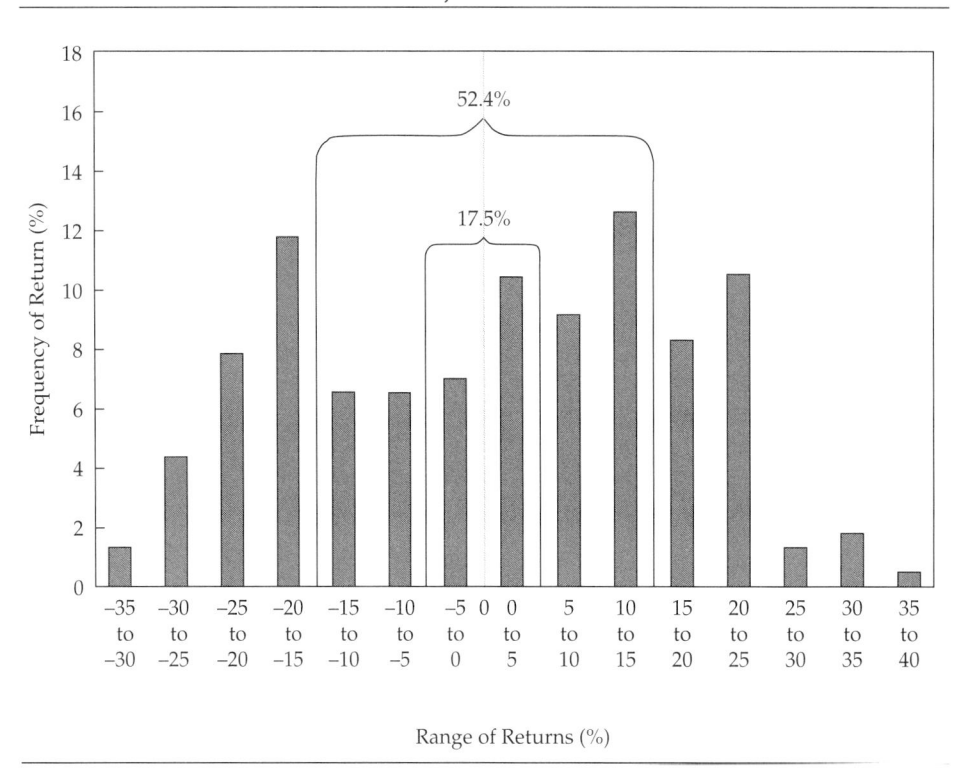

Figure 3. Distribution of Rolling Five-Year Returns from Currency Surprise Moves for U.K. Investors, 1974–97

Moving on to the 10-year rolling returns in **Figure 6**, one can see that the probability of the return being less than ±10 percent is only 23 percent. So, although U.S. funds may not be subject to MFR rules, they still face substantial risks from currency movements.

Use of Historical Data. Manager expectations for returns on underlying assets and on their respective currencies frequently differ. Given those different expectations, does it make sense to construct the underlying asset portfolio using historical data derived from unhedged asset returns? If managers are going to separate the currency and underlying asset decisions, one might wonder whether they should construct their portfolios of underlying assets using hedged data so that the currency effects are completely excluded.

To show how much difference the use of hedged versus unhedged historical data makes in an actual portfolio, I constructed correlation matrixes, shown in **Table 3** and **Table 4**, using rolling five-year returns for the seven major equity markets with both unhedged and hedged data. The tables show three time periods (ending in February 1998, February 1997, and February 1996) to demonstrate how correlation data have varied during the past three years. These differences can have a profound influence on mean–variance optimization and, ultimately, country allocations.

Figure 7 shows five-year rolling correlations of the U.K. equity market with non-U.K. equity markets as of February 1998. Although the use of hedged versus unhedged data does not appear to change the correlations much, portfolios constructed using mean–variance optimization provide different results. Assuming equal expected returns for all markets, **Figure 8** shows two optimal portfolios (hedged and unhedged) for a U.K. investor. Notice that the allocation to foreign equities increases by more than 10 percent, from 65 percent to roughly 76 percent, when using the hedged rather than the unhedged data. Also, the allocations to each market have changed significantly, particularly for the U.S. and Canadian markets. Some of the increase can be attributed to hedged foreign equities having lower volatilities than unhedged foreign equities. So, despite the fact that the correlations with the U.K. market are more or less unchanged, the changes in cross-correlations for the non-U.K. markets and their lower volatilities have been large enough to create some substantial differences between the portfolios.

The results for the U.S. investor, shown in **Figure 9**, indicate some noticeable differences in the correlations between U.S. and non-U.S. equity markets. When looking at the optimal hedged and unhedged portfolios generated in the same way as in Figure 8,

Dealing with Currencies

Figure 4. Distribution of Rolling 10-Year Returns from Currency Surprise Moves for U.K. Investors, 1974–97

one can see some differences, although they are not as large as those for the U.K. investor. As seen in **Figure 10**, the decrease in the allocation to domestic equities is not as pronounced as for the U.K. investor, but the individual holdings in foreign equities have changed substantially, particularly in the German, French, and Canadian markets. So, the changes in the correlations and volatilities have had more of an impact on changing the mix of non-U.S. equities than on their total allocation.

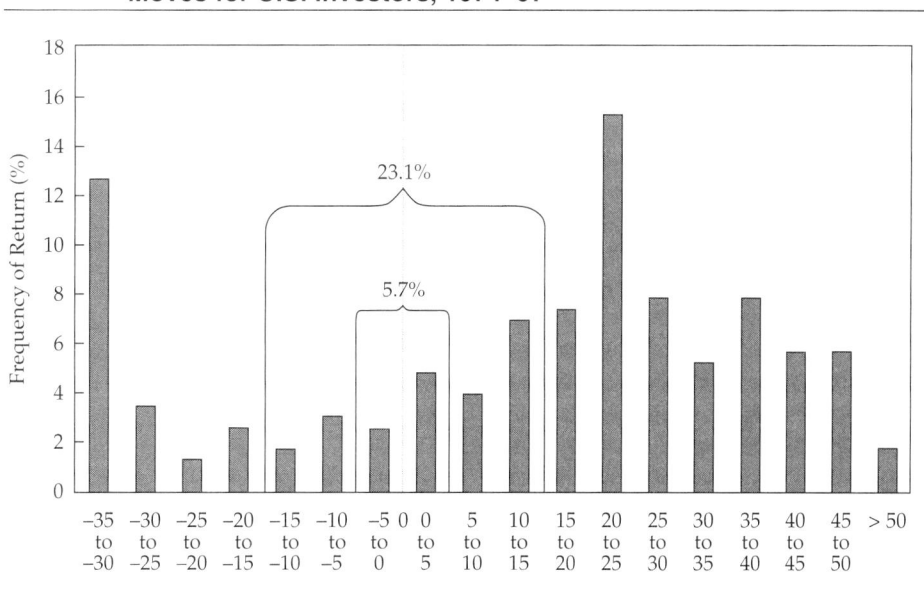

Figure 5. Distribution of Rolling Five-Year Returns from Currency Surprise Moves for U.S. Investors, 1974–97

©Association for Investment Management and Research 51

Asset Allocation in a Changing World

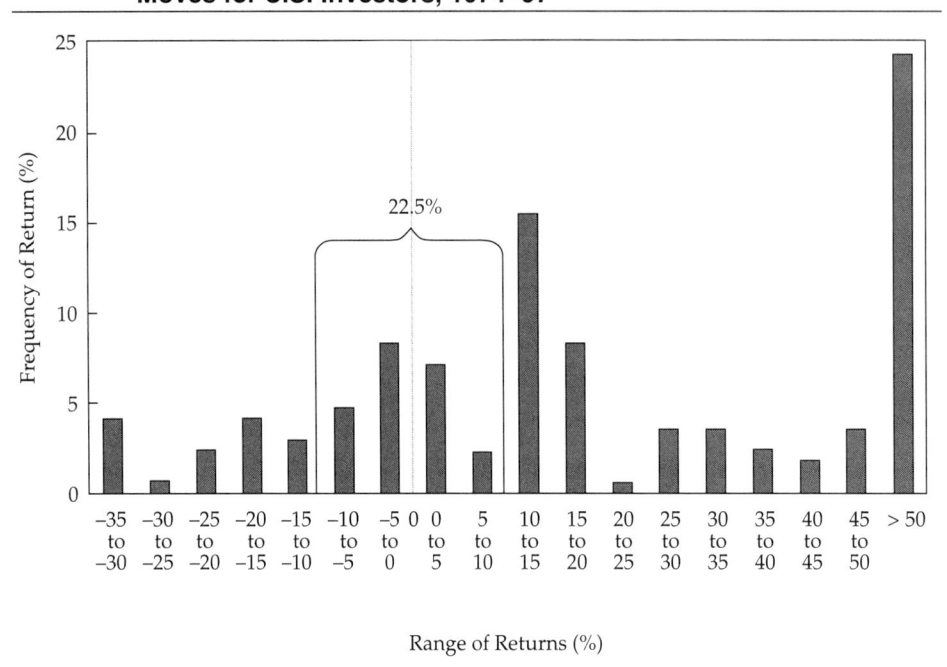

Figure 6. Distribution of Rolling 10-Year Returns from Currency Surprise Moves for U.S. Investors, 1974–97

With the hedged data, the allocations for both investors are virtually identical, which is exactly what one would expect. The allocations exclude currency effects, and thus, the optimal portfolio is the same regardless of the base currency of the investor. So, a manager should be buying the same portfolio of hedged, underlying assets for all clients in all base currencies, provided they have similar guidelines and risk profiles. Thus, using hedged rather than unhedged data makes a substantial difference to the final portfolio allocations for both U.K. and U.S. investors, but it also simplifies the asset allocation process for managers because it becomes base-currency independent.

Overlay Management

In the United States, some plans have turned to currency overlay managers to help them manage currency risks. In the United Kingdom, however, one sees very little separate currency overlay management. Nevertheless, if a plan does decide to appoint an overlay manager, the trustees are faced with the job of selecting a manager and understanding the overlay management approach.

Manager Selection. Selecting an overlay manager is a decision that many trustees find difficult. The market for overlay business is very concentrated compared with other asset classes. The top 10 firms account for more than 80 percent of overlay contracts awarded in the United States. Relatively few mandates are awarded each year, and the competition to win them is intense. Understandably, trustees have less experience with currency than other asset classes and, therefore, find it more difficult to assess the subtle differences between the various styles. We, the managers, do not make it any easier. Most of the top firms have spent years refining their marketing stories, and as one trustee said, "They all sound very plausible."

Risk Control. In the currency overlay market, managers are charged with the management of pre-existing currency risk. Risk is a word that can be defined in different ways but is most commonly used to mean volatility or the standard deviation of a series of returns. Most trustees, however, are not primarily concerned with the volatility of currency returns. Their main objective is more selective—to avoid losses from adverse currency moves. Thus, currency overlay managers interpret the expression "managing risk" to mean "avoiding losses." Therefore, the objective of most programs is to reduce exposure to foreign currency selectively. The plan wants to keep the upside risk when foreign currencies are rising and avoid the downside risk when they are falling. Consequently, the performance of the perfect overlay looks like a zero-cost option.

The payoff to such an option, shown by the Perfect Active Overlay line in **Figure 11**, provides 100 percent participation in gains from upward currency

Dealing with Currencies

Table 3. Five-Year Correlation Matrix of Equity Returns Hedged and Unhedged into U.S. Dollars

<table>
<tr><th rowspan="2">Currency</th><th colspan="7">Hedged</th><th colspan="7">Unhedged</th></tr>
<tr><th>Australian Dollar</th><th>Canadian Dollar</th><th>German Mark</th><th>French Franc</th><th>U.K. Pound</th><th>Japanese Yen</th><th>U.S. Dollar</th><th>Australian Dollar</th><th>Canadian Dollar</th><th>German Mark</th><th>French Franc</th><th>U.K. Pound</th><th>Japanese Yen</th><th>U.S. Dollar</th></tr>
<tr><td colspan="15">*Ending February 1998*</td></tr>
<tr><td>Australian dollar</td><td>100.0%</td><td>59.9%</td><td>59.5%</td><td>56.9%</td><td>71.5%</td><td>45.9%</td><td>54.3%</td><td>100.0%</td><td>58.4%</td><td>48.1%</td><td>50.4%</td><td>61.3%</td><td>51.1%</td><td>42.8%</td></tr>
<tr><td>Canadian dollar</td><td></td><td>100.0</td><td>43.7</td><td>50.7</td><td>59.9</td><td>32.2</td><td>70.6</td><td></td><td>100.0</td><td>34.4</td><td>44.1</td><td>55.9</td><td>26.7</td><td>72.0</td></tr>
<tr><td>German mark</td><td></td><td></td><td>100.0</td><td>73.7</td><td>63.3</td><td>22.8</td><td>54.7</td><td></td><td></td><td>100.0</td><td>60.2</td><td>58.2</td><td>13.5</td><td>43.7</td></tr>
<tr><td>French franc</td><td></td><td></td><td></td><td>100.0</td><td>72.1</td><td>31.6</td><td>59.5</td><td></td><td></td><td></td><td>100.0</td><td>71.3</td><td>31.6</td><td>48.8</td></tr>
<tr><td>U.K. pound</td><td></td><td></td><td></td><td></td><td>100.0</td><td>25.0</td><td>57.7</td><td></td><td></td><td></td><td></td><td>100.0</td><td>37.0</td><td>51.1</td></tr>
<tr><td>Japanese yen</td><td></td><td></td><td></td><td></td><td></td><td>100.0</td><td>27.2</td><td></td><td></td><td></td><td></td><td></td><td>100.0</td><td>17.9</td></tr>
<tr><td>U.S. dollar</td><td></td><td></td><td></td><td></td><td></td><td></td><td>100.0</td><td></td><td></td><td></td><td></td><td></td><td></td><td>100.0</td></tr>
<tr><td colspan="15">*Ending February 1997*</td></tr>
<tr><td>Australian dollar</td><td>100.0</td><td>54.8</td><td>57.5</td><td>53.9</td><td>58.5</td><td>32.6</td><td>49.4</td><td>100.0</td><td>57.7</td><td>44.3</td><td>49.0</td><td>56.9</td><td>31.9</td><td>41.0</td></tr>
<tr><td>Canadian dollar</td><td></td><td>100.0</td><td>39.3</td><td>47.4</td><td>40.5</td><td>30.1</td><td>61.9</td><td></td><td>100.0</td><td>25.1</td><td>35.1</td><td>37.8</td><td>18.7</td><td>60.5</td></tr>
<tr><td>German mark</td><td></td><td></td><td>100.0</td><td>65.9</td><td>53.1</td><td>13.7</td><td>40.1</td><td></td><td></td><td>100.0</td><td>51.2</td><td>49.9</td><td>14.7</td><td>26.5</td></tr>
<tr><td>French franc</td><td></td><td></td><td></td><td>100.0</td><td>70.9</td><td>19.9</td><td>50.3</td><td></td><td></td><td></td><td>100.0</td><td>66.9</td><td>31.2</td><td>40.7</td></tr>
<tr><td>U.K. pound</td><td></td><td></td><td></td><td></td><td>100.0</td><td>13.7</td><td>50.5</td><td></td><td></td><td></td><td></td><td>100.0</td><td>31.5</td><td>42.4</td></tr>
<tr><td>Japanese yen</td><td></td><td></td><td></td><td></td><td></td><td>100.0</td><td>16.4</td><td></td><td></td><td></td><td></td><td></td><td>100.0</td><td>4.5</td></tr>
<tr><td>U.S. dollar</td><td></td><td></td><td></td><td></td><td></td><td></td><td>100.0</td><td></td><td></td><td></td><td></td><td></td><td></td><td>100.0</td></tr>
<tr><td colspan="15">*Ending February 1996*</td></tr>
<tr><td>Australian dollar</td><td>100.0</td><td>54.6</td><td>51.3</td><td>50.8</td><td>54.1</td><td>39.9</td><td>52.2</td><td>100.0</td><td>56.2</td><td>34.6</td><td>41.6</td><td>48.5</td><td>34.7</td><td>36.8</td></tr>
<tr><td>Canadian dollar</td><td></td><td>100.0</td><td>38.8</td><td>42.8</td><td>42.2</td><td>34.2</td><td>52.5</td><td></td><td>100.0</td><td>27.5</td><td>30.5</td><td>34.3</td><td>26.1</td><td>47.1</td></tr>
<tr><td>German mark</td><td></td><td></td><td>100.0</td><td>62.3</td><td>50.1</td><td>11.1</td><td>27.4</td><td></td><td></td><td>100.0</td><td>62.5</td><td>55.8</td><td>22.2</td><td>34.8</td></tr>
<tr><td>French franc</td><td></td><td></td><td></td><td>100.0</td><td>73.4</td><td>15.8</td><td>37.8</td><td></td><td></td><td></td><td>100.0</td><td>74.8</td><td>33.2</td><td>45.3</td></tr>
<tr><td>U.K. pound</td><td></td><td></td><td></td><td></td><td>100.0</td><td>19.5</td><td>54.7</td><td></td><td></td><td></td><td></td><td>100.0</td><td>40.3</td><td>57.4</td></tr>
<tr><td>Japanese yen</td><td></td><td></td><td></td><td></td><td></td><td>100.0</td><td>18.7</td><td></td><td></td><td></td><td></td><td></td><td>100.0</td><td>13.9</td></tr>
<tr><td>U.S. dollar</td><td></td><td></td><td></td><td></td><td></td><td></td><td>100.0</td><td></td><td></td><td></td><td></td><td></td><td></td><td>100.0</td></tr>
</table>

©Association for Investment Management and Research

Table 4. Five-Year Correlation Matrix of Equity Returns Hedged and Unhedged into U.K. Pounds

Hedged

Currency	Australian Dollar	Canadian Dollar	German Mark	French Franc	U.K. Pound	Japanese Yen	U.S. Dollar
Ending February 1998							
Australian dollar	100.0%	60.0%	59.6%	57.0%	71.6%	46.2%	54.4%
Canadian dollar		100.0	43.8	50.8	60.0	32.5	70.5
German mark			100.0	73.8	63.4	23.0	54.8
French franc				100.0	72.1	31.8	59.6
U.K. pound					100.0	25.3	57.7
Japanese yen						100.0	27.4
U.S. dollar							100.0
Ending February 1997							
Australian dollar	100.0	54.3	57.0	53.5	58.3	32.5	48.9
Canadian dollar		100.0	38.1	46.8	40.0	29.8	61.0
German mark			100.0	65.5	52.5	13.1	38.8
French franc				100.0	70.7	19.6	49.7
U.K. pound					100.0	13.6	50.3
Japanese yen						100.0	15.9
U.S. dollar							100.0
Ending February 1996							
Australian dollar	100.0	54.2	51.0	50.8	53.9	39.4	51.9
Canadian dollar		100.0	38.1	42.6	41.8	33.4	51.8
German mark			100.0	62.2	49.8	10.2	26.5
French franc				100.0	73.4	15.4	37.8
U.K. pound					100.0	18.9	54.6
Japanese yen						100.0	17.7
U.S. dollar							100.0

Unhedged

Currency	Australian Dollar	Canadian Dollar	German Mark	French Franc	U.K. Pound	Japanese Yen	U.S. Dollar
Ending February 1998							
Australian dollar	100.0%	66.3%	56.1%	57.6%	70.2%	50.5%	55.4%
Canadian dollar		100.0	47.8	54.5	64.9	26.3	80.3
German mark			100.0	65.8	63.7	11.4	56.5
French franc				100.0	75.0	28.4	59.3
U.K. pound					100.0	29.6	60.9
Japanese yen						100.0	18.8
U.S. dollar							100.0
Ending February 1997							
Australian dollar	100.0	67.7	55.2	59.6	65.2	35.6	58.3
Canadian dollar		100.0	45.9	53.2	48.3	25.3	77.5
German mark			100.0	61.8	51.8	15.8	54.3
French franc				100.0	72.0	33.4	62.7
U.K. pound					100.0	27.0	56.5
Japanese yen						100.0	20.5
U.S. dollar							100.0
Ending February 1996							
Australian dollar	100.0	69.5	42.8	50.9	57.4	35.9	58.7
Canadian dollar		100.0	40.8	45.1	42.3	28.4	74.0
German mark			100.0	61.7	47.4	11.5	44.4
French franc				100.0	72.4	26.5	55.1
U.K. pound					100.0	28.9	57.6
Japanese yen						100.0	19.2
U.S. dollar							100.0

Dealing with Currencies

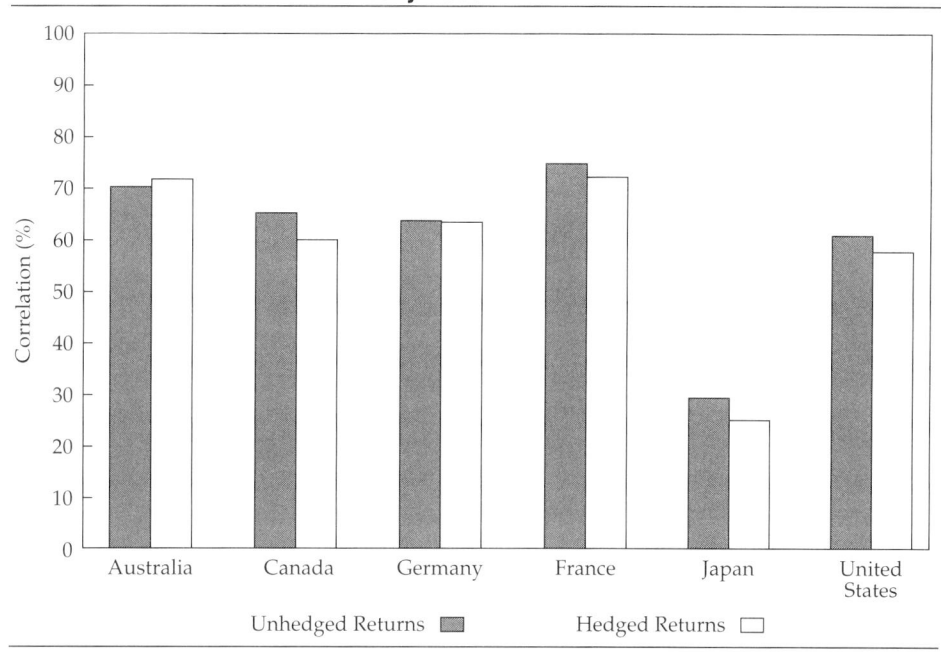

Figure 7. Five-Year Rolling Correlations between U.K. and Non-U.K. Equity Markets as of February 1998

moves and 100 percent protection from losses during downward moves. Despite the different philosophical styles of overlay managers, they all, in their own way, are seeking to achieve as closely as possible the payoff of this zero-cost option. The diagonal line labeled Underlying Assets shows the payoff from unhedged currency exposure. If the currency falls, the investor realizes a loss, and if it rises, he or she realizes a profit. One could protect against the downside by simply buying an at-the-money put option (the line labeled Option/Option Replication Strategy in Figure 11) on the foreign currencies, but for the vast majority of the time, this approach turns out to be an expensive way of avoiding losses. We overlay managers cannot guarantee the perfect payoff, but we have generally managed to outperform the passive strategy of buying and holding an option by capitalizing on inefficiencies.

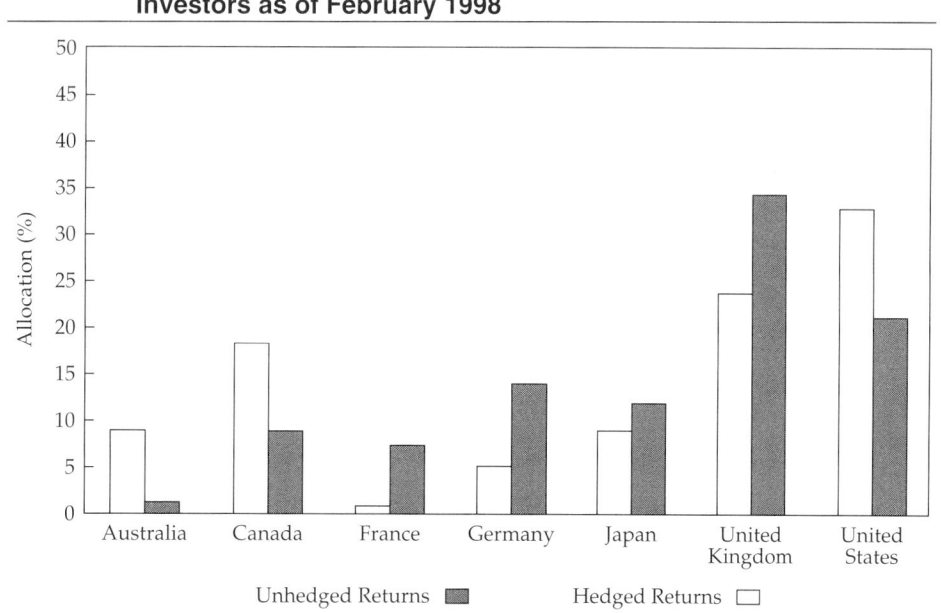

Figure 8. Optimal Portfolios of Hedged and Unhedged Equities for U.K. Investors as of February 1998

©Association for Investment Management and Research

Asset Allocation in a Changing World

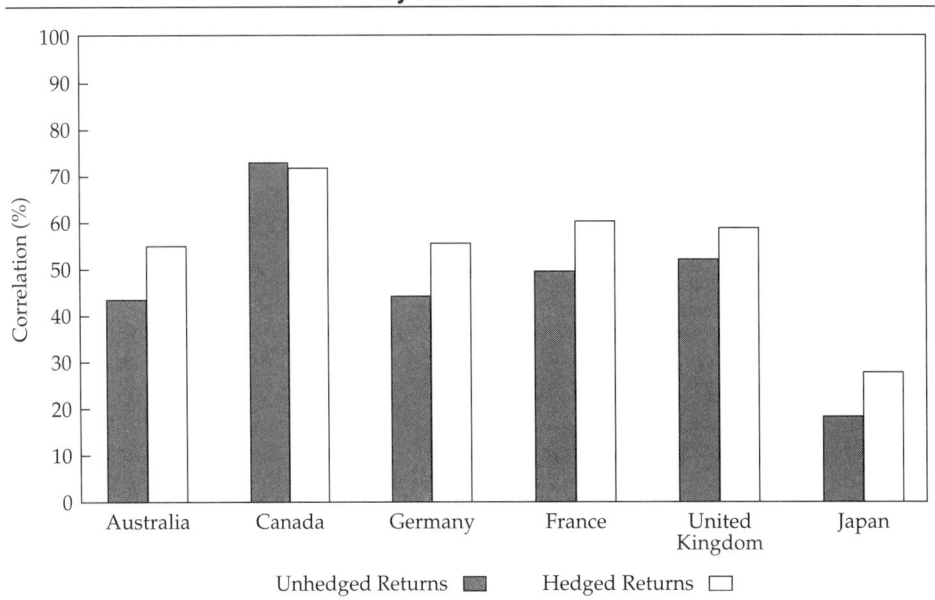

Figure 9. Five-Year Rolling Correlations between U.S. and Non-U.S. Equity Markets as of February 1998

Capitalizing on Inefficiencies. Active managers can identify and capitalize on inefficiencies in the foreign exchange market. The vast majority of managers use one of two sources. The first source is the nonrandom pattern of currency returns, which leads to clearly observable trends and other statistically identifiable patterns in measures such as volatility. This type of modeling is not founded on any economic theory but is by nature empirical, and the structure of the models will be driven purely by the statistical properties of the historical data. Critics of these technical trading approaches have been predicting their demise for years, claiming that increasing efficiency in the markets will eliminate these opportunities. The reality, however, is quite the opposite. More, rather than fewer, distinct trends have arisen in the past three years, and the market shows no sign of losing these characteristics.

The second source of "inefficiency" is the use of fundamental or macroeconomic data to predict cur-

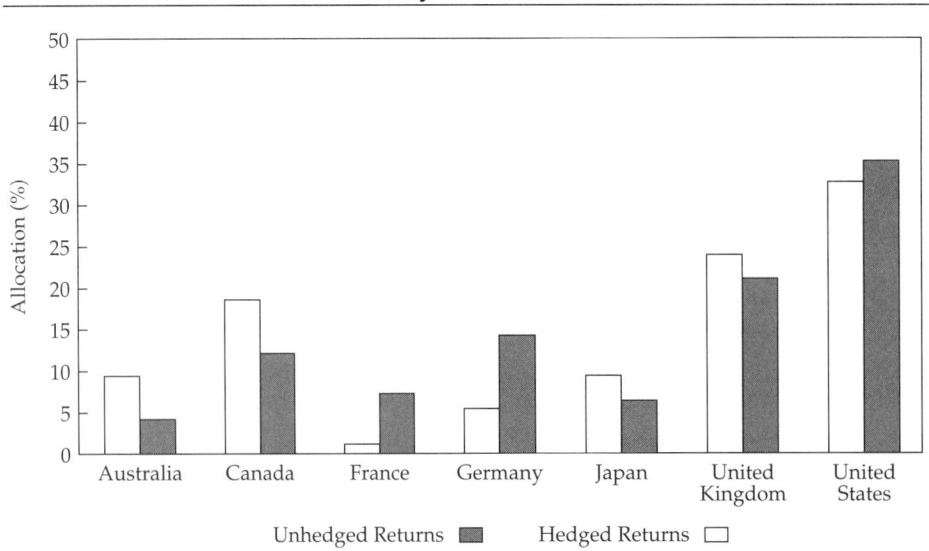

Figure 10. Optimal Portfolios of Hedged and Unhedged Equities for U.S. Investors as of February 1998

56 ©Association for Investment Management and Research

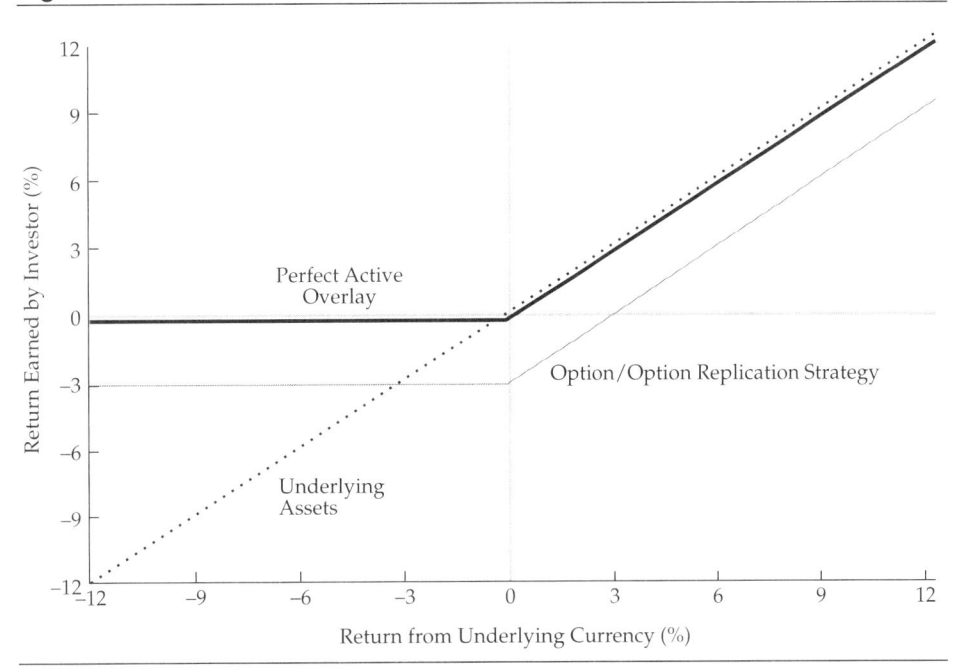

Figure 11. Active and Informationless Strategies

rency movements. This type of approach has the advantage that models can be based on economic theory. Theories such as purchasing power parity, the balance of payments model, and others postulate causality between exchange rate movements and macroeconomic factors. The use of these factors in currency models does create other challenges. For example, some data are available only monthly, but models and portfolios tend to have investment horizons that are longer term in nature.

Management Style. Broadly speaking, overlay management comes in two styles. Both styles attempt to capture one or more of the inefficiencies previously described. The first style has its origins in dynamic hedging, sometimes known as option replication, in which the level of hedging is increased as the exchange rate falls and decreased as it rises. The payoff of these strategies is asymmetric, similar to an option, but depends on how volatile prices are during the life of the strategy and also the degree of trending in prices. These strategies perform best when volatility is low and prices trend. Some managers who use this type of strategy also generate their own forecasts of factors such as volatility and skew. Additionally, some managers use several models in their processes, with each one focusing on a different time horizon. Regardless of the number of variables being forecasted in these types of strategies, all are based on technical analysis, in which the sole source of information is the historical price series of the exchange rate data.

The second style of overlay management forecasts the direction and/or magnitude of returns to determine the level of hedging required. The philosophy of this style relies on both fundamental and technical approaches for modeling exchange rate returns. In these strategies, technical analysis is used to identify trends and to measure price acceleration. Measures of price acceleration are useful because acceleration has mean-reverting properties. If an exchange rate reaches a high level, it always declines subsequently; therefore, it has the potential to be forecasted. Most of these types of indicators are directional, and the level of hedging can be adjusted to reflect the strength of, or degree of confidence in, the trend.

The second approach within this style models fundamental data. Most of the econometric theories previously described are used by one or more overlay managers. They can be very useful in identifying currencies that are grossly overvalued or undervalued, although the manager needs to have a mechanism to avoid buying a cheap currency that is still declining. This mechanism is needed because the signals from fundamental approaches tend to be leading indicators, which is the opposite of technical approaches (i.e., their signals are lagging indicators). The complementary nature of the two approaches means that most managers in this group use some combination of the two.

Managers are sometimes tempted to undermine the approach used by a competitor, citing academic articles as "evidence" of the folly of following such an approach. This practice should be treated with a degree of skepticism. Academic articles can be useful and have often opened up whole new areas of knowledge (e.g., modern portfolio theory), but these revelations tend to be general techniques rather than specific strategies. I would be very surprised if the details of an original and genuinely profitable strategy were openly published. In all likelihood, the authors would use it for their own benefit. Most successful managers devote considerable resources to researching and developing proprietary models with some competitive edge. So, one should not dismiss an approach used by an experienced manager just because some academics find that one simple application of the approach appears not to work. In fact, in many cases, subsequent articles justify the validity of a variation of an approach that was previously criticized. It clearly would be illogical to ignore a manager who had added value consistently because so-called academic wisdom holds the approach to be flawed.

Manager Considerations. If plan sponsors are thinking of hiring an overlay manager, they should really dig deep into the investment process and understand its workings. Some plan sponsors feel a degree of discomfort with quantitative processes, the so-called black boxes of the investment world. An experienced manager should be able to demonstrate that the black box is really a glass box. The investment process should be sufficiently transparent that the client can see how it works and how the inputs are analyzed and translated into hedging decisions for the portfolio. This transparency should leave a potential client with a feeling of comfort. Obviously, other considerations, such as strength and depth in the investment team, performance, and organizational stability, will also play a part in the decision-making process.

Conclusion

Before making a decision on how to manage currency risk, plan sponsors need to be able to break down and attribute performance in their global portfolios. They need to understand the impact of currency on their portfolios and assess how it will affect the plan's ability to meet its investment objectives. Pension plans need to be aware that they may not be able to wait a long time for adverse currency returns to wash out.

This analysis should lead to the selection of a strategic hedge ratio that is consistent with the other strategic allocations. Once the strategic hedge ratio has been determined, the plan sponsor can decide whether to use an active currency manager.

Selecting a currency overlay manager can be a problem for plan sponsors because of the difficulty of distinguishing among different overlay management styles. The important point to consider in dealing with currency risk is that the approach to managing currency risk and the objectives should fit well with the nature of the plan's liabilities.

Are U.K. Investors Turning More Conservative?

Martyn Hole, CFA
Managing Director, International Equity and Balanced Group
J.P. Morgan Investment Management

> Actuarial issues, historical effects, supply and demand, uncontrollable factors, and deliberate decisions contribute to the significantly high equity exposure for U.K. pension funds. But the introduction of the minimum funding requirement, plans' funding statuses, return expectations, and abolition of the Advance Corporation Tax credit may have led U.K. funds to take a conservative asset allocation strategy during the past few years—shifting assets from equities into fixed-income securities and cash. Anticipation of the European Monetary Union and pessimistic market views may also contribute to a conservative approach to equities, but whether U.K. investors are becoming more conservative is an open question.

Money managers are beginning to ask themselves whether U.K. investors are becoming more conservative. Of course, answering that question requires a definition of the word conservative. First, being conservative can be defined by attitude toward risk, but risk itself has a number of definitions. Risk can obviously be measured as the volatility of absolute returns. Investors might look at the equity–bond mix of their portfolios and move more toward fixed-income securities to lower the volatility of their absolute returns. But risk can also be seen as tracking error against some benchmark, as the possibility of not meeting liabilities, and as the chance of not meeting some statutory or regulatory requirement, such as the minimum funding requirement (MFR) in the Pensions Act 1995.

Second, being conservative can be defined by investment style. For the U.K. pension market, the conservative investment style is a traditional balanced manager approach. U.K. fund sponsors seem to be moving away from that conservative model. Typically, pension funds have had their portfolios managed in an active way, and now, some funds are moving away from active into passive management. In addition, some leading money managers are losing out to boutique-type firms.

This presentation focuses on the first definition of conservatism—risk—and addresses four main issues: where U.K. funds are today in terms of asset allocation, the reasons U.K. asset allocations differ from those in other countries, the causes of changes in asset allocations, and likely future developments.

U.K. Funds Today

U.K. funds have a high allocation to equities. **Table 1** shows the CAPS weighted-average distribution for U.K. pension funds. At the end of 1997, a typical U.K. pension fund had about 55 percent in U.K. equities and 18 percent in international equities, with only 25 percent in fixed income. The 1997 total equity weighting (73 percent) was actually slightly lower than in 1996 (76 percent); the reduction from 21 percent to 18 percent for international equities is largely explained by the declining prices of equities in the Pacific Basin ex-Japan.

Compared with other countries, the United Kingdom has one of the highest equity exposures. **Figure 1** shows the total equity exposures, separated into domestic and international allocations, for various countries.

Reasons for Differences

These differences among asset allocations in the United Kingdom and other countries are driven by a number of factors. First, financial factors may be affecting the asset allocation because of the nature of the liabilities. If liabilities are measured in real

Table 1. U.K. Asset Allocation

Asset	1996	1997
U.K. equities	55%	55%
International equities	21	18
Total	76%	73%
U.K. conventional bonds	6%	7%
Index-linked gilts	3	2
International bonds	5	6
Cash	8	10
Total	22%	25%
Property	2%	2%

Source: Based on weighted-average asset distribution data from CAPS Ltd.'s *1997 Pension Fund Statistics*.

terms rather than nominal terms, the investor might feel pressure to hold real assets, such as equities and real estate. For example, in the United Kingdom, postretirement benefits must rise by the lower of inflation or 5 percent, effectively introducing an element of indexation that is not present in some other countries' pension systems.

Second, legal, accounting, or actuarial factors may explain the differences. Some countries have restrictions on the amount of money that can be invested in certain asset classes, particularly in terms of the split between domestic and international. Legislative changes are occurring, however, that are loosening some of the restrictions that investors have faced in terms of where they can put their money. Also, sometimes the way assets and liabilities are measured by funds can influence the overall asset allocation within a country.

Third, cultural and historical factors play a part in asset allocation differences. For example, in the United Kingdom, many pension funds use the consensus asset allocation as their benchmark. They are less interested in benchmarks derived from an efficient frontier analysis or from asset/liability modeling; rather, they want to know and track the asset allocation and performance of the CAPS average or some other peer-group average or median. So, peer pressure can be very strong, as can be the so-called cult of equity. The belief that equity is the asset of choice is certainly well established in most Anglo-Saxon markets.

Sometimes factors that are completely out of the average pension fund's control can affect how asset allocations differ, and taxation is one such factor. Until very recently, for instance, U.K. pension funds realized some quite strong fiscal advantages from owning equities because of tax rules.

Finally, basic supply and demand can affect asset allocation. Sometimes the availability of assets determines to a large degree what pension funds and insurance companies can own.

Figure 1. Total Equity Allocation Broken into Domestic and International Allocations for Various Countries, December 1996

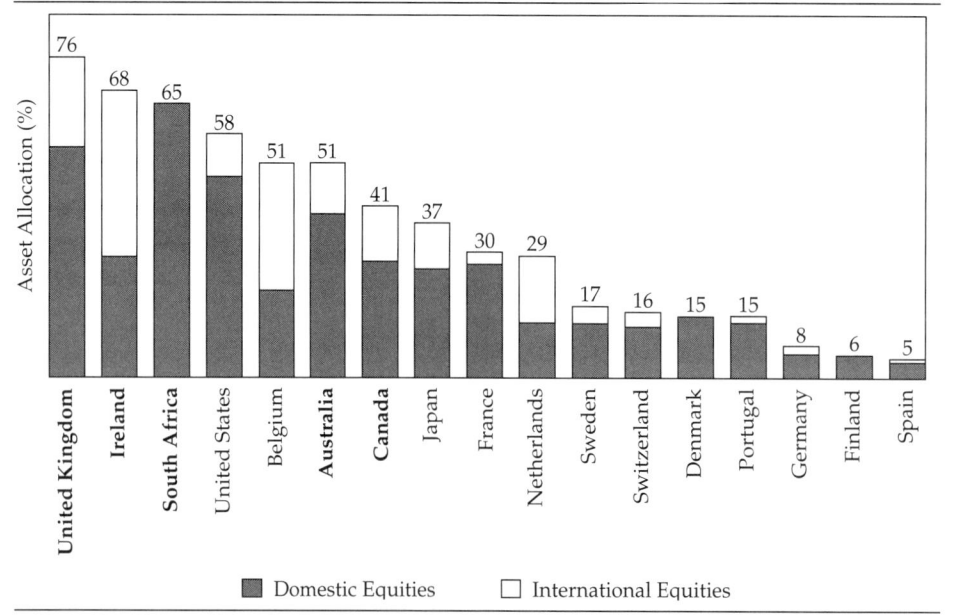

Country	Total
United Kingdom	76
Ireland	68
South Africa	65
United States	58
Belgium	51
Australia	51
Canada	41
Japan	37
France	30
Netherlands	29
Sweden	17
Switzerland	16
Denmark	15
Portugal	15
Germany	8
Finland	6
Spain	5

Note: Country names in bold indicate those countries that use the United Kingdom's actuarial assessed value approach of smoothed assets and liabilities.

Sources: Based on data from CAPS Ltd., Watson Wyatt Worldwide, InterSec Research Corporation, and Goldman, Sachs & Company.

Some of the reasons for the differences in asset allocation bear additional examination, particularly actuarial issues, historical effects, supply and demand, uncontrollable factors, and deliberate decisions by fund managers.

Actuarial Issues. Figure 1 helps to illustrate an interesting actuarial issue. Of the seven highest equity exposures shown in Figure 1, all but the United States and Belgium have an actuarial approach similar to that used in the United Kingdom, an approach that focuses on smoothing the volatility of the assets and the liabilities. Perhaps because these funds are looking at a measure of risk that uses smoothed data, rather than the very volatile data from market values, they have a tendency to have more money invested in equities than those funds that do not use smoothed data.

Historical Effects. The level of equity allocation and historical inflation appear to be linked, as shown in **Figure 2**. Countries that have experienced poor inflation performance during the past several years have a high exposure to equities. That finding should not be surprising; if a country has a problem with inflation, investors want to own real assets rather than nominal assets and, therefore, have high exposures to equities.

The "I told you so" argument also carries some historical significance. The data shown in **Figure 3** indicate the strong relationship between equity allo-

Figure 2. Asset Allocation as of the End of 1997 and Inflation for the 1980–97 Period

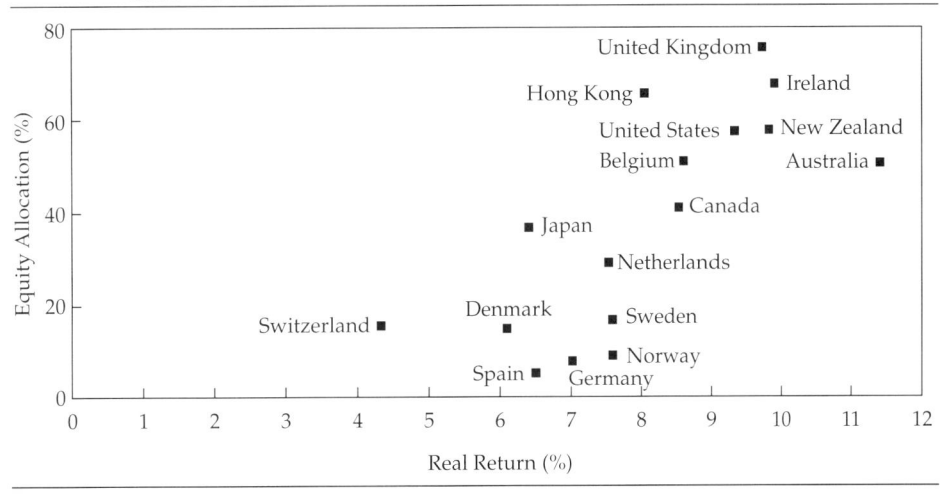

Figure 3. Asset Allocation as of the End of 1997 and Real Returns for the 1980–97 Period

cations and real return performance for the past several years. By having a high equity allocation, pensions funds in the U.K. and in other countries have achieved high real returns.

Supply and Demand. The potential impact of supply and demand on asset allocation is shown in **Table 2**. In the United Kingdom, the equity market is almost two and a half times as big as the bond market. At the other extreme are Italy and Germany, where the equity markets are only about one-fifth the size of the bond market. Sometimes the available investments can influence how assets are allocated, particularly in the case of a country such as the United Kingdom, where institutional investors dominate the equity market. Institutional investor dominance clearly does not exist in countries such as Germany and Italy, but nonetheless, the effect of supply and demand on asset allocation can be quite important.

Table 2. Market Capitalizations, December 31, 1996 (US$ billions)

Country	Equity	Bond[a]	Equity/Bond
United Kingdom	$1,740	$708	2.44
Australia	306	165	1.85
Switzerland	407	243	1.67
Netherlands	393	243	1.61
United States	7,836	10,018	0.78
Japan	3,071	4,626	0.66
France	601	1,057	0.57
Germany	648	3,132	0.21
Italy	253	1,297	0.19

[a]Includes corporate debt.
Sources: Based on data from Morgan Stanley Capital International and Salomon Brothers.

The question of supply and demand becomes particularly important in the context of the European Monetary Union. The expectation is that at some stage, the United Kingdom will become a member of the EMU, probably by 2002 or 2003. Thus, many people are starting to argue that in terms of equity benchmarks, U.K. investors should be looking at a Pan-European equity benchmark, rather than having a U.K. and an ex-U.K. benchmark. Consider the impact that such a change would have. At present, the average U.K. pension fund has about five times as much invested in U.K. equities as in European equities. Were allocations to move to a market-capitalization-weighted basis but with the overall amount in Pan-European (including the U.K.) equities staying the same, the proportions would shift to one third in the United Kingdom and two thirds in the rest of Europe. Some recent research has suggested that this change would result in the biggest program trade in history, with U.K. institutions selling US$250 billion of U.K. equities and buying a similar amount in European equities. But Table 2 and other market capitalization and capital flow data suggest that this hypothesis does not appear to be credible. Creating a Pan-European benchmark is likely to be a slow process because the supply of equity simply does not exist. Consider the relative sizes of European equity markets: Measured as a percentage of GNP, the U.K. stock market is worth a good bit more than 100 percent of GNP; the figure for Germany is roughly 50 percent, and for other European countries, it is similar. These data do not imply that the U.K. equity market is more highly valued than those other markets. The difference comes mainly from the fact that in Germany and many other European countries, an enormous number of companies are not quoted either because they are privately held (for example, the Mittelstand companies) or because they continue to be controlled by the government. As privatization continues and more companies come to the market, which should occur over time, the supply of equities will increase in these countries that traditionally have had a bond market orientation.

Uncontrollable Factors. Sometimes the overall asset allocation picture is driven by events that are largely out of the control of the funds themselves. **Figure 4** shows what has happened to the asset allocation of U.K. pension funds during the past 18 years. For example, the exposure to international equities grew sharply during the early 1980s. That growth was a function of the abolition of exchange controls. Also, domestic fixed income shrank quite rapidly during the late 1980s because the U.K. government was running a fiscal surplus and the supply of U.K. gilts was shrinking rapidly, a factor over which the typical pension fund had absolutely no control. At the same time the U.K. fixed-income allocation was shrinking, the international bond allocation was expanding, perhaps to compensate for the drop in domestic fixed income. Finally, cash exposure increased in the late 1980s, particularly after the 1987 crash. In recent times, the level of cash within institutional pension funds has been rising quite rapidly, which likely reflects the bearishness that some leading fund managers have about equities. Ironically, however, if liabilities are being measured in real terms, cash is probably the highest-risk asset a manager can hold.

Deliberate Decisions. On the surface, not many differences exist between the actual U.K. asset allocations in 1994 and 1997. **Table 3** shows that the international equity allocation fell by about 4 percent-

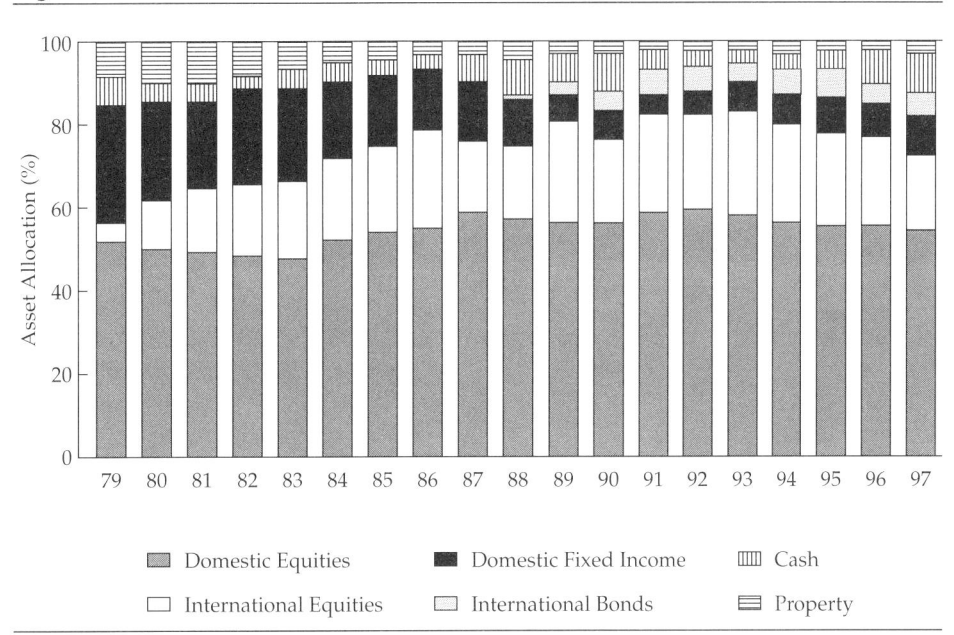

Figure 4. U.K. Pension Fund Asset Allocation, 1979–97

age points and U.K. fixed income rose by 4 percentage points. The interesting question is how many of these decisions were deliberate and how many simply reflect allowing the asset allocation at the beginning of the period to drift in line with market performance. The column for the weighted-average annual returns for that three-year period, for instance, shows strong returns from U.K., U.S., and European equities but poor returns from Japan, the Pacific Rim, and emerging markets.

To see if pension funds were simply letting their asset allocations move with the market, one can calculate what the allocation would have been if a buy-and-hold strategy had been followed. The first step is to take the asset allocation at the end of 1994. Then, take the performance of each asset class over the subsequent three years and calculate the implied weightings that would have resulted from these market movements assuming *no* rebalancing during this three-year period. These final simulated weights are shown in the "Implied Allocations" column. These implied allocations are substantially different from the actual allocations. If funds had let their allocations simply drift with the market, the allocation to equities in the United Kingdom would have been 8 percentage points higher than the actual allocation. So, quite a lot of selling of U.K. equities took place over this period. In addition, the U.S. exposure is much less—3 percentage points—and the exposures to fixed income and cash are substantially greater than what would have been implied by the movements in the markets. The "Net Change" column strongly suggests that funds have not simply been

Table 3. U.K. Asset Allocations and Weighted-Average Annual Returns

Asset	Actual Allocations End 1994	Actual Allocations End 1997	Weighted-Average Annualized Return	Implied Allocations End 1997	Net Change[a]
U.K. equities	55%	54%	21.0%	62%	–8
International equities	23	19	8.5	19	0
United States	5	3	26.6	6	–3
Europe ex-United Kingdom	8	10	19.1	9	+1
Japan	5	3	–12.8	2	+1
Pacific Rim ex-Japan	4	2	–6.5	2	0
Emerging markets	1	1	–2.5	—	+1
U.K. fixed income	5	9	14.0	5	+4
U.K. index-linked gilts	5	5	10.7	4	+1
International fixed income	4	4	6.6	3	+1
Cash and other	4	7	6.1	3	+4
Property	4	3	8.8	4	–1

[a]Net change from implied to actual allocations for the end of 1997.
Source: Based on CAPS Ltd. weighted-average fund data.

allowing their asset allocations to drift with the market. They have moved toward "more conservative" assets by selling equities and switching into fixed income and cash.

Causes of Change

U.K. investors have undertaken these recent asset allocation changes (i.e., moving somewhat out of equities and into fixed income and cash) in response to, among many possible influences, four major factors:
- The introduction of the MFR.
- The abolition of the Advance Corporation Tax (ACT) credit.
- Anticipation of EMU.
- Pessimistic market views by some market participants.

Introduction of the MFR. The MFR was introduced in the Pensions Act 1995 and became effective in early 1997. The basic strictures are that a plan's assets may be no less than its accrued liabilities, that trustees must obtain an MFR valuation every three years, and that if assets fall below 90 percent of liabilities, then the plan sponsor has to make short-term contributions. So, the MFR could potentially introduce an additional constraint on the activities of U.K. pension funds.

■ *Valuing assets and liabilities*. To determine compliance with the MFR, asset values are taken to be those given in a plan's accounts. Liabilities, however, are measured (or modeled) slightly differently. For pensioners, if the liabilities are stated in nominal terms, the benchmark is the long-term government gilt. If the liabilities are stated in real terms, then the benchmark is modeled using the index-linked gilt.

For nonpensioners, the calculation is a bit more complicated. For nonpensioners who are more than 10 years from retirement, effectively the plan must use U.K. equities as the modeling tool, with the assumption that equities will yield a 9 percent return. For nonpensioners who are less than 10 years away from retirement, the benchmark is a progressive mixture between equities and gilts. The fact that all of these liability measures are domestic may cause some problems in the future with respect to risk levels.

■ *Funding status*. The 1997 National Association of Pension Funds (NAPF) annual survey of the MFR positions of private and public U.K. pension funds is shown in **Table 4**. The weighted-average MFR valuation (assets as a percentage of liabilities) for the 237 responding U.K. private pension funds was about 125 percent. The majority (64 percent) of private funds reported MFR valuations in the 100–129 percent range. A higher response rate from public funds would likely have revealed a higher percentage of poorly funded plans; public pension funds, particularly in the local authority area, are much less well funded than those in the private sector. For the six public funds that responded, the average funding level was 105 percent. Although public funds are exempt from some of the MFR regulations that apply to the private funds, their funding level is important in relation to the ACT credit abolition.

Table 4. Percentage of Responding Private and Public Funds' MFR Funding Status

MFR Funding Level[a]	Private[b]	Public
Less than 90%	—	34%
90%–99%	1%	—
100%–109%	26	33
110%–119%	16	—
120%–129%	22	—
130%–139%	9	33
140%–149%	8	—
More than 150%	15	—

Note: Number of replies for private funds = 237; number of replies for public funds = 6.
[a] Assets as a percentage of liabilities.
[b] Does not total 100 percent because of rounding.
Source: Based on data from the *NAPF 1997 Annual Survey*.

■ *MFR return expectations*. The MFR establishes return expectations for calculating plan liabilities. **Table 5** shows a hypothetical plan that in order to meet its MFR liabilities allocated 60 percent to equities

Table 5. MFR and Average Fund Returns, March 31, 1997, through December 31, 1997

Asset	Allocation[a]	MFR Return	Average Fund Return
Equities	60%	20.2%	17.0%
Index-linked gilts	20	7.7	13.5
Fixed income	20	17.0	15.2
Overall (liability weighted)		17.1	15.9
Overall (actual median)		17.1	11.0

[a] As of April 1, 1997.
Source: Based on data from Bacon & Woodrow and CAPS Ltd.

(i.e., for beneficiaries who had not retired), 20 percent to index-linked gilts, and 20 percent to fixed income. The MFR-required returns that should have been achieved in the nine months ending December 1997 are 20.2 percent for U.K. equities, 7.7 percent for index-linked gilts, and 17 percent for fixed income.

The MFR-required returns are calculated in the following way. The 20.2 percent for equities shown in Table 5 effectively consists of two elements: rate of return and dividend yield. The expectation is that equities will earn a 9 percent return on an ongoing basis, so for three-quarters of the year, that amount becomes a required return of 6.75 percent (75 percent of 9 percent). On March 31, 1997, the dividend yield on the U.K. stock market, as measured by the FTA (Financial Times Actuaries) All-Share Index, was 3.64 percent. By December 31, 1997, it had fallen to 3.23 percent. When calculating the MFR-required return, the ratio of beginning and ending dividend yields is multiplied by the required return, 6.75 percent in this case. Thus,

$$\begin{aligned}\text{MFR return for equities} &= (3.64/3.23) \times 1.0675 \\ &= 1.127 \times 1.0675 \\ &= 1.202 \\ &= 20.2\%.\end{aligned}$$

The average fund shown in Table 5 did not do well in 1997. It achieved only a 17 percent return for equities, essentially because stock selection was poor, and therefore, the average manager underperformed the benchmark. For index-linked gilts, the average fund outperformed the MFR benchmark, but in fixed income, the average fund was slightly below the MFR benchmark. The liability-weighted total return for the average fund was 15.9 percent, compared with 17.1 percent for the MFR return. Overall, on a liability-weighted basis, the major negative was the fact that the performance on the equity side was below the MFR-required return. These liability-weighted returns reflect what this hypothetical fund would have earned had it been invested 60/20/20, but an actual average fund probably did not have those allocations and, in fact, might have looked more like the median fund. Performance for the median fund, however, was particularly bleak, returning only 11 percent compared with the MFR-required return of 17.1 percent.

Clearly, returns will vary from one fund to another. But having the MFR benchmarks should bring home to plan sponsors the fact that they need to think about their individual situations and circumstances, rather than worry about what other funds are doing in terms of consensus allocations.

Problems with MFR assumptions. In 1997, dividend growth was slow in the United Kingdom. The MFR assumption is that equities will return 9 percent over the long term, and the implication is that a certain rate of dividend growth will be achieved. Between March 31, 1997, and December 31, 1997, dividends in the United Kingdom, as measured by the FTA All-Share Index, grew by less than 2 percent. What seems to be happening in the United Kingdom is a change of corporate behavior. Companies are starting to use share buybacks much more actively than they have in the past, and dividend growth seems to have slowed down.

An additional problem is that the MFR liability calculations are based entirely on domestic assets. In 1997, the performance of international equities and bonds was depressed because of the weak performance from Far East markets and strong performance from the U.K. pound, which depressed the returns from international assets. The argument that many people put forward is that international assets are good because they are diversifiers, but in 1997, international assets did not work in investors' favor from an MFR perspective. In fact, from an MFR perspective, international markets could be considered risky.

One solution to these problems is to change the MFR rules. Another solution is for investors to reduce their international weightings. Finally, investors could strategically hedge the currency exposure back into U.K. pounds, which would reduce the risk from a U.K. perspective.

Abolition of ACT Credit. The idea behind the ACT credit was that it would avoid double taxation of dividends. Prior to 1997, if a company paid out £1 of net cash dividends, the U.K. tax authorities viewed the payout as being net of a 20 percent ACT. Therefore, pretax, the dividend was considered to be worth £1.25. Gross or tax-free institutions were able to reclaim that ACT credit, which resulted in a substantial uplift to the value of the dividend stream. For a few investors, the credit will apply until 1999, but for most investors, that credit no longer applies after 1997.

The implications of abolishing this credit are important. First, the gross value of dividends to tax-free institutions will be reduced by 20 percent. For the local authorities, which in many cases are not well funded, this reduction in the value of dividends is a dramatic effect. Consider a fund with £500 million invested in U.K. equities. Assuming a gross dividend yield of 3 percent, the effect of the ACT abolition would be to reduce the cash income from U.K. equities by £3 million per annum. Both public and private plan sponsors have already voiced serious concerns about the impact that abolishing the ACT credit will have on their overall pension fund returns. **Table 6** shows data from the NAPF 1997 annual survey on

Table 6. Percentage of Respondents Indicating Expected Effect of Abolishing the ACT Credit

Effect	Private Funds	Public Funds
Increased employer costs	88%	97%
Increased employee contributions	13	7
Reduced benefits	13	—
Reduced security	19	2

Note: Number of respondents for private funds = 471; number of respondents for public funds = 58.

Source: Based on data from the *NAPF 1997 Annual Survey*.

the reactions from roughly 500 pension funds, both public and private, on abolishing the ACT credit. Both types of funds see this change as having a major negative impact on their future costs, which will be a greater burden for the typically less-well-funded public funds.

Second, abolishing the ACT credit will reduce the attractiveness of U.K. equities relative to fixed income and international assets because the expected return has been reduced. The Frank Russell Company expects that abolishing the ACT credit will reduce the expected return on U.K. equities by as much as 70 basis points (bps) a year. Thus, abolishing the ACT credit will have a major impact on overall expected returns.

Third, abolishing the ACT credit will encourage a fundamental reappraisal of the balance sheets of U.K. companies. Paying out large dividends is, perhaps, no longer the fiscally most attractive or optimal way of returning value to shareholders. Therefore, companies will likely use more share repurchases than they have in the past and probably will move to increased balance sheet leverage.

One of the implications of this move is the potential development of a new asset class in the United Kingdom, corporate debt. The amount of corporate debt outstanding at the moment is limited. In **Table 7**, the current corporate debt structure in the United Kingdom is compared with those in continental Europe and the United States. The difference in leverage among these groups of companies is striking. In the United Kingdom, the net debt-to-equity position is about 30 percent. In continental Europe and the United States, the ratio is 63 percent and 66 percent, respectively. Similarly, U.K. pretax interest coverage is nearly two to three times that of the other groups. (Some may argue that these comparisons are distorted by differences in accounting systems. Although the accounting systems do differ, were the accounts to be reported on a common set of accounting principles, the differences could well be even larger. For example, in the United Kingdom, goodwill from an acquisition is written off immediately, but in the United States, it is amortized over a period of time, thereby depressing published shareholder funds or net equity in the United Kingdom relative to the United States and elsewhere.)

These statistics indicate that corporate balance sheets in the United Kingdom are substantially less debt laden than those in continental Europe and the United States. If the United Kingdom moves in the direction of more-leveraged balance sheets, the equity supply in the United Kingdom may shrink by as much as £100 billion and the supply of debt may expand by a similar amount. In March 1998, several U.K. companies announced share buybacks, some of which were very large, in the £1 billion to £2 billion range.

So, abolition of the ACT credit may already be shrinking the equity supply and increasing corporate debt, and those trends are likely to continue.

Anticipation of the EMU. Assuming that the United Kingdom joins the EMU four or five years in the future, certain key assumptions seem warranted:
- Cash returns will converge.
- Bond returns, from a government-debt perspective, will converge to reflect simple credit risk.
- Equity returns will continue the marked convergence already experienced.
- Intra-European correlations will increase.
- Sector factors across Europe will become more important relative to country factors.

The anticipation of the EMU has already affected both bond and stock markets. **Figure 5** shows that the convergence of markets is well under way. Panel A shows a marked decline in the spread between Italian and German long bonds; that spread is now measured in tens rather than in hundreds of basis points. Similarly, Panel B, which shows forward-looking stock returns as measured by expected dividend discount rates, illustrates the recent dramatic convergence of the Italian and German equity markets.

Table 7. Balance Sheet and Income Gearing for International Comparisons

Measure	United Kingdom	Continental Europe	United States
Net debt/equity	30%	63%	66%
Pretax interest coverage	6.0×	2.2×	3.7×

Note: U.K. data are for the largest 800 nonfinancial companies; European data are for the largest 1,500 nonfinancial companies; U.S. data are for the S&P Industrials.

Source: Based on data from UBS.

Figure 5. Convergence of Italian and German Returns, 1991–97

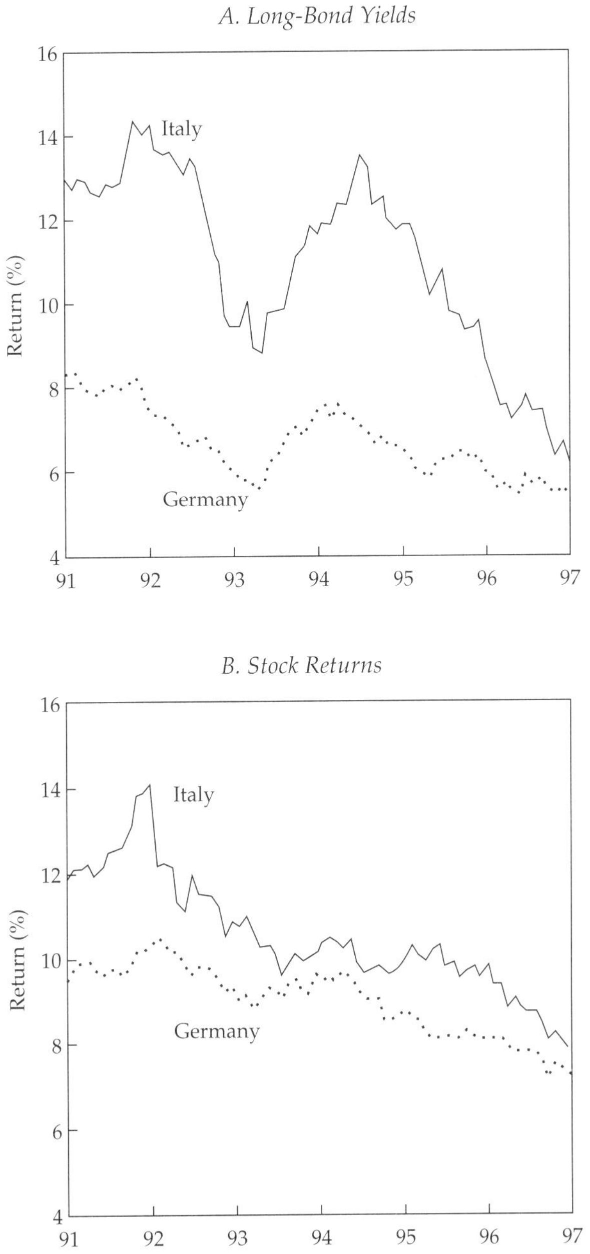

A. Long-Bond Yields

B. Stock Returns

Source: Based on data from Reuters.

The convergence of European markets has important implications for asset allocation. For investors in countries that are part of the EMU, the domestic market will include all the EMU countries. The downside is that investors will get lower diversification benefits for European bonds after establishment of the EMU. But currency risk will also disappear, so European equities should have lower risk. Using our (J.P. Morgan Investment Management's) own forward-looking assumptions on returns, risks and correlations, we can try to estimate the impact that these changes may have on optimal portfolio allocations. For the purposes of this exercise, we have assumed that the overall split between equities and bonds does not change, but as shown in **Table 8**, changes may well occur in the composition of those broad categories. European funds may reduce exposure to purely domestic equities in favor of increasing exposure to Pan-European securities and will increasingly favor non-European bonds over local debt. In the case of the United Kingdom, the impact on optimal asset allocation is minimal if the country remains outside EMU, but were the United Kingdom to enter the EMU, the results would be similar to those shown for the "European Perspective" in Table 8. Although in this analysis we have assumed that the equity/bond split remains the same pre- and post-EMU, we suspect that because U.K. pension funds have a high weighting in equities, certainly much higher than for funds in the rest of Europe, U.K. and European equity allocations will probably converge toward each other. The result will be that final equity levels will be somewhere in the middle of current U.K. and European levels. Essentially, peer-group pressure should cause U.K. equity weightings to fall and European equity weightings to rise.

Table 8. Implications of EMU for Asset Allocation

Asset	U.S. Perspective	European Perspective
Equities/bonds mix	Neutral	Neutral
Domestic bonds	Up	Down
European bonds	Down	Down
Other international bonds	Up	Up
Domestic equities	Up	Down
European equities	Down	Up
International equities	Up	Neutral

Pessimistic Market Views. Cash levels have risen in U.K. pension funds in the past few years, reflecting perhaps a degree of pessimism among some of the very large pension fund managers. Some U.K. funds have also shown quite strong weightings toward international equity, perhaps suggesting an aggressive stance grounded in pessimistic views of selected markets, namely the United States and Japan. Table 9 shows the international equity weightings of U.K. pension funds at the end of 1986, 1993, and 1997. At the end of 1986, the typical fund was neutral versus the U.S. benchmark, overweight Europe, and underweight Japan, thus reflecting the fact that most investors thought Japan was overvalued. The "bet size" is the sum of all the overweightings. So, in 1986, a 10 point overweighting in Europe and a 6 point overweighting in the Pacific Rim meant the bet size relative to the market-cap-weighted index was 16 percent. Some quite dramatic changes can be seen from the end of 1986 to the end of 1993. The U.S. weighting fell markedly, so managers had a bet of 21 percent against that market; Europe rose, Japan stayed about the same, and the Pacific Basin rose strongly. The total bet size more than doubled to 34 percent. At the end of 1997, the U.S. allocation fell even more from the 1993 level relative to the benchmark; managers had an overall 39 percent bet, essentially all against the U.S. market. Europe was very strongly overweighted, Japan was more or less neutral, and the Pacific Rim reverted to a smaller, 8 percent, overweighting—a change that largely reflects market movements rather than actual cash withdrawals.

Some observers have claimed that the asset allocation of a typical U.K. pension fund is totally consensus driven and cannot be explained by any rational investment policy. In the time period of Table 9, for instance, the consensus was that Pacific Basin markets were good value and that the U.S. market was bad value. Consider a hypothetical fund in the context of Table 9 whose benchmark is the peer-group average or consensus fund weightings. This fund shares the consensus view that the United States is expensive and that the Pacific Rim ex-Japan is cheap. The manager will, therefore, attempt to be underweight the United States and overweight the Pacific Rim relative to the consensus. But so will many other managers with similar benchmarks! Thus, as each quarter's estimate of the consensus weight is published, the manager will find that the fund is less underweight the United States and more overweight the Pacific Rim than it would want to be. So, the fund will sell a bit more U.S. exposure and buy more Pacific Rim; this response, repeated across time periods, creates momentum or positive feedback that causes the actual asset allocations to move away sharply from a cap-weighted benchmark. Furthermore, when that consensus view is wrong, the consequences can be dire. For example, in 1997, U.K. managers massively underperformed in international equities because of the strong performance in the United States, which they underweighted, and

Table 9. U.K. Asset Allocations to International Equities

	End 1986		End 1993		End 1997	
Country/Region	Average Manager	Index	Average Manager	Index	Average Manager	Index
United States	42%	43%	21%	42%	18%	57%
Europe ex-United Kingdom	28	18	41	21	54	25
Japan	21	35	15	28	16	14
Pacific Rim	9	3	23	9	12	4
Bet size		16%		34%		39%

the very weak performance in the Pacific Basin, which they overweighted.

Fortunately, more and more plans are starting to think that they should be determining their overall strategic asset allocation themselves. Table 9, in fact, suggests that U.K. institutions, as far as their international equity component is concerned, are actually turning more aggressive, not more conservative. The table certainly highlights the problem of consensus benchmarks, and other evidence suggests that more and more investors are moving away from a consensus approach and developing their own international equity allocation and indeed their own customized benchmarks.

At J.P. Morgan Investment Management, for example, we have a number of U.K.-based clients who have given us international equity mandates. Of these, about 20 percent have market-cap-weighted benchmarks, about 10 percent have consensus benchmarks, and the balance (70 percent) have some form of customized benchmark. For example, one client has a benchmark of 40 percent Europe, 20 percent Pacific Rim, 20 percent Japan, and 20 percent North America. The variations among customized benchmarks are great and increasing; within our group of customized international benchmarks, no two are exactly the same.

Future Developments

Whether U.K. investors are becoming more conservative must remain an open question. What is certain is that fundamental change will continue to occur in the U.K. markets; the move toward customized benchmarks that is already under way is but one example. U.K. equity will play a reduced role because of the abolition of the ACT credit and also because of the move to EMU and the impact of supply and demand. As a result, international, and particularly European, equities will assume a larger role in institutional portfolios. Non-European equity and bond currency exposures will be increasingly strategically hedged. Finally, the U.K. market will see a growing supply of, and increasing importance attached to, corporate debt.

Question and Answer Session

Martyn Hole

Question: Will the trend toward indexing continue in the United Kingdom and Europe?

Hole: The main factor that is pushing many funds into passive management is disappointment with active managers. For the typical U.K. pension fund, active managers have underperformed the cap-weighted benchmark in international equity for three of the last four years. One could argue that much of that underperformance comes from asset allocation, which perhaps will be corrected at some point in the future. But the performance data suggest that the underperformance goes well beyond merely asset allocation.

In 1997, the CAPS median for U.K. pension fund managers managing U.S. assets was about 700 bps behind the index. In Europe, the average U.K. manager lagged the Europe ex-U.K. benchmark by about 300 bps. Performance numbers were somewhat better for Japan and the Pacific Rim, but managers' stock selection in the two very large markets (United States and Europe ex-United Kingdom) was clearly quite poor. Even in the United Kingdom in 1997, the typical U.K. pension fund manager underperformed on the order of 100 bps and more.

So, investors are wondering why they are paying high active fees and getting bad performance; justifying active management is difficult. The drift toward passive management is largely driven by performance, and that drift will continue as long as performance is poor.

The lesson for us, as active managers, is that we must convince pension funds that we are able to deliver an information advantage and then use that advantage to deliver good active returns. Perhaps the key determinant of being able to deliver is knowing what we are and are not good at doing; some managers are good at particular areas of asset allocation and some are good at stock selection. We must be aware of the areas in which we can add value with an acceptable level of risk and those areas in which we cannot; underperformance often comes from lack of such awareness.

Question: Why should EMU have a negative implication for U.S. investors with respect to European equities?

Hole: At J.P. Morgan, we did an efficient frontier analysis recently and looked at our expectations in terms of forward-looking correlations, returns, and risks. Those forward-looking expectations are obviously our own assumptions, and some people might disagree with us. But essentially, we found that both European bond markets and European equity markets are becoming more correlated. If you combine this trend with a dramatic reduction in the number of investable currencies under EMU, then the effect from a U.S. perspective is to lower the attractiveness of European equities and hence to reduce the allocation.

Question: What benefits from EMU do you see for European companies?

Hole: We are optimistic that one of the consequences of EMU will be that European companies will become much more focused on shareholder well-being. We are starting to see evidence of that trend already, particularly in Germany. We are seeing in many countries across Europe the start of such shareholder-friendly actions as share buybacks. Although these buybacks remain illegal in some countries, legislative changes will increasingly favor such activity.

European companies are beginning to talk seriously about economic value added—the whole concept of focusing on the shareholder. One motivation is that increasingly, the interests of management are being brought into line with the interests of shareholders through profit-sharing and option schemes. In addition, companies in continental Europe have a big problem, in the form of unfunded pension liabilities, that needs to be addressed. Funding those liabilities will probably lead to a lot of money going into equities during the next few years. Therefore, companies will want to make sure that their equities are delivering decent returns. To do that, they will have to earn substantial returns on equity and capital and improved profit margins; these changes are starting to happen. In Germany, for example, unit labor costs are falling because companies are implementing more-flexible work practices. In other countries, these changes may be taking place more slowly. But we believe that EMU will lead to greater corporate restructuring in Europe, which will help profitability and overall returns.

Question: What is the time frame for the development of a European corporate debt market, and what factors will enable that development?

Hole: A European corporate debt market is already starting to develop and should emerge full blown during the next 5–10 years. Favorable factors include fiscal changes (such as the ACT credit abolition in the United Kingdom), increasing stock buybacks and recapitalizations of balance sheets with more leverage, the realization on the part of European companies that they can borrow directly from markets more cheaply than from banks, and increasing privatization of companies from both government and family ownership. The process of developing the corporate debt market is long term in nature, but it is inexorable.

Question: What is your opinion of GNP-weighted indexes?

Hole: GNP-weighted indexes are often suggested when people are uncomfortable with the country weights that result from using market capitalizations (such as Japan in 1989 or the United States today). But GNP-weighted indexes themselves can lead to some questionable allocation decisions, particularly if we include developing markets; we might get 20 percent of a portfolio in China, for instance. A second problem is that the companies may not actually exist in which to invest. One advantage of market-cap indexes is that they represent the universe of available, investable companies. Although GNP measures the size of the economy, it does not capture the available investment universe particularly well. A third problem with GNP is measurement. GNP is revised frequently, so keeping up with GNP weights adds another dimension of difficulty to the management process. I think these disadvantages present some very difficult obstacles for using GNP-weighted benchmarks.

European Pension Funds: Turning More Aggressive?

Daniel Witschi
Economic and Market Analysis
UBS Brinson

> Assessing whether pension funds are becoming more aggressive requires a serious look at current European Union pension provisions in terms of structure, demographics, costs, and recent pension reforms. Taken together, these factors argue for a modest shift into equity by European pension funds. A number of factors influence a pension fund's equity allocation—accounting standards, funding rules, taxes, and regulations. Despite shortcomings, a simple asset allocation model can provide some sense of a plan's equity capacity if it assumes a multiyear horizon, changing risk premiums, and constant rebalancing.

This presentation focuses on two crucial issues affecting European pension funds and their portfolio compositions: how quickly might European social security systems move to fully funded private pension systems and to what extent will portfolio allocations shift to higher equity exposures.[1]

First, the financial burden Europe's unfunded pension systems face because of demographic trends is examined and a possible scenario of reform is outlined. Changing demographics are widely seen as a major issue that will eventually require fundamental reform of Europe's social security systems and force a wholesale shift from state-run pay-as-you-go to privately funded pension systems. Although one element of such a scenario is the switch to privately funded plans, such a switch is likely to be both partial and gradual. Of course, other elements of reform, such as preferential tax treatment of life insurance plans, are currently being debated in the press and by European Union (EU) governments.

Second, the equity capacity of pension plans is analyzed by using a simple pension fund asset allocation model. The long-run nature of the liabilities of private pension plans along with reforms in portfolio regulation are expected to induce pension fund managers to invest a meaningful share of their funds in equities. Because most of the fundamental considerations for equity exposure that are made for private pension funds also apply to life insurance companies, the focus of this presentation is not restricted to pension plans.

EU Pension Provisions

To analyze whether European social security systems are moving to fully funded private pension systems and whether portfolio allocations are shifting to higher equity exposures, one needs to analyze current EU pension provisions in terms of structure, characteristics, dependency ratio and cost projections, policy adjustments, and recent pension reforms.

Structure. The current structure of the EU pension system includes three "pillars." Pillar 1 of the pension provision includes statutory public pensions that are mostly provided by the government out of current revenues on a pay-as-you-go basis. State pensions within Pillar 1 presently account for the bulk of pension payouts: 88–90 percent. Most of the Pillar 1 provisions are earnings-related schemes. Pension income in retirement is usually indexed to inflation or to current wages. The link between contributions made during working life and benefits received after retirement varies substantially from system to system.

In contrast to state schemes, most Pillar 2 schemes are funded. Pension schemes in this cate-

---

[1]*Author's note*: I would like to thank my colleagues Guenter Schwarz and Christof Kessler for their helpful comments and suggestions in preparing this presentation.

gory are generally linked to employment or the exercise of a profession (i.e., industry-wide schemes). Membership in a particular scheme is limited to those working in a sector, industry, profession, or company. Pillar 2 schemes are administered by private institutions, and benefits are not guaranteed by the government. Contributions are generally shared by employers and employees. With the notable exceptions of some French and German schemes, Pillar 2 plans are generally funded (with contributions accumulated and invested to provide benefits in the future, rather than to pay benefits to those who have already retired). Pillar 2 schemes account for about 7.0 percent of the total pension payout.

Pillar 3 schemes predominantly include life-insurance-based pension savings plans that account for only 0.9 percent of total payout. Although the contribution of these schemes to the total pension payout is currently relatively small, the funds invested to meet future pension liabilities are sizable.

Characteristics. Two types of social security (i.e., government) pension systems are prevalent in the major EU countries: universal basic and insurance based. Universal basic systems, which usually offer flat-rate pensions, seek to provide a minimum standard of living for all pensioners. Insurance-based systems, in contrast, offer earnings-related pensions that aim to provide a standard of living similar to that enjoyed during working life and are financed by earnings-based contributions. In some countries, such as the United Kingdom, pension schemes are mixed, or hybrid, systems that involve both basic and insurance-based elements. As **Table 1** shows, total pension spending as a percentage of GDP was 11–19 percent in the first half of the 1990s. Replacement ratios (i.e., the ratios of pensions to preretirement salaries) for low-income earners (US$20,000) were similar in most countries, with outliers being Spain (exceptionally high) and the United Kingdom (relatively low). For upper-middle-income earners (US$50,000), replacement ratios were generally lower across countries, with Italy, Spain, Germany, and France being much more generous than the United Kingdom.

Dependency Ratio Projections. The age structure of a population is a key determinant of the likely future strain on a social security system. The populations of EU countries are already aging, but future developments are likely to be even more dramatic, as shown in **Figure 1**. Elderly dependency ratio projections can be made with a reasonable level of precision. Projections for the 1990–2030 period indicate that the demographic shift will be particularly marked from 2010 onwards. In the Netherlands, Germany, and Italy, the elderly dependency ratio (population younger than 14 and older than 65 as a proportion of the population between ages 15 and 65) will be more than 45 percent in 2030. Health care costs are also projected to rise substantially as a result of the increase in the very elderly ratio (i.e., the population aged 75 and older as a percentage of the population aged 65 and older). This demographic pattern largely results from declining birth rates. The fertility rate has been below the replacement level (the fertility rate needed to stabilize a country's population) of about 2.2 percent a year since the late 1960s in most EU countries. In the mid-1990s, the fertility rate stood at 1.4 percent in the 15 nations of the EU. Reflecting this decline in fertility, the generation born in the late 1970s is 17 percent smaller than that of the 1960s, and the 1980s generation is 25 percent smaller than that of the 1960s. Greater longevity and a decline in immigration have also played roles in the overall pattern of aging. Aging is expected to be accompanied by a fall in the total population in a number of EU countries, notably Germany and Italy, but in countries

Table 1. Characteristics of Social Security Pension Systems in Major EU Countries

Country	Type	Ratio of Pension Expenditure to GDP[a]	Ratio of Pension Expenditure to Government Expenditure[a]	Ratio of Total Pension Spending to GDP[a]	Replacement Rate[b] (Final Salary US$20,000/ US$50,000)	Contributions as a Proportion of Earnings (Salary US$20,000/ US$50,000)
Germany	Insurance	9.1%	16.0%	14.3%	70%/59%	37%/37%
Spain	Insurance	7.1	16.2	11.2	90/60	38/27
France	Insurance	10.7	19.3	14.4	67/45	59/59
Italy	Insurance	12.7	22.3	17.1	77/73	56/54
Netherlands	Basic	10.2	18.1	19.1	66/26	32/26
United Kingdom	Mixed	10.7	25.3	14.2	50/26	18/16

[a]1993 data.
[b]1992 data from The Wyatt Company.
Sources: Based on data from "Social Protection Expenditure and Receipts 1980–1993," Eurostat (1995) and "1993 Benefits Report Europe—USA," The Wyatt Company (1993).

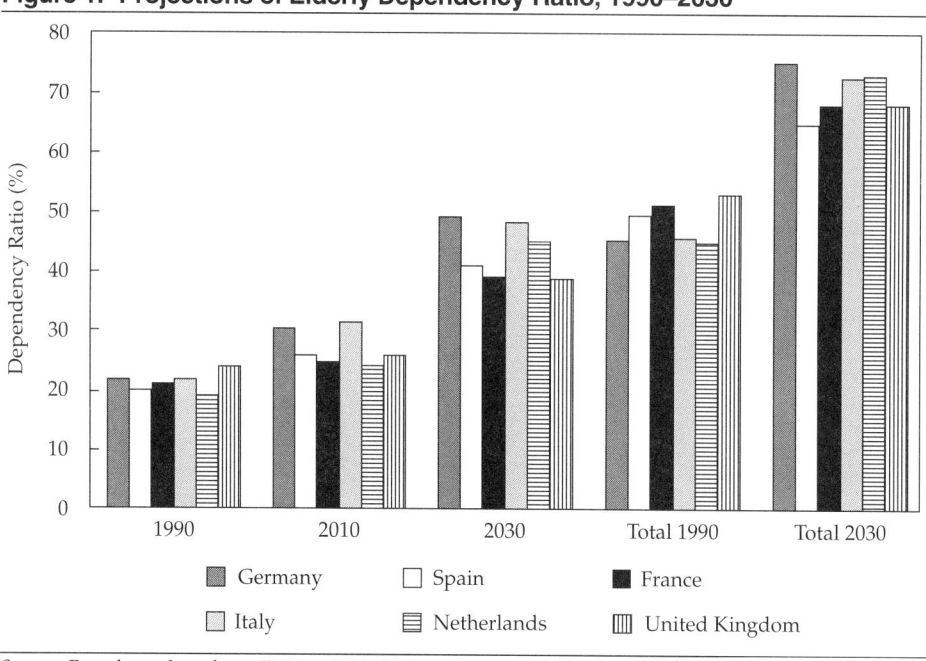

Figure 1. Projections of Elderly Dependency Ratio, 1990–2030

Source: Based on data from E. Bos, "World Population Projections 1994–95" (Washington, DC: The World Bank, 1994).

such as France and the United Kingdom the population is expected to rise until 2030 before stabilizing. By itself, aging may entail a slowing of potential economic growth, reduced tax revenues, and exacerbated effects on public finances.

Cost Projections. With current trends, demographic problems will impose difficulty for social security systems; pension expenditures as a percentage of GDP are expected to rise significantly between 2000 and 2030 for Italy, Germany, France, and Spain. For example, pension expenditures as a percent of GDP for Germany and Italy are expected to rise from about 12.5 percent to about 18.0 percent for Germany and to about 21.5 percent for Italy.

If state-run systems remain unchanged, the problems just outlined will tend to boost the intergenerational redistribution of wealth, with workers and employers paying higher contributions for the same pension. In a recent analysis, the Organization for Economic Cooperation and Development (OECD) estimated future pension expenditures for EU countries and took into account the impact of the most recent reforms. Their estimates suggest that pension expenditures will rise by 7 percent or more of GDP between 1990 and 2040 with Italy, Germany, and France facing the heaviest burdens and the United Kingdom remaining in a relatively comfortable position.

Policy Adjustments. Given demographic projections, the pension problem will worsen substantially from the year 2010 onwards. Until then, countries have a window in which to reduce the burden. If they fail to act in a timely manner, political opposition to reforms is likely to strengthen as the electorate ages. Several policy options are currently being discussed within the pay-as-you-go framework. The main options are (1) changing the ratio of beneficiaries to contributors by such measures as raising the retirement age, (2) reducing the benefit levels, and (3) increasing revenue. In another analysis, OECD researchers calculated the effects of these options on pension net liabilities as a percentage of GDP. **Figure 2** demonstrates the effects of an increase in the contribution rate by 3 percentage points, a 10 percentage point reduction in the replacement ratio, and extending the retirement age by five years. In each case, the situation shows some improvement, and except for the United Kingdom, the retirement age has the largest effect. As mentioned earlier, the demographic distribution in the electorate and efficiency of reforms prevailing in the "window" until 2010 (before demographics worsen) could facilitate reform.

Recent Pension Reforms. One should not assume that state-run pension systems cannot be reformed as a result of widespread resistance in the electorate. For instance, **Table 2** highlights selected recent pension reforms in the EU within the pay-as-

Figure 2. Effects of Policy Adjustments on Net Pension Liabilities

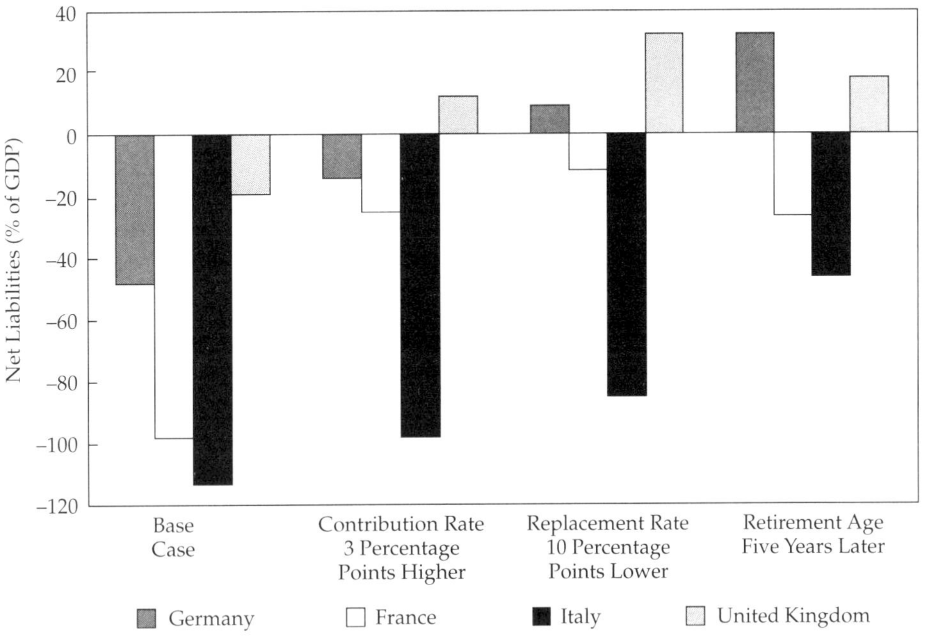

[Bar chart showing Net Liabilities (% of GDP) for Germany, France, Italy, and United Kingdom across four scenarios: Base Case, Contribution Rate 3 Percentage Points Higher, Replacement Rate 10 Percentage Points Lower, and Retirement Age Five Years Later.]

Source: Based on data from "Economic Outlook" (Paris: OECD, 1995).

you-go framework. Steps toward increasing the retirement age have been taken in several countries. Another major reform on the benefit side involves curtailing the indexation of pensions. For example, the temporary suspension of indexation, or a link to prices rather than to wages, would not be as noticeable to pension participants but has major short-term financial effects. An alternative adjustment to indexation may be to link pensions to net (i.e., after-tax) rather than to gross wages, as recently instituted in Germany and some smaller EU countries. As for reforms related to contributions, so far only Spain and Germany have increased contribution rates.

One should note that the process of adjusting EU pension systems to the new demographic conditions has already begun. In the discussions of reforming pay-as-you-go systems, a switch to funding is being widely debated. Funding clearly has a number of advantages. It increases the actuarial fairness of the system, given its closer link between benefits and contributions than in pay-as-you-go systems. Thus, contributions are more likely to be viewed as a form of saving than as taxation. Funding may, therefore, reduce distortions to labor and financial markets and may in itself reduce the overall economic impact of aging by boosting labor force participation, thus potentially raising aggregate savings and increasing the stock of fixed capital (from which future pensions must be paid). Funding allows for risk diversification and reduces the vulnerability of retirees to the overall performance of the domestic economy. Assets accumulated under funding schemes may be more secure against future political developments than are promises under pay-as-you-go systems.

Table 2. Selected Recent Pension Reforms in the EU within the Pay-As-You-Go Framework

Reform	Germany (1989)	Spain (1984/85)	France (1993)	Italy (1992/95)	Netherlands	United Kingdom (1986/95)
Change to benefit indexation rules	•		•	•	•	•
Increase in retirement age	•			•		•
Cut in replacement ratio		•	•	•	•	•
Increased contribution period		•				
Lower incentive to early retirement	•			•		
Public employee privileges reduced				•		
Lower eligibility for disabled pension		•			•	

Source: Based on data from D. Franco and T. Munzi, "Pension Expenditure Prospects in the European Union: A Survey of National Projections," *European Economy*, no. 3 (1996):1–126.

A wholesale switch to funding is extremely unlikely in the EU because funded pension schemes are widely seen as ill-suited to low-income workers or those with broken career patterns and because funding cannot redistribute income to retired persons facing poverty. Also, with a gradual switch to full funding, generations in the transition period will be forced to "pay twice" for pensions—once for the previous generation via pay-as-you-go and once for its own generation via funding—and will hence resist such a change in pension regimes. Moreover, funded pensions do not relieve pressure on public finances in the short run. Existing pension promises need to be met and tax relief granted on contributions and asset returns with little tax revenue from the initially low amounts of funded pension payments to offset these costs. Hence, a somewhat contractionary fiscal stance and a likely increase in the fiscal burden on current workers is needed to finance the existing unfunded systems and the proposed funded systems.

The polar opposite to the gradual switch to full funding is to recognize the implicit government debt that is represented by the accumulated benefit obligation of pay-as-you-go and convert it immediately to explicit debt. Given the scope of the current accrued obligations under pay-as-you-go, which are typically well more than 100 percent of GDP, converting the accumulated benefit obligation to explicit government debt may not be feasible without having severe effects on financial markets and on confidence in the domestic economy. In the EU, this solution would also seem to be ruled out by the current state of government finances and the ceilings on government debt imposed by the Maastricht Treaty.

In light of these problems, EU governments are likely to focus largely on scaling back their benefit promises and opt for a partial and gradual switch to funding.

Private Funding Determinants

In general, the current provision of private pension funding in the EU is dependent on the scale of social security provisions, taxation and regulatory provisions, and the maturity of funded schemes.

The scope and growth of private pension plans is directly related to the scale of state pension provisions. In particular, if government plans have a generous provision for individuals at high income levels, the incentives for providing private sector plans are limited. **Table 3** outlines some replacement ratios in key EU countries to highlight the inverse relationship between replacement rates and the coverage of funded schemes. If social security provides high replacement ratios to high-income earners, as in Italy and Spain, little incentive exists to develop private pension plans. On the other hand, countries with large funded sectors, such as the United Kingdom, have low replacement ratios for both high- and low-income earners.

For taxation, a clear correlation is found between generous tax treatment of private pensions and the size of the privately funded sector. For example, in the Netherlands and the United Kingdom, where funded sectors are large and offer generous "expenditure tax" treatment, pension contributions and asset returns are tax exempt and only pension distributions are taxed. Such a regime is denoted as EET. (The abbreviations in Table 3 refer to taxation of contributions, returns, and benefits; hence, EET means contributions and returns are tax exempt and benefits are taxed.) In Germany, where employers' contributions are taxed as wages and employees' contributions and asset returns are tax exempt (TET), funded plans are not as prevalent as in countries with favorable tax treatment.

Finally, the maturity of funded schemes influences the current and prospective scope of accumulated pension assets. In the United Kingdom and the Netherlands, funded plans are largely mature, and

Table 3. Determinants of Scale of Private Pension Funding

Country	Replacement Rate[a] (Final Salary of US$20,000/ US$50,000)	Form of Taxation	Coverage of Funded Schemes	Maturity of Funded Schemes
Germany	70%/59%	TET	42% (voluntary)	Immature
Spain	90/60	EET	8% (225,000 pension funds, 875,000 personal pensions)	Immature
France	67/45	E(E)T	Less than 10% (voluntary)	Immature
Italy	77/73	EET	5% (voluntary)	Immature
Netherlands	66/26	EET	83% (voluntary)	Mature
United Kingdom	50/26	EET	50% company, 25% personal (voluntary)	Mature

[a]1992 data from The Wyatt Company.
Sources: Based on data from "1993 Benefits Report Europe—USA," The Wyatt Company (1993) and E. Phillip Davis, *Pension Funds, Retirement-Income Security and Capital Markets, an International Perspective* (Oxford, United Kingdom: Oxford University Press, 1995).

hence, the asset-to-GDP ratio is near a peak. In Germany, France, and other continental European countries, immaturity of company plans suggests that further growth is likely.

Status at Year-End 1993. Privately funded pensions in European countries could be encouraged by reducing replacement ratios and switching to expenditure tax treatment of pensions. More generous tax treatment also appears to be the key ingredient to boosting demand for individual life insurance plans. Such moves would lead to a substantial rise in the stock of accumulated assets and coincide with higher demand for fixed-income and equity investments. As **Table 4** shows, at the end of 1993, generous tax treatment in the Netherlands and the United Kingdom, as well as high labor force coverage, may have contributed to the high equity market capitalization as a percentage of GDP.

Scope of Pillar 2 Investments. To reach a highly tentative estimate of the potential additional demand for European securities, one can focus on Pillar 2 investments and assume that privately funded pension plans in continental European countries reach either half the size (measured in percent of GDP) or the total size of pension plans in both the United Kingdom and the Netherlands. As **Figure 3** demonstrates, if continental European pension plans reach half the combined size of U.K. and Dutch plans, the market value of the aggregated assets will be about US$6.2 trillion. If they reach the whole size of U.K. and Dutch plans, aggregate assets would total about US$10.4 trillion, which is comparable to the current US$11.5 trillion market cap of the European bond and equity markets. These figures give a feel for the additional demand financial markets in Europe may eventually face should a number of structural reforms be adopted in the years ahead. Although a rapid and wholesale shift to fully funded private pensions is highly unlikely, one should expect to see gradual and partial reforms.

Portfolio Composition

An examination of the portfolio composition of European pension funds reveals that continental funds' asset allocations are heavily biased toward domestic fixed-income investments and against equity holdings. As **Table 5** shows, German pension funds hold less than 10 percent in domestic and foreign equities. France, Italy, and Spain show a similar pattern in the portfolio weights of asset classes. Dutch funds' equity exposures are significantly higher than but still far below the equity share of U.K. pension funds. Since the early 1990s, however, portfolio weights of equities have been rising moderately in most continental European funds.

Determinants. Several factors have contributed, to varying degrees, to such a small equity allocation for continental European funds in comparison with their U.K. and U.S. counterparts.

■ *Accounting standards.* With respect to accounting standards, several studies suggest that in Germany, the strict application of accounting principles, which are considered more appropriate for banks than pension funds, restrain equity holdings by funded plans independently of the legal portfolio regulations. These accounting conventions, for example on positive net worth of the fund at all times, carry equities on the balance sheet at the lower of book or market value and calculate returns net of unrealized capital gains. In contrast, the U.K. accounting standards permit long-run smoothing and focus on dividends rather than market values and, therefore, enable funds to accept the volatility of equity returns.

■ *Funding rules.* Minimum funding regulations make holding a large proportion of bonds optimal to protect against shortfall risk, despite bonds' weakness as an inflation hedge. In the United Kingdom, such funding rules are well below actual liabilities and have traditionally fostered large equity holdings. In countries such as Germany, the effect of minimum funding rules may be overwhelmed by tight account-

Table 4. Private Pension Funding, Year-End 1993

Country	Labor Force Coverage	Characteristics	Supplementary Pensions (percent of total pensions)	Stock of Assets (billion ECU)	Stock of Assets (percent of GDP)	Equity Market Cap (percent of GDP)
Germany	46%	Voluntary, both book-reserved and funded	11%	106	5.8%	22%
Spain	15	Voluntary, both book-reserved and funded	3	10	2.2	24
France	90	Quasi-mandatory, pay-as-you-go	21	41	3.4	36
Italy	5	Voluntary, partially funded	2	12	1.2	16
Netherlands	85	Company funds, funded	32	261	88.5	42
United Kingdom	48	Voluntary funded	28	717	79.4	79

Source: Based on data from "Supplementary Pensions in the Single Market, a Green Paper," European Commission (1997).

Asset Allocation in a Changing World

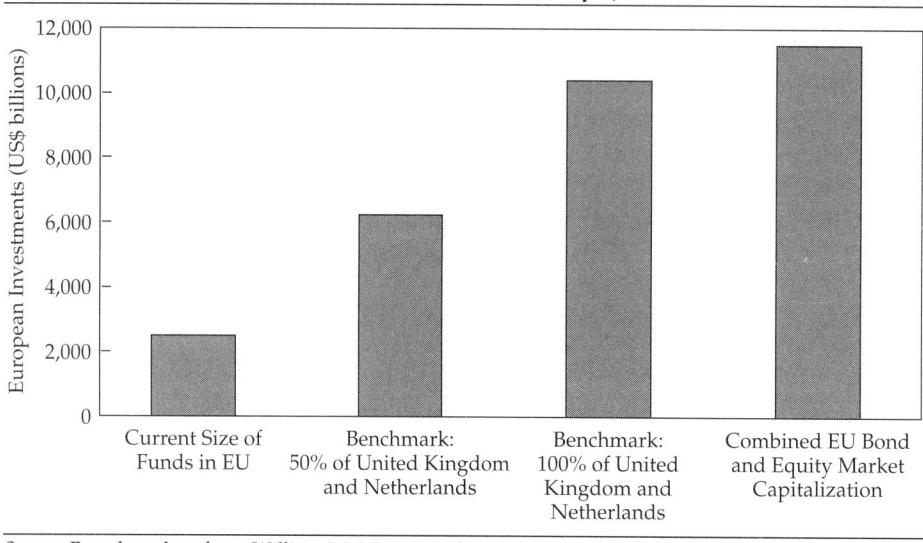

Figure 3. Scope of Pillar 2 Investments in Europe, 1997

[Bar chart showing European Investments (US$ billions):
- Current Size of Funds in EU: ~2,500
- Benchmark: 50% of United Kingdom and Netherlands: ~6,200
- Benchmark: 100% of United Kingdom and Netherlands: ~10,300
- Combined EU Bond and Equity Market Capitalization: ~11,400]

Source: Based on data from William M. Mercer and the European Commission.

ing and portfolio regulations.

■ *Portfolio regulations.* Portfolio regulations have a clear and widespread influence on asset allocation. In several continental European countries, funds are forced to hold a certain minimum proportion of assets in government bonds. In France, for example, pension funds are required to invest at least 50 percent of assets in EU government bonds.

■ *Structure of fund management.* In some countries, the structure of fund management may have been counterproductive to efficient fund management. This finding is particularly true for Spain, where delegating to foreign fund managers is forbidden, and in Germany, where *Pensionskassen* (German pension funds) are obliged to internally manage their funds. Low equity exposures may also be influenced by restrictions on the transferability of shares, lack of market transparency, entrenched management, and lack of information on a firm's development and prospects.

■ *Higher taxation.* Historically, the higher taxation on bonds than on equities has made bonds an attractive investment to tax-exempt investors in many countries.

■ Ex post *asset returns.* Finally, historical, or *ex post*, asset returns are a key influence on the structure of any portfolio. In Germany, absolute and real returns on bonds and other fixed-income assets have been historically higher than on equities. In the United Kingdom, in contrast, bond returns have been historically low, and pension funds correspondingly hold few bonds.

National Regulations. Regulations on pension fund portfolios are a key determinant of a pension fund's asset allocation, as shown in **Table 6**. Most EU countries have restrictive rules that generally limit the maximum exposure of a fund to a particular asset, asset class, or currency. In Germany and France, national regulations require fund managers to hold a sizable share of their funds in fixed-income investments. But, as mentioned before, the limits imposed on equity holdings have so far not been used, and sizable room for increases still exists. Only the United Kingdom and the Netherlands have so far adopted liberal Prudent Man-type regulations.

National regulations and current EU rules on asset allocation for life insurance companies are very similar to those for the pension fund industry. As Table 6 shows, the United Kingdom and the Netherlands are more liberal than other EU nations. Current EU rules on life insurance investments are also much less restrictive than most national regulations. The European Commission recently stated in a research paper that any restrictions imposed on prudential grounds must be proportional to the objectives they may legitimately pursue. In an effort to harmonize national regulations on pension funds and life insurance companies, the European Commission is currently considering proposing common EU standards for both pension fund and life insurance schemes or making pension fund schemes subject to the current EU rules governing life insurance companies. Whatever decisions are made, EU-wide regulations will probably shift to Prudent Man Rules and eventually be adopted throughout the EU.

Equity Capacity

Assuming that tight regulatory restrictions for equity

Table 5. Pension Funds' Portfolio Compositions by Country, 1994–97

Country/Asset	1994	1995	1996	1997
Denmark				
Domestic equities	14%	19%	17%	17%
Domestic bonds	70	71	67	65
Foreign equities	3	5	5	7
Foreign bonds	2	1	1	1
Real estate	9	3	9	8
Cash/other	2	1	1	2
Germany				
Domestic equities	6	6	6	6
Domestic bonds	72	71	71	71
Foreign equities	3	3	3	3
Foreign bonds	4	4	4	4
Real estate	13	13	13	13
Cash/other	2	3	3	3
Netherlands				
Domestic equities	9	10	11	15
Domestic bonds	49	50	50	47
Foreign equities	20	19	18	19
Foreign bonds	7	7	8	10
Real estate	13	13	12	7
Cash/other	2	1	1	2
Portugal				
Domestic equities	3	8	6	14
Domestic bonds	58	67	78	72[a]
Foreign equities	6	3	2	4
Foreign bonds	7	1	1	1
Real estate	1	3	3	2
Cash/other	25	18	10	7
Switzerland				
Domestic equities	8	10	11	10
Domestic bonds	54	46	46	25
Foreign equities	5	3	3	5
Foreign bonds	5	6	6	7
Real estate	19	20	19	16
Cash/other	9	15	15	37[b]
United Kingdom				
Domestic equities	56	57	54	53
Domestic bonds	7	7	8	9
Foreign equities	26	24	23	22
Foreign bonds	5	6	6	6
Real estate	4	2	2	2
Cash/other	2	4	7	8

[a]50/50 fixed and floating issues.
[b]Money market instruments.
Source: Based on data from AP Fonden.

behind the optimal share of equity holdings.[2]

In this simple model, shown in **Figure 4**, four key variables determine a fund's equity capacity: the required assurance of full funding (which defines the desired probability that assets will suffice to meet obligations at a specified horizon and, therefore, is a measure of a plan's risk tolerance), the horizon of liabilities, the equity risk premium over liabilities, and the initial funding ratio (defined as initial assets divided by liabilities). The signs above the arrows indicate the impact individual factors have on a pension fund's equity capacity: The higher the required assurance of full funding, the higher the required probability that assets will equal or exceed the liability and hence the lower a plan's equity capacity; the higher the initial funding ratio, the higher the probability that the fund can meet its obligation and invest in more-risky assets. Finally, the impact of the equity risk premium on equity capacity is straightforward: A higher equity risk premium justifies a higher equity exposure.

Mechanics. This simple pension plan asset allocation model allows for the analysis of the cumulative performance of a plan over a specified period. The liability of the plan is the discounted value of a benefit stream that begins at the measurement horizon. Of course, pension plans face benefit payments before their long-term measurement horizons are reached. Such plans, however, may regard certain assets or incoming cash flows as dedicated to meeting their benefit payment obligations over a limited horizon while the balance of the fund is invested more aggressively. One can assume that the horizon liability will be discounted at 8 percent, representing the growth rate or liability return, and that the annual volatility of the horizon liability is 10 percent.

The model incorporates two asset classes: a riskless asset (e.g., a dedicated bond portfolio that matches the liability cash flow and is priced using an 8 percent discount rate) and a risky asset (e.g., equity, which has annual returns that are lognormally distributed). The assumed distribution of equity reflects an expected return of 10 percent (i.e., a risk premium over liabilities of 2 percent), a volatility of 16 percent, and a correlation of 35 percent with the liability return. On the basis of these model assumptions, the equity capacity of the model plan can now be examined under the assumption of a continuous rebalanc-

holdings and other administrative hurdles are eventually abolished, one might find it interesting to address pension plans' equity capacity from a theoretical perspective. A simple pension plan asset allocation model developed by Leibowitz provides a useful conceptual framework to illustrate the mechanics

[2]Martin Leibowitz, Lawrence Bader, and Stanley Kogelman, "The Opportunity for Greater Flexibility in the Bond Component," *Journal of Portfolio Management* (Summer 1995):51–59. See also Martin L. Leibowitz, *A New Perspective on Asset Allocation* (Charlottesville, VA: The Research Foundation of the Institute of Chartered Financial Analysts, 1987).

Asset Allocation in a Changing World

Table 6. National Regulations

Country	Pension Fund Portfolios (Pillar 2)	Life Insurance Companies (Pillar 3)
Germany	Maximum 30% EU equity, 25% EU property, 6% non-EU shares, 6% non-EU bonds, 20% overall foreign assets, and 10% self-investment limit.	Maximum 30% domestic equity, 25% property, 6% foreign equity, 5% foreign bonds, 10% unlisted securities, 50% combined limit for mortgages and loans.
Spain	5% limit in securities issued by any one enterprise; 90% of assets must be invested in quoted securities, bank deposits, property, or mortgages, and 1% must be invested in current accounts or money markets.	No specific limits.
France	At least 50% to be invested in EU government bonds, less than 33% in loans to sponsors.	65% combined limit on domestic equity, unlisted securities, and foreign equity, 40% limit on property, 10% combined limit on mortgages and loans.
Italy	No pension law for self-administered schemes, but investment policy determined by the board of directors and usually restricted to government bonds, bank deposits, insurance policies, and property.	Maximum 20% domestic equity, 20% unlisted securities, 20% foreign equity, 50% foreign bonds, 50% property, 50% mortgages, and 0% loans.
Netherlands	5% self-investment limit; Prudent Man Rule.	10% combined limit on unlisted securities and mortgages, 8% limit on loans.
United Kingdom	5% self-investment limit; Prudent Man Rule.	10% combined limit on unlisted securities, mortgages, and loans.

Source: Based on data from "Supplementary Pensions in the Single Market, a Green Paper," European Commission (1997).

ing strategy. This model assumes pension funds determine their maximum allowable equity exposures and subsequently maintain these exposures over the entire horizon. This model framework can now be used to find out how pension funds can identify their maximum allowable equity exposures.

Multiyear Horizons. As **Figure 5** shows, the expected funding ratio return (i.e., the difference between the initial and terminal funding ratio divided by the initial funding ratio) rises both with rising equity exposure (as depicted by moving to the right along individual equity risk–return lines) and longer horizons (as depicted by moving to the same equity allocation on a "higher" line). The equity risk–return lines viewed in isolation, however, do not help to define the maximum allowable equity exposure of the model fund. To reach this exposure for various time horizons, the funding constraint line is needed. The funding constraint is defined as the portfolio risk and return profile for various funding targets. The area to the left of the funding constraint line allows pension funds to exceed their expected funding ratio return requirements. For a given time horizon, the intersection of the funding constraint line and the equity risk–return line defines the maximum allowable equity capacity. The assumptions used regarding the volatility of liabilities and stocks, the correlation between stocks and bonds, and the risk premium of stocks over bonds can produce different results from those depicted in Figure 5. A rise in the assumed volatility of stocks, for example, reduces the slope of the equity risk–return lines and accordingly reduces the maximum allowable equity exposures. A decline in the assumed risk premium has the same effect. In all of these alternative scenarios, however, the maximum equity exposure does not increase but declines with longer time horizons.

Figure 4. Pension Plan Equity Capacity

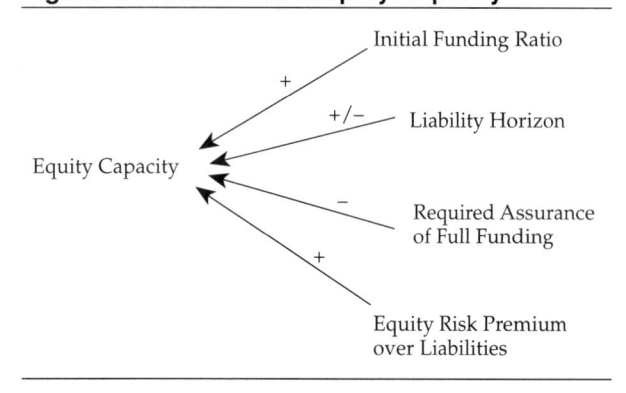

Equity Capacity
- + Initial Funding Ratio
- +/− Liability Horizon
- − Required Assurance of Full Funding
- + Equity Risk Premium over Liabilities

This drop is understandable but may be counterintuitive. The plan surplus is unlikely to vanish quickly but could be wiped out by a prolonged bear market. Assuming constant rebalancing and a 2 percent risk premium, a plan with a 110 percent funding ratio, as shown in **Figure 6**, invested entirely in equity can almost certainly meet its liabilities if it matures in a week. What is more surprising, however, is that the decline in the maximum equity holding continues out to the 15-year horizon under the previous assumptions. Even a 25-year horizon implies no more

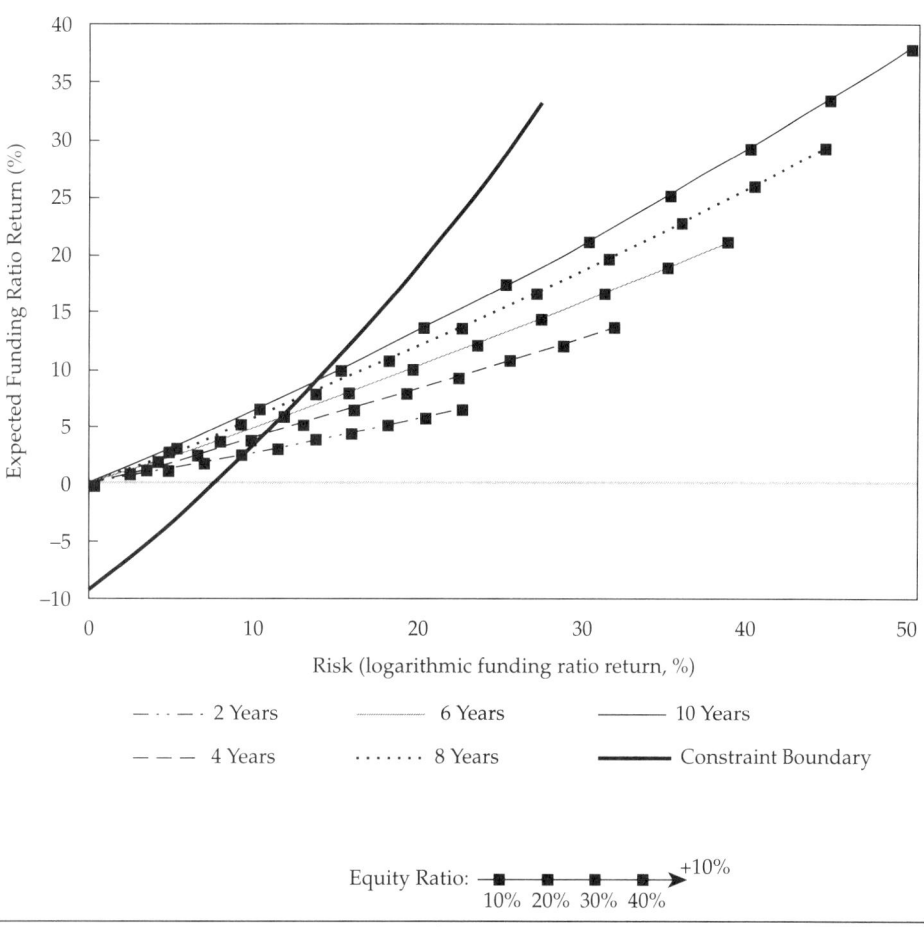

Figure 5. Maximum Allowable Equity Exposure for Multiyear Horizons Based on Expected Funding Ratio Return

Note: Assumes rebalancing and risk premium of 2 percent.

equity capacity than a 2-year horizon. Note that under the assumptions used in this example, the maximum allowable equity exposure broadly matches the typical equity exposure of U.S. pension funds.

Changing Equity Risk Premiums. The maximum allowable equity exposure for multiyear horizons changes as the risk premium changes. **Figure 7** demonstrates the consequences of different assumptions of risk premiums for pension fund asset allocation decisions. Keeping all other assumptions constant, a rise from 2 percent to 3 percent in the expected risk premium increases the maximum allowable equity exposure of a fund with a 20-year horizon from 28 percent to about 36 percent. Assuming a 4 percent risk premium and a 20-year horizon, the maximum equity capacity would be 100 percent.

Model Shortcomings. Of course, this model framework suffers from a number of important shortcomings compared with the reality in which pension funds operate. Funds' liabilities often cannot be easily defined, and crafting a bond portfolio that perfectly matches liabilities is difficult. The model's investment universe is defined too narrowly, and the assumed investment strategy may appear too simplistic. Most of all, the model parameters used to run the simulations do not remain constant in reality. The maturity of liabilities, risk premiums, rates of return, volatilities, and correlations are also interdependent. Despite all these caveats, using the model gives a feel for the most important issue facing European pension fund managers—deciding the optimal asset allocation.

Equity Risk Premium. The long-run patterns in the relative performance of stocks versus bonds are shown in **Figure 8**. Because consistent performance data running more than 50 years are scarce, the following tentative considerations are limited to Germany, the United Kingdom, Switzerland, and the United States. Except for Germany, which has no clear discernible trend for a 25-year horizon, equity

Asset Allocation in a Changing World

Figure 6. Maximum Allowable Equity Exposure for Multiyear Horizons

Note: Assumes rebalancing and risk premium of 2 percent.

Figure 7. Maximum Allowable Equity Exposure for Multiyear Horizons for Various Risk Premiums

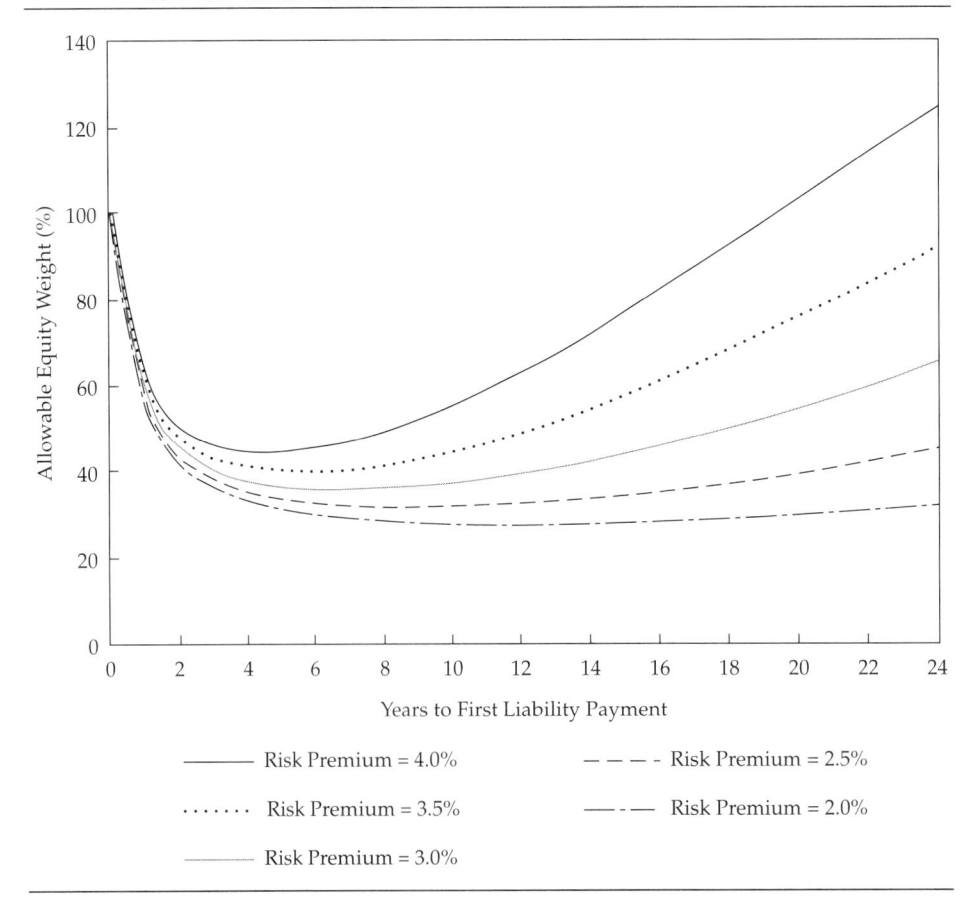

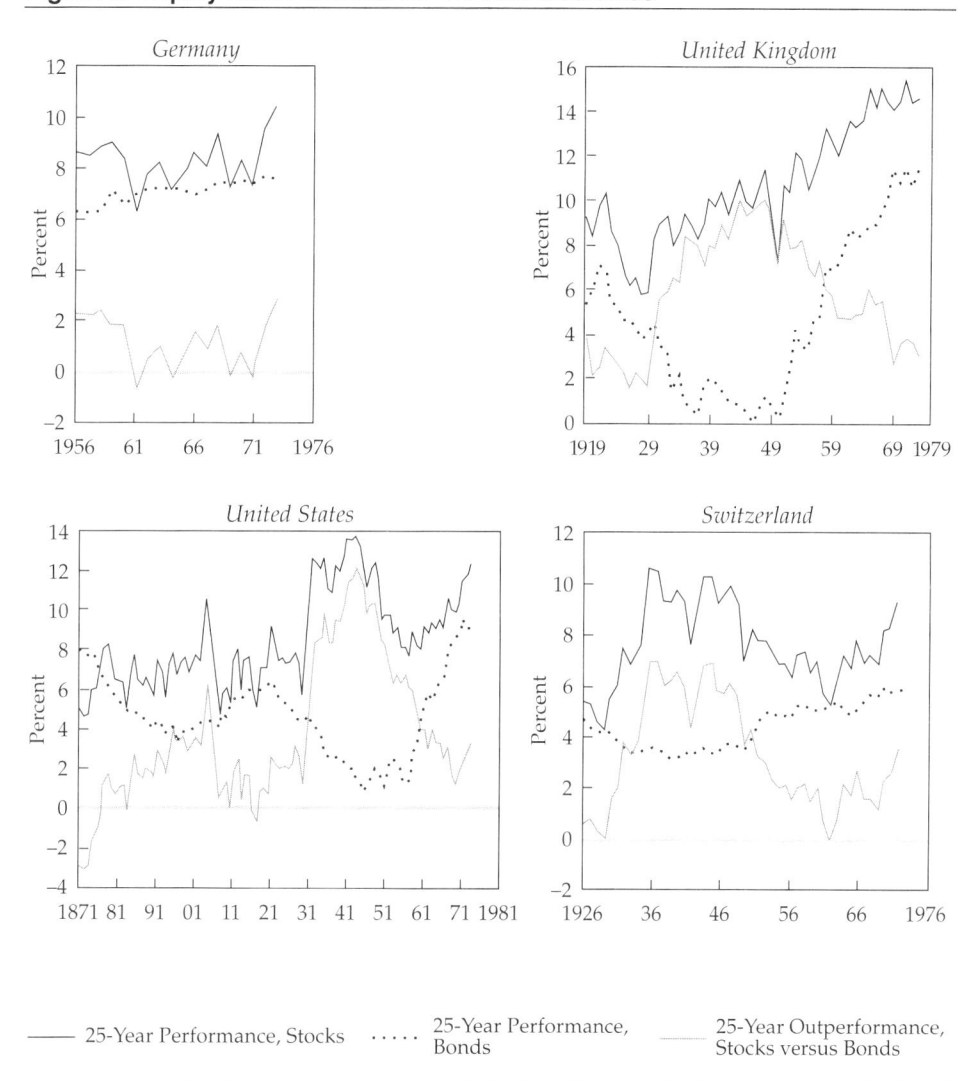

Figure 8. Equity Risk Premium for Various Countries

risk premiums tended to decline during the post-World War II period and rebounded marginally during the past five years. Apparently, several decades had to pass before the risk premium declined to the levels recorded before the 1929 stock market crash. It remains to be seen whether the moderate rebound registered in the past few years will continue over the coming years or whether the secular decline in the risk premium was just an interruption in the general trend of the 1990s.

Tentative Considerations. Two key issues come to mind with regard to the future trends in equity risk premiums. These considerations are, of course, highly tentative and warrant further research. As Europe's investment universe broadens and liquidity improves, new segments in European fixed-income markets (such as high-yield corporate debt) may become particularly interesting for pension funds, possibly drawing money that was traditionally allocated to equity. For example, index-linked bonds and long-maturity bonds might match funds' long-run liabilities better than the current European fixed-income universe. On the other hand, European equity markets will also broaden and deepen, which may stimulate higher equity exposures.

Conclusion

Transformation of Europe's social security system will be gradual and partial. Arguments in favor of increasing the equity exposure of pension schemes appear strongly overstated by many analysts. Substantial near-term shifts to privately funded pension plans are extremely unlikely. A rapid and massive rise in private pension funds' investment needs is, therefore, improbable.

Equity capacity of pension plans is a multifaceted and complex issue. According to tentative simulations based on a simple asset allocation pension plan model, the maximum allowable equity capacity may roughly match the equity exposure of U.S. pension funds.

A key determinant of European pension funds' equity capacity is the equity risk premium over bonds; several concurrent factors will shape long-run trends in the equity risk premium. These factors need to be addressed in more detail.

Finally, portfolio regulations on pension funds will shift to Prudent Man Rules and will eventually be adopted throughout the European Monetary Union, thus allowing equity pension managers to conduct their investments more freely than under the current binding regulations.

Client Expectations and the Demand to Minimize Downside Risk

Mark Tapley, CFA
Chief Investment Officer
WestLB Asset Management

> People often wonder why equity allocations of U.K. and continental European investors are so different. Structural reasons—legislative, regulatory, and contractual sources of differences—provide much better answers than cultural reasons, but pension surplus explains the most significant differences in asset allocations. Large surpluses tend to lead to risky asset allocations; small surpluses foster loss aversion, which leads to asset allocation policies that produce option-like payoffs (i.e., downside risk protection and upside return participation). Important questions remain, however, about how to assess manager results, how to set the floor return, and what can go wrong.

When people outside the United Kingdom are discussing asset allocation in the United Kingdom, one frequent question is why U.K. pension funds have such a high percentage of their assets in equities. By comparison, long-term savings institutions in continental Europe typically have little in equities. The other Anglo-Saxon countries have equity allocations somewhere between those in the United Kingdom and those in continental Europe. Even within the U.K. community, actuarial consultants are asking a slightly different asset allocation question: "Why is there is so little differentiation in asset allocation practice between mature and immature pension funds?" By contrast, U.K. investors are wondering why "euroland" investors (i.e., those eventually using the euro) seem so afraid of high equity allocations; U.K. investors believe that equities (obviously) provide superior long-term returns.

Answers

Answers to those questions are needed. Wherever you come from, without good answers the possibility exists that *you* are wrong. In other words, diversity of outcomes disturbs everyone. Can both outcomes be "right" in some way? Is one set of investors making serious misjudgments, for which they will one day pay the price? On whose side is rationality?

Some people may be interested in better answers for another reason, namely the globalization of the investment management industry. If continental European investment managers want to start offering their services in the United Kingdom and vice versa, then they should try to find out something about investment practices abroad before they decide what they can sell and how they can sell it. Looking at the stereotypes of investors can be helpful in this regard. Anglo-Saxon and euroland investors seem to differ remarkably along a number of dimensions. For example, eurolanders tend to have a short-term investment horizon (annual return targets instead of three- or five-year targets), have a bond market culture, focus on nominal liabilities because of historically low inflation rates, and develop strategies that focus on absolute returns. On the other hand, Anglo-Saxons have a long-term investment horizon, have an equity culture, focus on real liabilities because of inflation concerns, and develop strategies based on how a peer group might perform (such as is done in the United Kingdom) or based on comparisons with passive benchmarks (such as is done in the United States). These are cumulatively big differences. Failure to understand them might mean that a globalizing investment management firm wastes much money pursuing the wrong strategy.

People tend to provide cultural and structural explanations to the "why different" asset allocation question.

■ *Cultural*. This reasoning suggests that practice is determined in light of that group's historical experience. U.K. investors experienced relatively high inflation during the 1970s and 1980s. They remember the negative returns on bonds. In particular, they remember that bonds failed to match their pension funds' liabilities. As a result, trustees and managers have an aversion to fixed-income securities. By contrast, the Bundesbank has for many years provided eurolanders with confidence in their currency and, therefore, in bonds. Real returns have been satisfactory and volatility low. Under "cultural" answers, I would add the mountaineer's response: U.K. investors hold more equities because they are there. In other words, the United Kingdom has a relatively large equity market and euroland a relatively small equity market.

Cultural explanations, and more exist than are described here, are deeply unsatisfactory. Investors do not invest in things just because they are there; investors are not permanent prisoners of their past; they can look forward as well as backwards. Finally, restating a consensus view sheds no light on why it is the consensus.

■ *Structural.* This group of answers is much more interesting than the cultural ones. This rubric looks at the legislative, regulatory, and contractual sources of differences. For example, a German *Spezialfonds*—a fund set up under Germany's *Kapitalanlagegesellschaftgesetz*, which is the law governing special investment companies—enjoys certain tax advantages and is regulated by the *BaKred* (*Bundesaufsichtsamt für Kreditwesen*). If the assets of the *Spezialfonds* fall below book value, the parent company must itself take the write-down in its own books. That requirement discourages heavy equity investments.

German life assurance companies provide a good example of structural explanations for asset allocation differences. These companies are required by law to provide a minimum return to policyholders. This rate, known as the *Rechnungszinsfuß* (literally the "accounting rate foot"), applies to all new policies for their lives. The rate stands today at 4 percent; the yield on the 10-year government bonds stands at 3.95 percent and has been falling. The equity market is relatively narrow and illiquid, with a gross yield of 1.3 percent. In fact, competition within the industry has pushed typical bonus rates, which are credited annually, to 7 percent; bonus rates are now in part funded out of fixed-income capital gains as interest rates have fallen. Savings via life assurance policies, however, also enjoy tax benefits as long as policies cover a minimum term of 12 years. The tax advantages make this means of saving popular among private investors.

The point is that the regulatory backdrop to institutional savings will influence asset allocation as much as expectational or specific asset/liability circumstances. In this case, with inflation officially estimated at 0 percent, the regulations impose a 4 percent real return threshold. These "structural" factors exert a two-way pull on equity exposure. They *discourage* heavy equity investments because of the minimum required rate of return but also *encourage* equity investment in order to achieve a competitive rate of return and to build a cushion of reserves.

By contrast, a U.K. pension fund in part defines its liabilities by reference to a long-term dividend stream. The asset class that best matches this liability is—guess what—an equity portfolio. Moreover, dividends are remarkably stable compared with market levels. As a result, market setbacks increase the dividend yield and, therefore, increase the appetite and tolerance for equities. Never mind the losses; feel the yield. (Note that U.K. regulations are changing. Apart from the Pensions Act 1995, which imposes for the first time a minimum funding requirement, international accounting standards may soon impose recognition of pension assets' market levels on parent company accounts.)

Structural reasons for differences in investment practice are significant and are frequently neglected or poorly understood by investors. A study by Goldman, Sachs & Company explains the influence on asset allocation practice that arises from the wide variety of pension legislation.[1] These reasons, however, may be insufficient in an important way.

Surpluses

The missing link in most explanations of asset allocation differences is the surplus—the excess of assets over liabilities. In the remainder of this presentation, I will explore how rational, wealth-maximizing behavior can lead to different asset allocation outcomes when similar outcomes are expected (and vice versa). Such outcomes are not explained purely by reference to the structural or legislative framework within which the institutional investor is operating or by reference to past experience. Relatively small surpluses foster loss aversion (i.e., an asymmetric valuation of the utility of gains relative to losses). Consequently, loss aversion leads to asset allocation policies with an asymmetric or option-like payoff. Such asset allocation policies need frequent rebalancing and are, therefore, dynamic in nature rather than static. By contrast, investors with large surpluses of assets over liabilities will tend to adopt more-stable asset allocation policies than those who do not have large surpluses. In addition, investors with large surpluses will tend to hold more of their assets in risky

---
[1] Mark Griffin, "The Global Pension Time Bomb and Its Capital Market Impact," Goldman, Sachs & Company (May 28, 1997).

categories. My second objective is, therefore, to show that when managers and clients discuss asset allocation strategies, the dialogue often works best when both parties see the asset allocation decisions within an option-replication framework.

U.K. Experience

Asset allocations in the United Kingdom can be examined by making comparisons with allocations in non-U.K. countries and by looking at peer-group pressure within the United Kingdom.

Comparisons with Other Countries. U.K. pension fund exposure to equities can be compared directly with exposures in other countries. **Table 1** shows the relationship between the percentage of assets invested in equities and the maturity ranking of pension liabilities for 11 countries.[2] Two groups emerge: countries with immature pension liabilities (Hong Kong, Australia, Canada, the United States, and Ireland) and countries with mature pension liabilities (Japan, France, Germany, the Netherlands, the United Kingdom, and Switzerland). Most of the countries with immature pension liabilities rightfully (according to common sense) have a high percentage of assets invested in equities. The countries with mature pension liabilities—with one glaring exception, the United Kingdom—have a relatively low percentage of assets invested in equities. The idea is that if a plan's liabilities are short term in nature, it should have lots of fixed-income assets. If a plan's liabilities are long term in nature (i.e., it has an immature pension fund), then it should allocate more funds to risky assets, such as equities. The United Kingdom is the anomaly because it has such a high percentage of assets in equities and relatively mature pension liabilities.

Examining the diversity in asset allocation practice within the U.K. pension fund community is also useful. One might expect, for example, that the exposure to equities will vary with maturity of the liabilities, as was expected in the international comparisons. **Figure 1**, based on data from The WM Company, divides pension funds in the United Kingdom into three groups—immature, mature, and supermature—and looks at the percentage of assets invested in equities and real estate. Immature funds are defined as having more than 60 percent of their members active or employed, mature funds have 40–60 percent of plan participants employed, and supermature funds have less than 40 percent of their members currently

Table 1. Percentage of Assets in Equities for Various Countries

Country[a]	Assets Invested in Equities
Immature liabilities	
Hong Kong	79%
Australia	51
Canada	41
United States	58
Ireland	68
Mature liabilities	
Japan	37
France	30
Germany	8
Netherlands	29
United Kingdom	76
Switzerland	16

[a]Ranked from least to most mature pension liabilities.

Source: Based on data from Watson Wyatt Worldwide's *Global Asset Study*.

employed. This mix of active members and deferred, or retired, members determines the actuarial valuation of a plan's liabilities and might, therefore, also be expected to influence the asset allocation policy.

The WM survey does not support this hypothesis. Of the immature funds, 16 percent had more than 90 percent of their assets invested in equities and real estate, as expected. The vast majority—74 percent—had between 70 percent and 90 percent of their assets so invested, and relatively few—10 percent of such funds—had 60 percent or less of their assets invested in equities and real estate.

The pattern for the mature funds in Figure 1 is surprisingly similar to that of the immature funds. In fact, 93 percent of the mature funds had more than 70 percent of plan assets invested in equities and real estate. Surely then, the supermature funds, in which more than three members out of five are no longer employed by the sponsoring company, will have shifted their assets to fixed-income securities. Wrong again; 88 percent of such plans had more than 70 percent of their assets in equities and real estate. One would expect the supermature funds to have much less in equities than immature funds because the duration of their liabilities is much shorter and because they will be paying out benefits much faster, but that is not the case. A mismatch appears to exist.

Peer-Group Pressure. One explanation of why U.K. managers fail to differentiate between mature and immature funds in their asset allocation policies is quite unflattering. The hypothesis is that the pension management business has two forms of risk—business risk and financial risk.

---

[2]The same study shows that U.K. pension funds are generally well funded with only a small percentage of plans at risk of failing the government-prescribed solvency tests.

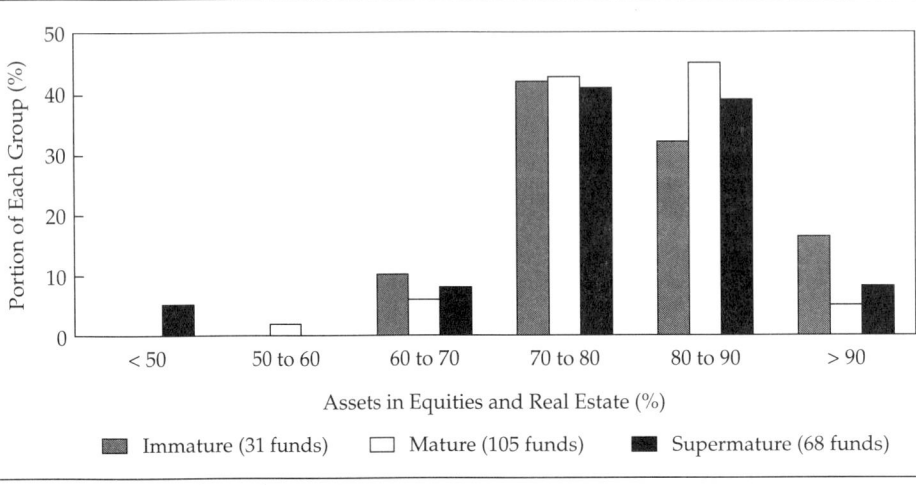

Figure 1. Percentage of U.K. Pension Funds' Assets in Equities and Real Estate by Maturity of Fund

Source: Based on data from The WM Company.

■ *Business risk.* If performance tables are easily available, and influential in manager selection, and if equity markets outperform, then investment management houses that tailor asset allocation policies to client liabilities might see lower average returns than a management house that stays with a uniform, but more aggressive, asset mix. In the absence of adjustments to the raw return figures, managers are encouraged to maintain high equity allocations. Otherwise, they risk underperforming the peer group and losing assets under management.

■ *Financial risk.* This risk is carried by the pension fund sponsors and might be measured as the probability of having to make unplanned contributions into the pension fund because, for example, the fund has too much in equities and experiences a setback.

Critics of the current situation suggest that this situation is possible in the United Kingdom because

- returns are not risk adjusted. (Ideally, the adjustment should be in the form of surplus volatility, not just in the form of return volatility.)
- managers are unwilling to stray too far from the consensus asset mix, whatever the nature of their clients' liabilities. (This is an agency–principal type problem. The way in which performance is currently measured will not encourage differentiation of client asset mixes, even by in-house managers.)
- the focal point of performance comparisons is the balanced fund, not the component subfunds.
- actuarial consultants and trustees do not take charge of the long-term asset mix decision. (In fact, the Pensions Act 1995 seems to have brought about more active involvement by consultants and trustees.)

Those who argue that managing business risk dominates client financial risk may be ignoring a vital aspect of the U.K. investing scene. There has been a long bull market, which has generally increased surpluses in spite of contribution holidays and early retirement programs. (In the United Kingdom, workforce participation rates for those 55 and older are particularly low.) Although taxation rules should in theory limit surpluses, the U.K. tax code has considerable flexibility as to how assets and liabilities are measured. Unless one assumes that strong past returns from equity markets have now eliminated the equity risk premium—a controversial assumption—the surpluses encourage per se a riskier asset mix (and a more stable asset mix[3]) and even a more homogenous asset mix. Furthermore, chief financial officers of sponsoring companies may encourage a riskier asset mix in such circumstances to reduce the long-term funding cost, with the risk of disappointment largely transferred to the sponsoring company's shareholders.

Euroland Experience

In terms of equity exposure, Table 1 shows Germany to be as much an exception on the low side as the United Kingdom is an exception on the high side. Of course, Germany does not have funded pension schemes to anywhere near the same extent as the United Kingdom. As mentioned earlier, in recent years, German companies have made great use of *Spezialfonds* (a tax-favored corporate vehicle) in order to defer corporate taxes. Compared with pension

---

[3]See Table 7 of Randall and Satchell, Discussion Paper PI-9714 (London: The Pensions Institute, November 1997).

funds in the Anglo-Saxon countries, the need to flow losses through the parent company's income statement is particularly onerous. Also remember that German life assurance companies are affected by legislated minimum return requirements.

The result of these legislative structures is a much greater emphasis in Germany, and indeed in the rest of euroland, on absolute portfolio returns but against a background of increasing interest in, and use of, equities. Clients seek both protection against downside risk and upside return participation, and what clients seek, managers frequently offer. Whether managers can realistically deliver both protection and participation is the subject of the rest of this presentation.

Three Important Questions

When dealing with downside risk and upside participation, the manager and client should ask themselves three questions:
1. How can we assess the manager's results?
2. How high should we set the floor return?
3. What can still go wrong? In other words, in what market conditions will it be difficult to meet expectations?

The key to a good client/manager relationship is exploring these issues in as open a manner as possible.

Manager Assessment. The benchmark for performance cannot reasonably be the equity market if performance rises and cash if performance falls; a benchmark must be both investable and known in advance. A "protect and participate" strategy seeks to provide the higher of two outcomes—the equity market if performance rises and a floor return if performance falls. Because an option is an instrument designed to deliver to the holder the better of two outcomes, then to assess the manager, the client needs to think in terms of option replication. Option replication is simply a disciplined buy–sell strategy designed to protect against falling markets. It does so by systematically selling into down markets and buying into up markets. How much is to be sold or bought is determined by an option delta calculation, in which the delta determines the proportion of the portfolio exposed to the risky asset.

One simple way of assessing a manager in these circumstances is to set as a benchmark the combination of the index plus a one-year put on the market (or, equivalently, a one-year deposit plus a call on the market). Checking with the OTC market shows what the market value of an asymmetric payoff might be worth. Fixed-income markets are less volatile than equity markets, and some evidence exists that fixed-income markets trend. As a result, downside protection in these markets should be less costly. Seven or eight percent per annum for an equity investment is typical. In volatile periods, the price of this asymmetry rises sharply. Clients might think that their managers can so cleverly time their exposure to market risk that this cost can be recovered through active management. But clients should be more cynical. If managers could reliably achieve such high excess returns, they would normally do so with their own assets and would, therefore, exit third-party asset management.

An alternative to OTC options is a simple rebalancing algorithm that aims to replicate an option. A paper portfolio of cash and equities is maintained, in which a simple delta-hedging strategy is followed. The manager's task is to outperform this paper portfolio. This model is analogous to the classic circumstance in which an index is set as a benchmark; the manager's job is to add value to a simple alternative that is available to the client. In fact, the rebalanced cash and equity portfolio is a much fairer assessment of the manager than the OTC option, for reasons that are explained later under the heading "What Can Go Wrong?" Of course, this discussion covers only how to assess the manager. It presupposes nothing about how the manager adds value and certainly does not presuppose a quantitative approach.

Setting the Floor. In a sense, eurolanders are *protectors* of assets. The stereotypical U.K. pension fund, on the other hand, with 80 percent invested in equities, is a *participator* in the risky asset class. The 100/100 investors—100 percent participation when the market is rising and 100 percent out when the market is falling—incorrectly think they can be both a protector and a participator. The way in which the floor affects the participation rate is the subject of an article by Garcia and Gould.[4] Setting the floor too high will lead to disappointing participation rates.

The retail market in many countries offers a wide choice of guaranteed investment funds, and another way of studying the trade-off is to look again at what the market offers—through the marketing literature from the insurance companies. **Figure 2** provides an example from some recent U.K. marketing literature about how the floor value for downside protection affects the participation rate on the upside. The retail investor had the choice of 11 percent participation in the risky asset—the return on the FTSE (Financial Times Stock Exchange) 100 Index and 100 percent capital protection; that is, the investment guarantees the client's money back. The other choice was 47 percent participation and 95 percent capital protection. The retail investor in these cases takes a haircut.

---
[4] C.B. Garcia and F.J. Gould, "An Empirical Study of Portfolio Insurance," *Financial Analysts Journal* (July/August 1987):44–54.

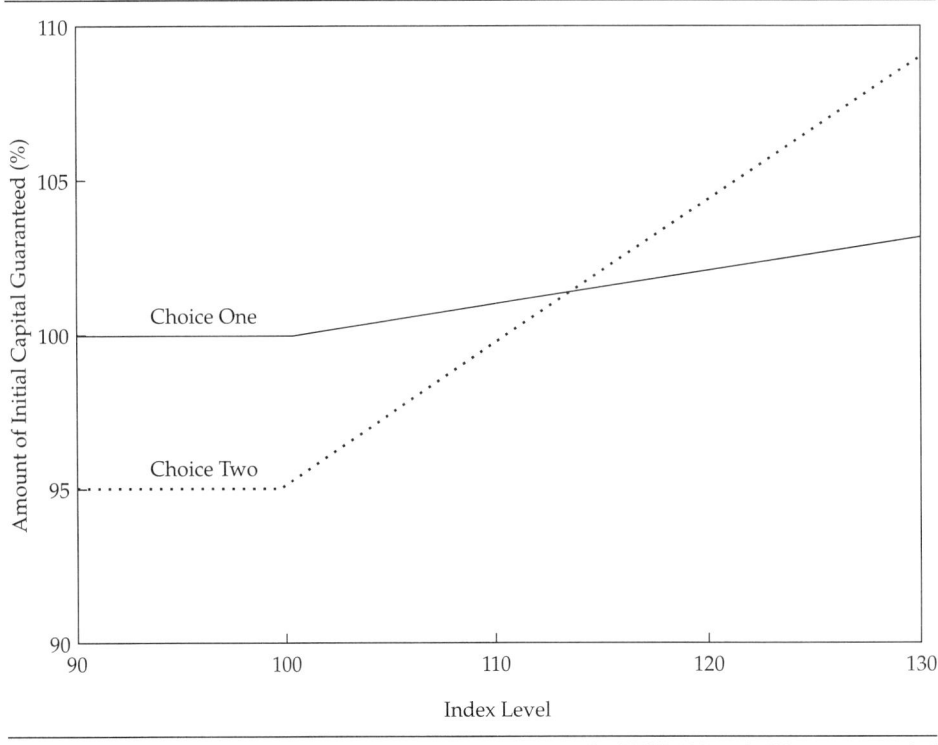

Figure 2. Effect of the Floor on the Participation Rate

Note: Choice One gives the client 11 percent participation in the FTSE 100 and 100 percent capital protection. Choice Two gives the client 47 percent participation and 95 percent capital protection.

For full capital protection, he or she loses 89 percent of the market return, and interest. For 95 percent protection, the haircut is 53 percent of the market return, and again, interest.

Obviously, in the retail example, distribution costs will be significant. In the earlier OTC option case, however, the institutional investor must also take a significant haircut. Why is the haircut so large relative to most client expectations? Why does a high floor reduce participation so sharply? To some extent, this is basic option mathematics, but Stapleton, Ho, and Subrahmanyam give some hope to those who believe they can manage a downside protection strategy more cheaply than the option markets.[5] They argue that the holder of an option has protection against misestimation of the hedging costs. The holder is, therefore, immune to changes in volatility levels. The writer of options typically charges more than the Black–Scholes model would suggest in order to receive a reward for the hedging risk that the option writer is carrying. When a client asks a manager to provide downside protection, the manager must delta hedge, but the guarantee is "soft." If the hedging program fails, the client pays. In other words, the "soft" guarantee offered by managers should be much less costly than the "hard" guarantee offered by an OTC option, but not by much. And it will depend significantly on market conditions. It is still wise for clients who seek a combination of protection and participation to look first at the price of insurance, as indicated in a free and competitive market between participants acting at arm's length. A market is first and foremost a source of information.

What Can Go Wrong? When clients and managers set absolute return targets, they should discuss what can go wrong. Clearly, the first thing that can go wrong is that expectations are unrealistic and that signals from the option markets are ignored. Second, the manager might fail to participate in market rises to the expected extent because of a poorly constructed delta-hedging program, with initial delta set too low.

The third, and most common, source of failure is misestimation of market volatility. Although the delta-hedging parameters might be set well, the market surprises investors by being more volatile than expected. Market volatility is the bane of the portfolio insurer. Delta hedging requires the manager to buy into rising markets and sell into falling markets. If the market is unusually volatile, then clearly there is a risk of being whipsawed (i.e., experiencing repeated

---
[5] R.C. Stapleton, T.S. Ho, and M.G. Subrahmanyam, "Idiosyncratic Risk and the Pricing of Options," Lancaster University Working Papers (1995).

losses in a mean-reverting market). It so happens that for three or four years—from the end of 1994 to mid-1998—Germany has experienced relatively strong trending equity and bond markets, which has helped portfolio insurers.

A fourth problem can arise if the manager's style is to act anticyclically. The management of downside risk requires the manager to buy high and sell low, which is a procyclical style. If the manager's instinct is to do the opposite—to buy low and sell high—then the policy is likely to be unstable and have high turnover as the two influences contest for the manager's attention.

Simulations

The market is one guide to what is reasonable. The past is another. Clients who seek downside protection from their managers should ask for a simulation of the managers' basic downside protection strategies. The time periods covered in the backtest should be as long as possible and should ideally cover periods with different market conditions.

A major difficulty when backtesting financial markets is that risk parameters are rarely stable. A manager can back test a model diligently, but the next period may not behave like the past. Markets that were mean reverting can temporarily turn mean averting, and vice versa. Yield curves that were downward sloping can turn upward sloping, thus affecting the results. The risk-free rate can fall to unprecedented lows. Finally, the results from any option-replication strategy can be very sensitive to incorrect estimates of the future level of volatility.

Summary and Conclusion

U.K. investment institutions look anomalous. They hold much more in "real" assets (i.e., equities and real estate) than equivalent institutions in other countries. The usual explanations of this situation refer to either cultural or regulatory reasons. A better understanding of the anomaly, which extends to variations within the universe of U.K. pension funds, would take into account the effect of surpluses. The high equity weighting, the relative stability of the asset mix, and the homogeneity of asset mix are all evidence of healthy surpluses of assets over liabilities.

By contrast, German institutions (and euroland institutions in general) often seek downside protection from their managers. This desire leads to nonlinear payoffs that are more difficult to manage, are likely to be more heterogeneous in their asset mix, and require more individual tailoring of the asset mix. Client and manager expectations need to be carefully thought out and communicated if disappointments are to be avoided. Simulations are especially helpful, even for managers who are not quantitative in their approach, as a means of establishing the cost of portfolio insurance. With reasonable expectations of what can be added through market timing, one would still expect managers who set out to protect a floor value to underperform markets when they rise and to underperform cash when they fall. Clients should not be disappointed, however, unless the manager has also underperformed a simple paper portfolio rebalanced monthly to reflect the client's desire for a nonlinear payoff.

Strategic Asset Allocation and Total Portfolio Returns

D. Don Ezra
Director of European Consulting
Frank Russell Company

> Strategic asset allocation has its place in the investment decision-making process and reflects a trade-off between opportunity and safety that only the investor should make. The asset allocation decision should take into consideration basic issues: determining which systems to model, identifying goals and fears, modeling the future, making decisions based on model results, and knowing what to do next. Ultimately, the impact that asset allocation has on total return reflects judgmental departures from a naive alternative.

Strategic asset allocation has been the subject of discussion for some time, but that does not mean all the issues have been resolved. This presentation reviews the importance of strategic asset allocation, including where it fits in the range of decisions required for investing a pool of money, explains some basic issues related to modeling and the decision-making process, and finally, provides a review of some historical studies that demonstrate the impact of the asset allocation decision on total fund returns.

Importance

The investment return is far and away the most important feature of institutional investing. For instance, think about the accumulation of wealth during the lifetime of a participant in a typical pension fund. The numbers are quite startling. The amount that goes in as contributions ultimately accounts for no more than 20 percent of the aggregate fund wealth. The investment return starts off small but accelerates very rapidly and, over time, completely dominates the contributions. Ultimately, more than 80 percent of a fund's wealth tends to come from the investment return. Thus, for pension funds, the investment return tends to be at least four times as important as contributions. So, investment policy is much more important than funding policy, which addresses the pace at which the contributions should be put into the fund.

Because investment returns are so important, the sources of those returns in the marketplace are a critical determinant of investment performance. **Figure 1** shows the annual returns for three U.K. investment categories and demonstrates clearly that asset classes have different risk patterns and different reward patterns. That realization is very important for understanding the role of asset allocation policy. Assets have two desirable features, high returns and low risk. Unfortunately, those features are not available together: They are at opposite ends of the risk–reward spectrum.

At one end of the spectrum is opportunity (i.e., high returns) with risk. Equity investments have the highest average return in Figure 1, but unfortunately, they do not have much year-to-year predictability. Equities have a lot of risk because investors cannot be sure what the returns will be. The line for bonds shows generally lower returns than equities with lower (but still very noticeable) volatility. At the other end of the spectrum is safety: Whereas stocks and bonds fall and rally, the return for T-bills (the cash equivalent) goes gently along. So, T-bills tend to offer safety but with little opportunity; one would never see the headline "T-Bills Rallied Strongly Today."

Unfortunately, because opportunity and safety are at opposite ends of the spectrum, investors cannot get an investment that provides both (high returns and low risk) at the same time. What investors have to do is to make a trade-off between seeking opportunity and tolerating risk. Essentially, where the trade-off is made determines the strategic asset allocation. So, the strategic asset allocation becomes, in

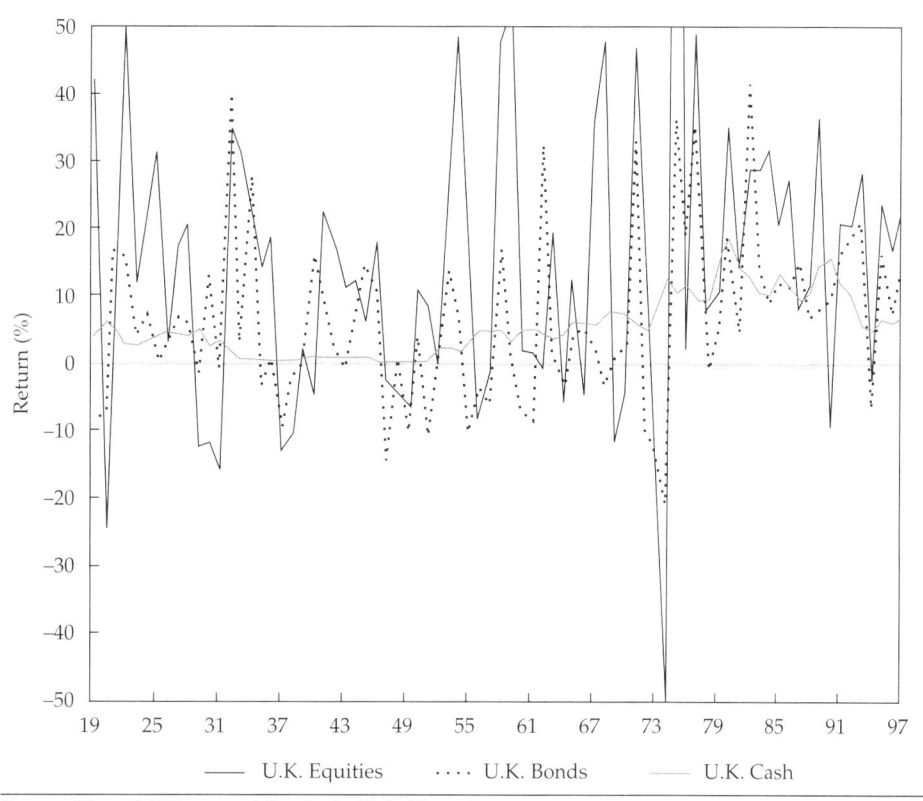

Figure 1. Annual Returns for U.K. Equities, Bonds, and Cash, 1919–97

Sources: Financial Times and Barclay's Global Investors.

essence, the way in which investors express the risk posture that they are most comfortable taking.

This risk posture relates more to the decision maker's personal comfort than to anything else. Investors do not have to be investment experts to make the risk tolerance decision, provided those jagged lines in Figure 1 can be translated into measures of comfort that investors understand.

Where the asset allocation decision fits in the entire panoply of investment decisions is the next consideration. **Figure 2** shows the scope of decisions that investors need to make. Everything starts with

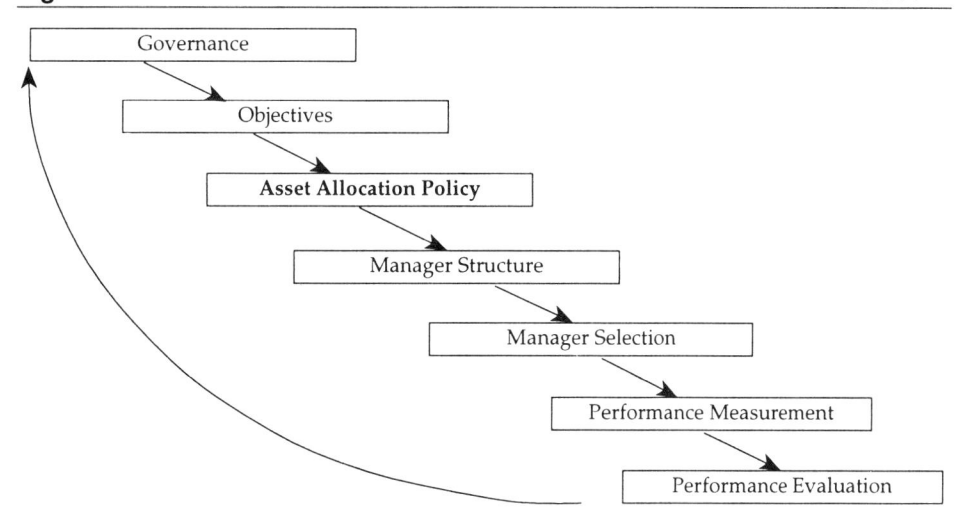

Figure 2. Placement of Asset Allocation in the Entire Investment Process

Governance → Objectives → Asset Allocation Policy → Manager Structure → Manager Selection → Performance Measurement → Performance Evaluation

©Association for Investment Management and Research

governance—deciding how a group of people will make decisions. It is a very important subject and one to which far too little attention has been paid.

Objectives and asset allocation policy are the big-picture decisions. These decisions start with what the trustees are trying to achieve with this pool of assets. They end with setting the trade-off between being comfortable that returns will be fairly predictable and being comfortable that the long-term objectives can be met in a cost-effective manner.

After those big-picture decisions are the day-to-day details of actually placing the money in the markets. Who are the managers who will make the day-to-day decisions? How are the trustees going to assemble a portfolio of managers, or if they have decided to have only one manager, what will be the characteristics of this one portfolio? Those are manager structure and manager selection decisions.

Remember that managers make many decisions, including not only security selection decisions but also tactical asset allocation (TAA) decisions. The latter are departures from the long-term strategy. Usually, the long-term strategic, or policy, position is arrived at by making the assumption that markets in various asset classes are in reasonable equilibrium with one another and the only way to get a higher expected return is to take more systematic risk. Markets, however, according to investment professionals, are almost never in complete equilibrium with one another, so some of them are temporarily considered overvalued and others undervalued. Therefore, if a manager thinks he or she can capture that overvaluation or undervaluation, departing from the strategic asset allocation temporarily makes sense until markets go back to equilibrium. These tactical departures, clearly, are made by managers after the asset allocation policy decision has been specified.

The last two boxes in Figure 2 are after-the-fact performance measurement and evaluation, which are two separate processes. Typically, measurement is done fairly frequently. Unfortunately, evaluation is also done frequently, although it should be done only when a whole stream of measurement data are available for evaluation purposes.

At the end of the whole process is an arrow that goes all the way back to the start because if measurement and evaluation are done well, new insights and new understanding should be generated. These new insights should help the trustees cycle through the process with greater knowledge the next time around.

Decision-Making Process

The decision-making process focuses on how a group of people (e.g., the plan trustees) make the strategic asset allocation decision. They must address five basic issues. First, what are the systems that are actually being modeled? Second, what are their goals and fears for the investment program? Third, how should the future be modeled? (No matter what is being modeled, inputs are needed to generate possible future scenarios.) The fourth, and typically the toughest, issue is how the trustees actually reach a decision using the data generated from these models. Finally, because this exercise is carried out only periodically, the trustees need to determine in advance what they will do between the time when they make the decision and the next time they address the strategic asset allocation issue. The world is going to change between those two times, and the trustees need a plan for anticipating those changes.

Modeling Issues. Before any asset allocation decision can be made, before any modeling can begin, the trustees need to decide what they are trying to model. The problem is, if the trustees do not discuss in advance what aspects they are modeling, they will end up with a poor model. In turn, any insights gained will be faulty.

This step is more of a philosophical than a numerical or financial issue. Often what happens is that someone says, "We have to make an asset allocation decision and run a study. What kind of model should we use?" Then, the context in which to place the study and the model are ignored. It is always best to make sure that the model is appropriate for the problem being studied. When deciding which aspects of the problem to model, the trustees have several choices to make.

- *Assets and liabilities*. If the trustees are going to make an asset allocation decision, they must model the assets. Liabilities, however, can be a tricky issue. Sometimes liabilities clearly exist—insurance liabilities, defined-benefit pension liabilities—but sometimes there may be none, as with defined-contribution pensions.

So, the trustees have to decide whether liabilities exist and, if so, how they are going to define those liabilities. For example, a defined-benefit pension scheme can have many different definitions of liabilities. Three that are often considered are as follows:
- *Wind-up liabilities*. Assuming the plan were to terminate today, what would the liabilities be? These liabilities would be based on current membership and salary histories and measured using current market conditions, such as interest rates.
- *Point-in-time liabilities*. Assuming the plan is not going to be wound up but is going to continue, what do the liabilities look like at this point in time? The answer is not necessarily the same as for the wind-up liabilities.

- *Ongoing liabilities.* Assuming that the plan will be ongoing, the trustees may want to model not only the present liabilities but also any possible changes or improvements that might occur in the benefits.

Because liabilities can be defined in a number of ways, how they are measured must be considered explicitly.

- *Changes in asset and liability valuations.* When modeling assets, one can easily determine their values because markets exist in which new assets are issued and in which existing issues are traded. Valuing liabilities is much more difficult. Typically with liabilities, although a new issue market might exist, one in which liabilities are traded does not. So, the reference points for measuring liabilities occur infrequently at best. As a result, estimating the value of liabilities is done by a group of experts called actuaries. Actuaries have a natural tendency—built right into their educational system—to smooth things out. Market participants, however, know that nothing is smooth in the real world. So, the way trustees model changes in liability values is important because the smoothing phenomenon can distort the problem they are trying to solve.

- *Taxation.* Taxation varies by incidence and amount in different countries. If it is relevant, trustees must ensure that it is built into the model.

- *Externalities.* Aspects beyond the assets and liabilities may be relevant for the model. For example, in the case of a defined-benefit pension plan, the financial status of the sponsor is very important because, in effect, the sponsor may be the underwriter of the benefits. So, the sponsor's goals become relevant and also the sponsor's financial position because that financial position may dictate the sponsor's ability to underwrite the benefits. The trustees must decide to what extent, and how, these issues will be modeled.

Defining Goals and Fears. Trustees have many goals and fears for the plan. Recognizing these multiple goals and fears is important; some models cannot cope with numerous goals and fears and instead artificially try to capture those multiple aspects in a single input.

A discussion of goals and fears is always helpful. During this discussion, members of an investment committee or board of trustees will realize they have different goals and fears. Unless they discuss them before making the asset allocation decision, they will make inappropriate decisions and will suffer a lot of grief when things go wrong.

Another issue with goals and fears is that they relate to different time horizons. Some of the goals may be short term, some intermediate term, and some long term. The same is true with fears. Realistic models will differentiate among them. Other models can cope with only a single time horizon.

Goals and fears are also difficult to specify in advance. Who can predict accurately what issues will be troubling in the future? In practice, people have vague thoughts about the kinds of issues that bother them; precision is rare. It is useful to start a discussion in which one person says, "You know, there really is a chance this might happen." Someone else says, "Well, that is not too bad, but how about this? This could happen." From that simple start, an important dialogue begins about the amount of bad news (what experts call "downside risk") that can be tolerated.

In particular, something that is rarely specified in advance is what behavioral finance theorists have labeled "regret," which everyone wants to avoid in practice. Regret is the after-the-fact feeling that an obvious alternative course of action would have worked out better. It is, unfortunately, after the fact. At the time the decision was made, the obvious alternative course of action did not look as appealing as the action that was taken. Regret occurs all the time. One should try to anticipate regret, although doing so is admittedly difficult. Even the mere fact of discussing the possibility of future regret is useful because then it can be built into the problem that is being modeled.

Remember that a poor discussion will inevitably lead to poor problem specification because a model can only be used to solve the problems that have been identified.

Modeling the Future. So, how does one actually model the future (i.e., make forecasts)? Whether the forecast is right or wrong is less important than whether it is credible, because one can only tell after the fact what was right and what was wrong. Before the fact, one can do nothing more than have a defensible set of forecasts. No one has a crystal ball. How one group decides what is credible may be different from how another group decides what is credible. That word "credible" or "defensible" needs to be included as an attribute in the model.

Many models lack balance. Of course, a model necessarily simplifies the real world because no one can possibly anticipate all the real-world complexities, and even if someone could, modeling them would be far too complicated mathematically. So, simplification is the answer. The problem is that the degree of simplification built into assets and the degree of simplification built into liabilities are rarely the same. Actuarial firms tend to focus more on the liabilities, possibly even modeling every participant, with assets covered in broad categories. Conversely, investment firms often model the assets in detail but use only a broad treatment of liabilities.

Having equal simplicity on both the asset and liability sides is a desirable feature of a model so as to avoid building a bias into the specification of the problem. An investor using a sensible model will get sensible projections.

Making a Decision. After running the model, an individual or group of people have to make a decision. *This step is the most difficult one in the process.* The model churns out reams of numbers. But what do all those numbers mean, and how does one go from all those numbers to saying the portfolio should be 75/25 equities/fixed income or 60/40?

■ *Modeling approaches.* Three approaches can be used for modeling: simulations, mean–variance optimization, and multistage stochastic programming (MSP). **Table 1** shows the characteristics of these different modeling approaches.

A simulation, as the word suggests, models the future in different ways. The modeler can project any number of measures of good and bad outcomes. Sometimes the model generates a complete probability distribution. Sometimes the model has a limited number of scenarios. In either case, a simulation models ways in which the future might develop.

Mean–variance optimization, as its name suggests, uses the mean as the measure of good news and the variance as the measure of bad news—just a single measure of each. It also uses a single balance of good and bad news, called risk tolerance. In essence, risk tolerance balances all the considerations of different goals, different fears, and different time horizons. It becomes the mathematical definition of the decision maker's comfort. The model runs all possible asset allocations through this formula for comfort and finds the point at which comfort is maximized. That point of maximum comfort is the asset allocation that the investor should adopt.

One of the limitations of mean–variance analysis is that because it operates over only one time horizon, it is not amenable to building a disaster recovery scenario. Such a scenario can be simulated, however, by saying that at the end of the period, if a certain event happens, then a new analysis starts from that point and a mean–variance analysis is conducted on that event in the future. Such an analysis can be done piecemeal, and in skilled hands, it probably imparts a fair understanding of the disaster scenario, but the final product will still be just a simulation of different mean–variance horizons as opposed to a single optimization over multiple horizons.

MSP is similar to mean–variance optimization, albeit somewhat more complex. MSP allows for multiple time horizons and many different ways of expressing good news and bad news. Of course, if specifying one measure of good news and one of bad is difficult, specifying multiple measures of each is even more difficult! But sometimes multiple measures fit more naturally with the real world. MSP is, in fact, an extension of mean–variance analysis that incorporates a more complex description of comfort. If, in fact, a single asset allocation held constant over all periods were the optimum, MSP would specify this allocation. If not, it would produce a series of allocations as optimal—in essence, not a single asset allocation strategy but instead a strategy for asset allocation. MSP is simply an extension of mean–variance analysis that incorporates several pieces of good news with different weights and several pieces of bad news with different risk tolerances all over multiple time horizons.

Simulations do not purport to indicate the optimal asset allocation. They just show the possibilities and leave the modeler to decide. Both of the optimizers (mean–variance optimization and MSP) attempt to indicate the optimal asset allocation position to take given the goals, fears, possibilities, and time horizons that have been built into the model. In taking this potentially valuable extra step, an optimizer ironically takes on the ability to mislead.

One interesting characteristic of the word "optimizer" is that it is such an optimistic word. An optimizer sounds like a good thing. If someone were to say, "Let's run that through the error maximizer," that would sound like a bad thing. In fact, every optimizer is also an error maximizer. In 1989, Richard Michaud wrote a wonderful article in the *Financial Analysts Journal* in which he looked at the

Table 1. Characteristics of Modeling Approaches

Characteristic	Simulations	Mean–Variance Optimization	Multistage Stochastic Programming
Multiple measures of good and bad outcomes	√	X	√
Guidance as to optimal asset allocation	X	√	√
Error-maximizing potential	X	√	1/2
Different degrees of risk aversion	Intuitive	X	√

error-maximizing capabilities of all optimizers.[1] He pointed out that an optimizer is only as good as its inputs. The optimizer tends to recommend those asset classes with particularly high expected returns, particularly low variances, and particularly low correlations. Similarly, it rejects asset classes with the opposite characteristics. But the most extreme inputs are exactly the ones for which errors are most likely. And the optimizer, seeking the best possible solution, will incorporate forecast errors to the greatest extent possible.

In this sense, an optimizer is an error maximizer, which is one reason why people do not automatically do whatever the optimizer says. They know the optimizer leads to extreme solutions, and they know the solutions are very sensitive to the inputs. Mean–variance optimization certainly is an error maximizer, and MSP, to the extent that it is an optimizer, is also an error maximizer. For MSP, however, the range over which the modeler can maximize the error is smaller than for mean–variance analysis because if the modeler puts enough real-life goals and fears into the model, they will automatically cut back the range of possible outcomes (hence, the "1/2" in Table 1 for that item).

The degree of risk aversion taken into account also varies among the three types of modeling approaches. With simulations, the modeler does not make any decisions explicitly, but he or she can do so intuitively. The modeler can look at different outcomes and say, "I am less happy about this than about that." So, the modeler has some intuitive way to apply risk aversion. MSP gives the modeler the chance to build in many degrees of risk aversion. Mean–variance optimization permits risk aversion based on only one measure of good or bad news.

Mean–variance optimization is the standard modeling tool that is used today by investment professionals. In experienced hands, the error-maximizing potential is greatly reduced because experienced modelers know how to cope with error-maximizing situations. Through its complexity, MSP offers the chance of dealing with some of the intricacies of multiple inputs automatically, but because of that complexity, it is much more difficult to use than mean–variance optimization. Simulations are particularly useful in simple situations or to help confirm a decision already made.

▪ *Other considerations.* Modeling gets the decision makers (e.g., the trustees) only so far in making the asset allocation decision. Other considerations, besides strictly numerical issues, need to be taken into account.

The trustees must consider what is the lowest risk portfolio, with risk defined in whatever way makes sense to the trustees. If the plan has no liabilities at all, then typically, T-bills are the lowest risk portfolio. If the plan has liabilities, then the best matched portfolio, and thus the lowest risk portfolio, is whatever asset allocation most closely mirrors the short-term changing characteristics of the liabilities or keeps the gap between assets and liabilities the least volatile.

The trustees also usually look at what everyone else does—that is, the consensus or average portfolio reported by various measurement studies. Then, they think about how their situation is different. The naive starting point, therefore, is to do what everyone else is doing, but everyone's situation is at least slightly different from the average position. The question is, is it different enough to depart from what everyone else is doing, or do the trustees want to depart from the lowest risk portfolio? This is the point where all the discussion and modeling and intuitive feelings come in.

What is important to remember about making a decision is that it is not a mathematical exercise, an exercise in engineering, or an exercise in investment specificity. It is an exercise in personal comfort. Because it is an exercise in personal comfort, the most appropriate person to decide if he or she is comfortable is that person. Therefore, when trustees are making a decision, they should not ask someone else to determine their comfort level. These days in the United Kingdom, about half of the pension trustees are making the asset allocation decision for themselves based on comfort. The other half still do not. They rely on someone else to tell them when they feel most comfortable.

Revisiting the Decision. Most plans revisit the asset allocation decision periodically, whether that period is every year, two years, or five years. The question then becomes what to do in the interval between the decision-making periods. Trustees generally use one of two broad approaches. The first is based on the fact that the policy allocation represents the position of greatest comfort. If the asset allocation policy is determined based on being the most comfortable, then whenever the trustees feel uncomfortable, they should rebalance back to the level of comfort. So, if the market moves the allocation away from the comfortable position and the trustees are unhappy with the extent it has moved, then the fund should be brought back in line with the comfortable position. If many things change, including the plan's circumstances and the way the trustees feel about the comfort level, then they should redo the whole asset allocation study. The important point is that the

---

[1]See also Michaud (1998) for a way to reduce the error-maximizing effect.

trustees need to decide explicitly on a rebalancing policy; otherwise, the danger is that the fund can stray far away from comfort.

The second approach is to anticipate major changes, which is something that the MSP methodology allows. The trustees say, "We can anticipate that the world will change, and if it changes in this direction, we will change the policy in this way. If it changes in that direction, we will change in another way." The trustees can build in changes in the plan's circumstances and their own forecasts and anticipate their actions. The fund ends up not with a single asset allocation that is deemed to be right for all time but, rather, a strategic asset allocation. The asset allocation strategy is, in fact, dynamic. With this approach, the trustees can actually ask themselves how they will react if things go dreadfully wrong (and they can define "dreadfully wrong" in many ways).

Impact on Total Return

The asset allocation decision is more than a theoretical exercise. Research has confirmed the significant impact of asset allocation on a plan's total returns.

Two studies in particular are absolutely fundamental: Brinson, Hood, and Beebower (1986), who are justly famous for the results that were revealed in their study, and Brinson, Singer, and Beebower (1991), who updated the 1986 study with more-rigorous analysis using better information but which came to broadly similar conclusions as the first study. Additionally, Hensel, Ezra, and Ilkiw (1991) presented a conceptual extension of the framework used by Brinson, Hood, and Beebower.

The basic premise of these studies is that investment performance is mathematically the result of two factors: the return in each asset class and how much of each asset class the investor has. The asset allocations can be based on various characteristics, three of which are defined conceptually in **Table 2**. The X characteristic is the naive allocation, which can be either the lowest risk portfolio or the average of what everyone else does—that is, what the trustees would do if they did not have thoughts of their own. The Y characteristic is the sponsor's, or the trustees', strategic choice of asset allocation policy. The Z characteristic is the manager's actual allocation, which might, for tactical reasons, depart from the strategy that the manager was told to follow.

Similarly, the security weights in Table 2 are defined as "1" for the market weight, "2" for the sponsor's normal weight, and "3" for the manager's actual weights.

So, for example, $X1$ represents a portfolio with market weights in a naive asset allocation; $Y2$ means that the sponsor has a strategic asset allocation policy and has decided to introduce permanent tilts relative to the market in each asset class; and $Z3$ is the manager's actual weights from time to time combined with the actual asset allocation.

Table 2 is important in understanding the work of Brinson, Hood, and Beebower because they did not consider either Row X, the naive allocation, or Column 2, representing tilts in the definition of the asset classes. So, their framework essentially consisted of four cells, shown in **Table 3**. $Y1$ is the strategic allocation with market weights of securities, which they called the policy; $Y3$ is the strategic allocation with the manager's actual security holdings, which they called policy plus security selection (SS); $Z1$ is the manager's

Table 2. Conceptual Portfolio Asset Allocations and Security Weights

	Security Weights		
Asset Allocations	1 (Market)	2 (Sponsor's Normal)	3 (Manager's Actual)
X (Naive)	X1 (basic naive)		
Y (Sponsor's strategic)		Y2 (sponsor's departures)	
Z (Manager's actual)			Z3 (manager's departures)

Table 3. Brinson, Hood, and Beebower Conceptual Portfolio Asset Allocations and Security Weights

	Security Weights	
Asset Allocation	1 (Market)	3 (Manager's Actual)
Y (Sponsor's strategic)	Y1 (policy)	Y3 (policy + SS)
Z (Manager's actual)	Z1 (policy + TAA)	Z3 (total portfolio return)

actual allocation with indexed security weights in each asset class, which they called policy plus TAA; and Z3 is the actual portfolio with the manager's actual weights and the manager's actual securities, which generates the actual portfolio return.

Brinson, Hood, and Beebower analyzed data on all the pension funds for which SEI Corporation had results available for a 10-year period. **Table 4** shows their results. The policy portfolios, on average, had a 10.11 percent annualized return. The policy plus SS portfolios returned 9.75 percent on average, and the policy plus TAA portfolios returned 9.44 percent; the average actual return of the funds was 9.01 percent.

Table 4. Average Returns in Brinson, Hood, and Beebower

Asset Allocations	Security Weights	
	Market	Actual
Strategic	Policy = 10.11%	Policy + SS = 9.75%
Actual	Policy + TAA = 9.44%	Actual = 9.01%

Source: Based on data from Brinson, Hood, and Beebower.

Table 5 shows these data in another way. The policy return was 10.11 percent. The impact of tactical departures from policy was, on average, a cost of 67 basis points (bps) a year. The impact of SS relative to policy was a cost of 36 bps a year. Other factors, most of which today would be termed interaction effects, cost 7 bps a year. These costs reduce the policy return to the 9.01 percent that the funds actually earned.

One of the most quoted, or actually misquoted, results in the investment literature is that Brinson, Hood, and Beebower concluded that the policy return accounts for 94 percent of total performance. In other words, that 10.11 percent is 94 percent of 9.01 percent. Clearly, that is not the case because the policy return is 112 percent of the actual return. But the erroneous conclusion is what most investment professionals tend to remember; even the pundits get this fact wrong.

So, what did Brinson, Hood, and Beebower actually say, and what did they really explain? What they explained was the variability of performance, not the average level of performance. The jagged line for U.K. equities in Figure 1 shows the same pattern of returns that a fund might generate if one were to look at the fund's return month by month or quarter by quarter. Brinson, Hood, and Beebower did exactly that (looked at the data quarter by quarter) and noticed huge similarities when they plotted the return of the policy portfolio and the actual return. In fact, they got a 94 percent R^2, which really says that the shape and level of the policy portfolio explains 94 percent of the shape and level of the actual return.

They then went further and said that if they were looking at variability of actual return, the policy return explained 94 percent of the changes in the actual return, and the policy plus tactical portfolio explained 96 percent. So, tactical deviations must explain the difference, or 2 percentage points of the variability. Similarly, policy plus SS explained 98 percent of the variability in return, so 4 percentage points must be what was left to be explained by SS.

What is interesting is that they obtained the TAA 2 percentage points explanatory power and SS 4 percentage points explanatory power by measuring them as deviations from something that was already established, namely the policy portfolio. But they did not measure the policy portfolio itself as a deviation from anything, or implicitly, they measured it as a deviation from zero.

In effect, what Brinson, Hood, and Beebower did was to imply that a sponsor's naive alternative to having a policy was not to make any investments at all. This assumption was not realistic because other naive alternatives existed—either the lowest risk portfolio or a portfolio equivalent to what everyone was doing—that at least got the investor into the markets.

Hensel, Ezra, and Ilkiw recast the Brinson, Hood, and Beebower framework in terms of these two other naive alternatives. They postulated that if the policy return itself was measured as a departure from the lowest risk portfolio, typically the lowest risk portfolio would be a single asset class portfolio, such as T-bills or index gilts, then the variation in return that the lowest risk portfolio, or any single asset class, explains is typically tiny (3 percent or less); the mere fact that the investor has a naive alternative for getting money into the market, if it is in a single asset class, explains very little of the shape of the return pattern. The specific policy that the investor chooses explains most of the return pattern, which is exactly consistent with what Brinson, Hood, and Beebower said.

Looking at a single asset class portfolio explains almost nothing in the pattern of returns, but looking at the consensus policy—the average of what every-

Table 5. Attribution of the Actual Return

Item	Average Return
Policy return	10.11%
Impact of TAA	−0.67
Impact of SS	−0.36
Impact of other interactions	−0.07
Actual portfolio return	9.01%

Source: Based on data from Brinson, Hood, and Beebower.

one does—explains almost all (about 99 percent) of the variation in the policy portfolio's return. Typically, the specific policy departure that the trustees make accounts for almost nothing. So, if a plan has decided to base its asset allocation on the consensus and then asks whether its circumstances are sufficiently different from the consensus to warrant a significantly different allocation, typically the amount of difference has about as little effect in explaining the return variability as tactical departures or security selection. Suddenly, those issues become just as important in explaining the return pattern as the policy decision.

Summary

Consideration of strategic asset allocation centers on three messages. First, the strategic asset allocation decision reflects the investor's risk policy. It is a position of comfort, and the investor is trading off two desirable goals—safety and opportunity—that cannot be achieved at the same time. Therefore, no one but the investor should make this decision. Second, the traditional attention to modeling reflects an engineer's focus, not an investor's. If a model must be used, MSP comes the closest to taking real-life problems into account. Third, most pension funds depart from the minimum risk position. Typically, if a plan sponsor looks at the consensus as the starting point for asset allocation, then strategic policy departures from the consensus asset allocation, tactical departures from the strategic position, and security selection departures from index weights—all explain very little of the return pattern. They are, in a sense, equally important or equally unimportant. The fact that the plan sponsor has an asset allocation at all is the factor that explains most of the return pattern.

References

Brinson, Gary P., Randolph L. Hood, and Gilbert L. Beebower. 1986. "Determinants of Portfolio Performance." *Financial Analysts Journal* (July/August):39–44.

Brinson, Gary P., Brian D. Singer, and Gilbert L. Beebower. 1991. "Determinants of Portfolio Performance II: An Update." *Financial Analysts Journal* (May/June):40–48.

Hensel, Chris R., D. Don Ezra, and John H. Ilkiw. 1991. "The Importance of the Asset Allocation Decision." *Financial Analysts Journal* (July/August):65–72.

Michaud, Richard O. 1989. "The Markowitz Optimization Enigma: Is 'Optimized' Optimal?" *Financial Analysts Journal* (January/February):31–42.

———. 1998. *Efficient Asset Management*. Boston, MA: Harvard Business School Press.

Question and Answer Session

D. Don Ezra

Question: Many of the theories and methodologies you discussed have been around for a few years, so why are U.K. pension funds just now starting to take control and build their own asset allocation policies?

Ezra: I think plan trustees are beginning to understand that they do not have to be investment experts to do this work. Also, they realize that the single most important part of the asset allocation policy decision is not at the detail level but simply how much to have in equities and how much to have in fixed income. They are beginning to get comfortable with making those decisions themselves. Also, as they do asset-liability modeling, they are beginning to find that maybe their fund is not the same as the consensus (that their situation is at least a little bit different), and they are more willing to reflect that realization in a policy.

I also think trustees are realizing that if they do not make the asset allocation policy decision, the decision will implicitly be made for them, typically by a balanced fund manager, and often with the manager's business-risk considerations driving it. That's not properly carrying out the role of trustee.

Question: Does Frank Russell have any evidence that fund managers have systematically added value (i.e., created alpha) through TAA?

Ezra: Let's agree that by "systematically added value," we mean that we are fairly convinced that managers are more skillful than lucky. No, that is not what we find. TAA is not an area in which it is easy to distinguish luck from skill. Security selection decisions, with perhaps 100 securities in a portfolio, involve making bets for or against each of them, and this multitude of bets permits skill to show through much faster than with TAA. The reason is that the same manager who is making many security decisions in a year may make only one or two tactical decisions in the same period because the trigger for TAA moves comes in long cycles of time. Without the multiplicity of bets to analyze, we can't be convinced that a manager's right or wrong bets reflect the manager's skill.

For example, the equity market has been going up for some time. Most tactical decisions are to underweight equities, assuming that a fall is more likely than a continued rise. Until a fall occurs, these tactical decisions look wrong. But we have not had a cycle change since 1991, which is much too short a period to decide. The mere fact that most tactical allocators today are losing value with their tactical departures does not mean that they do not have skill. It is just that market conditions have been too uniform, too one-sided, to judge whether any skill is there or not.

Question: You demonstrated that the allocator's departure from the consensus policy is generally trivial and that asset allocation and stock selection have a negative impact on returns. So, given the study results, what is the benefit of investment management?

Ezra: Table 5 showed that most active departures from a neutral position explain relatively little of the *shape* of the return pattern. Just because they have little effect on variability does not mean they don't affect the absolute level of the actual return. Unfortunately, the impact of managers' active decisions is more often negative than positive. So, what's the benefit of active management?

Well, active management affects two aspects of investment management: the fund under consideration and markets as a whole. The impact on markets as a whole is a public good. The public good arises because active management requires a lot of investment research, which helps markets become more efficient. And everybody benefits from markets allocating resources more efficiently.

The impact on specific funds is, of course, more negative than positive. But remember that for many funds, active management is positive. For them, active management has been unambiguously good. The losers must decide what to do about a game in which the odds are stacked against them. One sensible response—always justifiable—is to say, "I choose to no longer play the game" and to go passive. Another response is to say, "I want to keep playing the game, but I recognize that I have to find a winning strategy."

There will always be a role for active management. The less it exists, the more inefficient markets will get, and the more opportunity there will be for a good manager to make money for clients by exploiting the inefficiencies.

Tactical Asset Allocation

William A.R. Goodsall
Managing Director
First Quadrant, Limited

> Plan sponsors need to shift out of the old paradigm of balanced management, acknowledge the catalysts for change, and accept the new focus of asset allocation—the movement toward asset-liability modeling—as the pension fund movement matures. Tactical asset allocation has its benefits and drawbacks, but it has the potential to add value over drifting and passive rebalancing, where subjective judgment can fail. Managers should understand behavioral issues, key assumptions underlying TAA, the investment style, and the quantitative approach before implementing a TAA approach.

Once a fund-specific benchmark for strategic asset allocation is set, sponsors must decide on a clear policy for managing asset allocation going forward. The basic choices are passive (some form of mechanistic rebalancing) or active, in the form of tactical asset allocation (TAA). The global investment puzzle is too complex to rely on subjective judgment, and a systematic tactical process can offer potential added value at acceptably low risk. This presentation discusses several aspects of TAA: the choices available for managing the asset mix away from the strategic policy benchmark, the not-so-subtle behavioral influences on the TAA process in general and on modeling in particular, the nature and composition of the TAA process in place at First Quadrant, and some pros and cons of TAA.

Managing the Asset Mix

Numerous pressures for change have resulted in the old paradigm for pension fund management being replaced by a new focus on asset allocation.

Old Paradigm. The pension investment business in the United Kingdom has been dominated for the past 15–20 years by a consensus type of philosophy—balanced fund management often pegged to a specific consensus benchmark. Although for a long time that consensus philosophy seemed to serve quite a few people quite well, actually it did a lot of damage, the results of which are now beginning to show. For example, the consensus approach encourages all funds to have a similar asset distribution, regardless of the fund's liability profile. In addition, because of the consensus approach, the asset allocation issue was sidestepped. Sponsors certainly did not want to make asset allocation decisions at the tactical level, so they passed them off to their investment managers, who really did not want to make them either. A few traditional investment houses made gutsy, off-benchmark decisions, and more often than not, those tactical decisions were correct. They did, however, follow a narrow path around the benchmark for some very good reasons. If an investment manager goes long Japan in a big way and is wrong or even just early, people will notice. If an investment manager adds another stock to a well-diversified portfolio and it does not do well, people may not notice. So, real active asset allocation can look like a high-profile, lonely thing to do, unless the manager has the tools to do the job.

A curiosity of this consensus approach is that trustees and fund sponsors often give traditional managers very wide permitted asset allocation ranges, but then they really do not expect the managers to use them. For example, in a traditional mandate, managers might have the latitude to allocate +20 or –20 percent of the plan's assets to U.K. equities in relation to the plan's strategic benchmark. But those same trustees would be rather shocked if they were to receive a note from the managers saying they had deviated from the benchmark by 20 percentage points. So, wide allocation ranges have been permitted but largely have gone unused.

Another manifestation of the culture of consensus is the similarity of holdings across diverse funds. The WM Company looked at three tiers of maturity for pension funds (immature, mature, and supermature), where maturity level has to do with the inflow versus the outflow of cash. So, a mature fund is one in which cash inflows and cash outflows are roughly equal. In a supermature fund, the outflow far exceeds the income of the fund. WM found a surprising and disturbing characteristic of all three maturity levels: The percentage exposure to real assets (i.e., equity-type assets) is, with the exception of a few outliers for supermature funds, about the same for all three types of funds. An immature fund has very good reason to hold a lot of equities, but what about a supermature fund with a strong outflow? A mature or supermature fund certainly needs some exposure to equities to protect assets from inflation, but whether such a fund should have 80 percent in equities is extremely questionable.

Someone might reasonably wonder what has created such a situation in which funds have the same exposure to real assets across the maturity spectrum. At least a partial explanation is certainly found in the culture of consensus that has dominated the industry. Having these high exposures to equities may have been acceptable during a long bull market, but if a fairly sudden and particularly a prolonged pullback in the markets takes place, some of these funds could be in severe financial difficulties.

A final consequence of the old paradigm has been that the investment management community has often focused on what suited them rather than what necessarily suited the client. Of course, one might wonder whether the client really knew what he or she wanted, given the lack of focus on maturity profile.

New Focus. A new focus on asset allocation has been slowly emerging during the past few years, and it will pick up speed for some fairly clear reasons. The whole pension fund movement is becoming more mature. The minimum funding requirement (MFR) in the Pensions Act 1995 has imparted an increasing sense of urgency to the asset allocation issue. The statement of investment principles, Section 35 of the Pensions Act, is clear that the assets of a fund should be run specifically in relation to the liabilities of that fund. The plain man's view of Section 35 might be that demonstrating compliance, at least with the spirit of that section, is hard if one follows a consensus policy.

Much more asset-liability modeling is taking place than in the past, and out of that asset-liability modeling comes an emphasis on fund-specific benchmarks, which is a proper long-term policy for the set of assets most likely to deliver the financial results the plan sponsor wants. A nice exercise to go through is to imagine a world where that asset allocation decision can be made only once and can never subsequently change. Fortunately, plan sponsors are not constrained in that manner, but thinking along those lines is a good exercise and forces sponsors to put a lot of effort into getting that best set of assets. Institutionally, this process is quite demanding, as anyone who has gone through it knows well.

Pressures for Change. All of those changes just mentioned are slowly but surely eroding the philosophy of consensus. The potential problems that can come from the Pensions Act's MFR have concentrated the minds of corporate finance professionals. Treasurers and finance directors have realized that because of their pensions funds, they could be put in a position of having to go to their boards with a large negative surprise, which is generally not a career-enhancing move. Volatility will certainly be less acceptable than has been the case historically, and many corporate officials, although not all by any means, have been thinking about possible protective measures.

Cash flow has, to a large extent, disappeared from pension funds, certainly compared with a few years ago. The way that the disappearance of cash flow reduces the opportunity set sometimes gets overlooked. If a pension fund has huge amounts of cash coming in, then directing that cash into one asset class or another as the cash comes along is easy. Although some funds still have large cash flows, most funds do not, and those that do not are finding it much harder to duck the asset allocation decision than in the past. In a poor cash flow environment, asset allocation requires serious attention.

Finally, specific benchmarks and the increasing number of specialist mandates also combine to make avoiding the asset allocation decision more difficult for sponsors. With a specialist structure, it becomes obvious that a decision is needed as to who will manage the asset allocation.

Available Choices. Given the slow demise of the old paradigm, the new focus on asset allocation, and the inexorable pressures to adopt that new focus, exactly what asset allocation choices does a sponsor have? Essentially, sponsors have only three choices:
- *Drift*. Drifting means letting the markets take the plan where they will, which is the least smart thing to do but which many sponsors have done in the past.
- *Use a passive approach*. Passive means some form of mechanical rebalancing, which is the equivalent at the asset class level of indexing stocks in an individual market.

- *Use an active approach.* Active means some form of TAA, by means of a traditional, subjective approach and/or a disciplined, quantitative process.

Currency is an important part of the whole investment decision-making process and complements nicely an active TAA process. If a sponsor has a currency forecasting process that can add value and operates it alongside the TAA process, the returns to the two—assets and currency—are pretty much uncorrelated, so adding the two processes together produces an attractive information ratio, which is calculated by dividing the added value by its standard deviation.

Tactical protection strategies have been created as an offshoot of TAA because some finance directors wanted insurance against a nasty MFR hit. The insurance comes from using an active TAA approach in one direction only—to protect on the downside, not to take bets on the upside—coupled with some out-of-the-money put options.

Figure 1 illustrates the decision process for asset allocation—a process that is evolving in the United Kingdom. The policy benchmark is at the top of the figure, the next level down is the policy for managing asset allocation (which is TAA in this figure), and the remainder of the investment decision-making process is at the bottom level of the figure. In the United Kingdom, sponsors seem to be reacting against the old consensus formula; they are taking asset allocation back under central control. TAA is being used to drive the real-time allocation for the entire fund. This pattern is in contrast to that in the United States, where TAA is being looked on as almost a different asset class. That is to say, a U.S. fund might put 5 percent or 10 percent of its assets into a TAA program. The U.K. approach runs in a rather more conservative way with narrower control ranges than would typically be seen in the United States. This evolving U.K. approach also addresses directly one of the problems with the old style of handling asset allocation (letting competing balanced fund managers do it). The old approach resulted in the actual real-time allocation at any point being some kind of random residual of what all those managers were doing.

Behavioral Issues

Certain behavioral issues, either explicitly or implicitly, form the context in which TAA is carried out. Chief among these are the Bernstein Paradox, culture clash, cognitive bias, and information mismanagement.

The Bernstein Paradox. Peter Bernstein tells long-term investors, particularly those with cash flow, that they should not mind if the market goes

Figure 1. Asset Allocation Decision Process

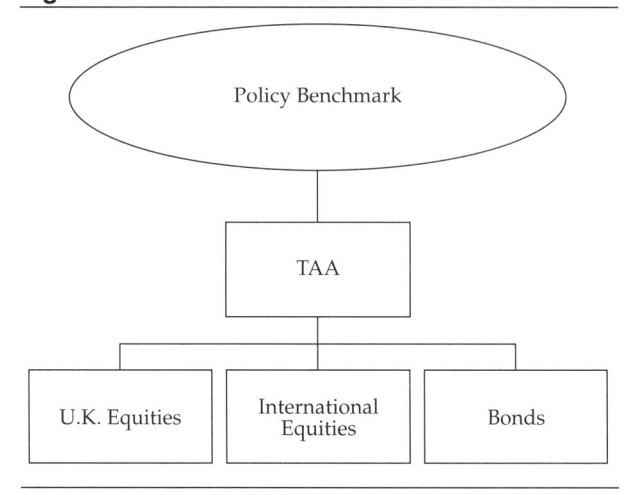

down. With money coming in and the need to continue investing, a down market gives better opportunities to invest for a higher future return. This paradox is a reminder of what must be one of the most basic tenets of good investment practice: If the price of an asset rises (falls), then all other things being equal at that new higher (lower) price, the asset is less (more) attractive than it was before because it is priced to give a lower (higher) return going forward. Of course, if an investor buys an asset today and its price goes up a little bit, the investor is not necessarily going to sell it tomorrow, but it behooves the investor to remember that every day that the asset's price does go up, it is becoming a little less attractive.

The behavior of market participants seems to imply that exactly the opposite is true. What happens when an asset's price goes up? Investors seem to like it more, not less, which is one of the reasons why bull markets run further than anyone thinks they are going to and why in a bear market the news gets even worse than people think it will. This attraction to rising assets is an important effect that should not be ignored.

Culture Clash. Another basic and pervasive behavioral issue is the culture clash between mainstream corporate life and the pension fund. If, for example, someone is running a division of a company and that person is successful, then he or she will probably get the resources to build a new factory to increase output further. If that person is failing, then that failure might be punished ruthlessly. A portfolio investor should do exactly the opposite. If an asset has done extremely well already, the investor should be thinking about paring back exposure to that asset, not adding to it. The clash between those two points of view is something that plays out in trustee meetings all around the world and will probably continue to do so. That clash, however, can quite often lead to bad decisions being made.

Cognitive Bias. Some convincing research has shown that humans have various cognitive biases. As decision-making machines, people are rather flawed. For example, the research shows that people pay far too much attention to the most recent pieces of information. One of the advantages of a systematic or quantitative approach is that it can keep those cognitive biases under control.

- *Framing*. The perceived significance of information is influenced by one's specific frame of reference. The way that a question is framed, for instance, can have a significant impact on the answer that people give. Studies have shown that when people are asked about making a bet, or what is effectively a bet, with a chance of winning a certain amount or losing a certain amount, 85 percent, for example, will go one way. But if that question is framed the other way around but with an identical mathematical outcome, almost as many people will go the other way. That finding is rather sobering because one can see how framing can affect the decisions that people make every day in the market.

- *Isolation effect*. Similarities between alternatives can be very important, and yet people will focus on the differences, especially when the information set is relatively complex. People tend to notice change more clearly than equilibrium. Someone might not know what the temperature is, but if it goes up or down 5 degrees, that person would probably know that it had changed and would have some idea by how much.

- *Certainty effect*. Some outcomes that have a measurable probability tend to be ignored because that probability might seem relatively low. If the probability of a certain sort of scenario developing is 60 percent, another scenario has a 20 percent probability, and a couple of scenarios each have a 10 percent probability, the tendency is to put too much focus on the one with the 60 percent probability and not enough on the others. As a fairly extreme example, what would the probability have been at the earlier part of this century that the value of German bonds would fall to zero? That outcome would almost certainly have been discounted. It had a fairly low probability by a number of criteria, but completely ignoring a possibility like that can have costly results. Again, a benefit of a disciplined and quantitative approach is that the investor can use probabilities in their real form to help in the decision-making process.

Information Mismanagement. The financial world is filled with a tremendous number of variables, and investors can and do mismanage all that information. One problem is sheer neglect: An investor's decision in the markets should usually be based on many interacting factors, some of which are quite subtle. More likely, the investor's decision is often based on just one thing—the most recent piece of information that the investor receives. If investors neglect the other factors and do not take them properly into account, how can they deal properly with unfolding events in the future?

Speed in information management is another important issue; being able to react quickly to new information is vital. A good example is found back in January 1990, when Japan was riding high. Japanese short-term interest rates went up roughly 150 basis points (bps) in about nine trading days. That increase of 150 bps may not sound like much, but it was a catastrophic rise at that time. A quantitative model would have shown an immediate collapse in the attractiveness of Japanese equities and suggested an instantaneous withdrawal from the market. Investors using more-traditional frameworks took a lot of time to accept that things had changed.

A third problem in information management is simple error, the misinterpretation of information.

Wealth Effects and Risk Tolerance. Risk tolerance and return prospects, including recent returns, can have a significant influence on the asset allocation decision. In an unpublished 1989 paper, William Sharpe wrote about the relationship between wealth and risk tolerance. Basically, his thesis is that as the price of a risky asset rises, the tolerance for risk rises. That effect is seen with equity markets all the time. If recent returns have been low, risk tolerance tends to be low. If returns have been high, investors feel good about the market, so their tolerance for taking on more risk by buying more stock goes up.

By combining Sharpe's hypothesis about risk tolerance with the basic investment tenet that low (high) recent returns should lead to high (low) future return prospects, one can get a sense of the wealth sensitivity of risk tolerance. Portfolio insurers, for instance, want to sell when the market falls; if returns have been low, the allocation to equities will be reduced because risk tolerance has plummeted. A drifting or buy-and-hold asset allocation mix will show a similarly low equity allocation; risk exposure declines with reductions in wealth, and the decline is rapid enough to outweigh the attraction of the improved return prospects brought on by newly fallen markets. Under a constant mix strategy, which is typical of the mechanical rebalancer who stays with the long-term policy benchmark, risk tolerance varies proportionately with wealth and declines partially—just enough to offset the attraction of improved return prospects. The active tactical allocator is exactly opposite to the portfolio insurer; risk tolerance does not change with changes in wealth, and if recent returns have been low, then the allocation to equities will be raised to take advantage of the future higher returns that should follow.

Rebalancing versus Drift. A 1994 First Quadrant study, based on data from The WM Company's performance survey, modeled returns for various allocation strategies applied to the U.K. market. **Table 1** shows the average returns to different asset classes and allocation approaches, with transaction costs included.

The annualized return for U.K. equities was slightly more than 15 percent a year; U.K. bonds returned roughly 12.6 percent. The last three columns are looking at a global fund with significant overseas content. With rebalancing, the ending mix and the starting mix are the same, so the starting allocation for the fund is 74 percent in equities and 26 percent in bonds. If an investor had done nothing but reinvest the income in each asset class and made no other asset allocation decisions (i.e., adopt a drifting strategy), the investor would have received a 13.98 percent annual return on that global mix. Excluding real estate, the investor would have ended up with 78 percent in equities. Because equities performed well, drift raised the exposure to equities by 4 percentage points. The actual average fund saw a 14.04 percent return, but its ending mix in equities was 87 percent. So, it did better than drift—6 bps a year more—but it raised the exposure to equities by another 9 percentage points. The final column shows that mechanically rebalancing every quarter back to that starting mix would have produced a 14.41 percent annual return, or about 40 bps a year more than the average fund and the drifting portfolio. On a large pension fund, that is a lot of money that pays a lot of benefits. The investor is still at 74 percent in equities, and the volatility of that return is lower than the average fund and the drifting portfolio.

Table 1 shows a sobering set of numbers that investment managers, trustees, and consultants would do well to ponder. Active management did not add much value over a drifting portfolio. If investors can get an equal or even better result with a passive approach, they have to think hard about doing something different and must have a firm basis for doing so. Compared with a passive approach, traditional active investment management increased the allocation to equities by 13 percentage points, which one might think was a good decision because equities have done well. But by taking a passive stance, investors could have had better returns with lower exposure and actually been in a stronger position to face the new conditions and the rigors of MFR.

Tactical Asset Allocation

The investment industry grew up around picking stocks to try and beat markets. Some people succeed some of the time, but beating the markets is very difficult; overall, of course, stock picking is a zero- or negative-sum game for the whole investment industry. Nonetheless, investors spend most of their time on stock picking; they do not spend much time on asset allocation. So, asset allocation provides a richer potential for value added than does stock selection, and it is something that can be exploited with the proper tools.

Key Assumptions. Three basic assumptions underlie TAA. First, the markets provide a lot of information about the rewards available. Market participants, for instance, can get a reasonable idea of the yield on cash by looking at the redemption yield on bonds, and the earnings yield on stocks gives an idea of what is available from the equity market. Second, investors can look at many variables, of greater or lesser use, but all of them have some sort of equilibrium or mean value, although those values can change. **Exhibit 1** shows some of the variables that First Quadrant uses in asset allocation models. For the most part, they are recognizable and widely followed items and have track records that give some sense of their normal or equilibrium values. Third, the further values get away from those equilibrium

Table 1. Drift versus Actual versus Rebalancing, January 1986–March 1994

	U.K. Equities	U.K. Bonds	Drift	WM Average Fund (Actual)	Quarterly Rebalance
Annualized return (%)	15.10	12.56	13.98	14.04	14.41
Standard deviation (%)	18.90	7.85	14.21	14.32	13.49
Information ratio	0.80	1.60	0.98	0.98	1.07
End mix for global equities (%)	100	0	78	87	74
End mix for global fixed income (%)	0	100	22	8	26

Source: First Quadrant study, based on WM AllFunds data.

Exhibit 1. Variables Used by First Quadrant

Pooled Models	Local Models
Normal equity risk premium	Equity risk premium
Equity risk premium	Equity dividend yield
Bond risk premium	Bond risk premium
Cash yield	Bond yield
Global short-term liquidity	Cash yield
Trend in maturity premium	Short-term liquidity
Trend in global equity risk premium	Trend in equity risk premium
Acceleration in global equity risk premium	Trend in maturity premium
Long-term liquidity	Long-term liquidity
Global equity volatility	Equity volatility
Sustained bond momentum	Trading effect

levels, the greater are the forces to pull them back in line. The equity risk premium is a prime example and still works in most markets around the world.

Investment Style. As quantitative investors, we at First Quadrant do the same thing as other investors, but we do it with numbers in a systematic and disciplined way based on fundamental theoretical principles. We want to know what drives the markets, but then using the tools at our disposal, we want to translate that knowledge into investment decisions. Those tools are value driven, generally contrarian and certainly unemotional, and multidisciplinary. They incorporate valuation, economics, and sentiment. One especially important issue is to make the process fact based, because if we have a systematic and disciplined approach, then using subjective opinion muddies the water; we will have destroyed the integrity of the process. Despite markets generally being reasonably efficient—certainly most of the bigger, developed ones are—we believe that investors can still make money using known, published facts.

Quantitative Approach. We use a quantitative approach to handle the ever-increasing complexity of the markets. Think about the number of markets around the world (stock, bond, and cash) and the number of variables that investors might want to look at to make well-founded decisions in any of those markets, especially if they are seriously trying to compare one market with another. The number of variables involved gets very large very quickly. The human mind is not well designed to cope with that degree of complexity, but computers are.

Being able to deal with complexity allows us to take advantage of a large opportunity set. By running a TAA program with many assets, we get a substantial diversification effect. If a manager is running a TAA program along traditional lines, that manager is probably limited to a relatively small number of major bets—perhaps the big regional bets (e.g., Spain versus France, Germany versus Hong Kong), which are hard to do day-by-day without a systematic framework. If a manager is limited to a few major bets and is wrong or simply a bit early, the discomfort can be acute. But having a dozen other bets with eight of them working can do a lot to ameliorate that discomfort.

The diversification benefits of using a large opportunity set are highlighted in **Figure 2**, which

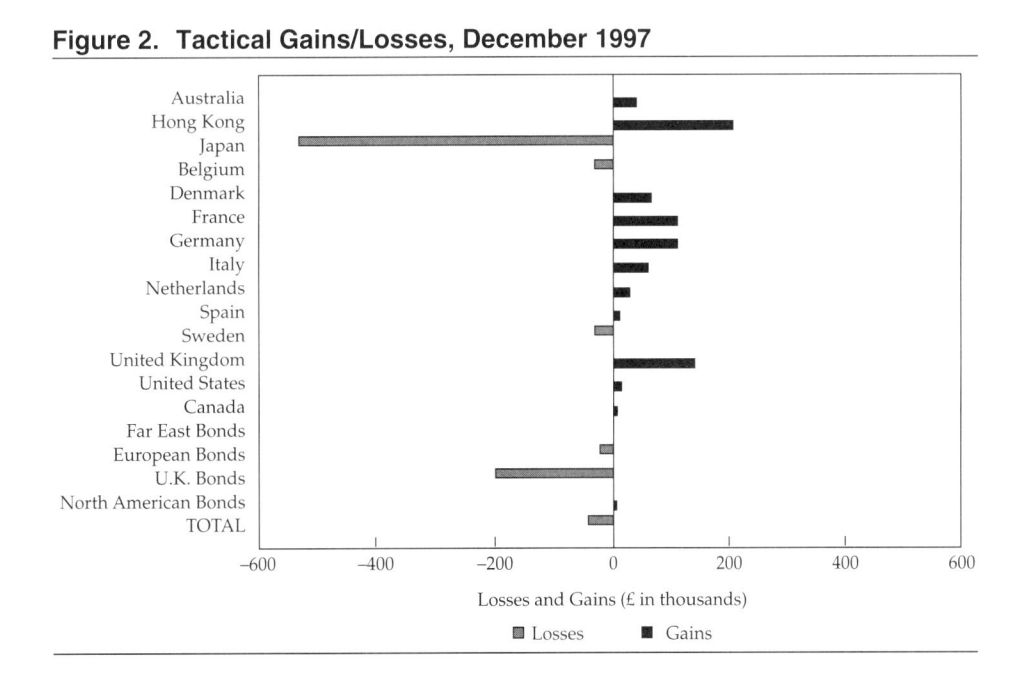

Figure 2. Tactical Gains/Losses, December 1997

shows the actual gains and losses for one of our U.K. TAA clients in December 1997. We were long Japan because it was very attractive, at least in our models, and remains so. But December was a particularly horrid month for Japan. Stocks went down 14 percent and bonds lost some money as well. A number of other bets were going right, however. Adding up the positive and negative bars produces a 2:1 ratio, which is actually quite nice. So, the diversification benefits almost canceled out the extraordinarily bad performance from Japan. Although the total return for the month was negative, it would have been a lot worse if we had not been able to diversify into other markets.

Using a quantitative approach also allows us to avoid popular but unprofitable trend-following behavior by mandating a regime that forces us to buy low and sell high.

Finally, a quantitative approach enables us, at least potentially, to minimize the slippage that almost inevitably occurs from the idea stage to the implementation state. If managers are going to use a quantitative process, then they should take it all the way through to implementation. Emotion should not get back into the picture at the output end. If they have built a complex, fairly sophisticated process to indicate what to do and then they "cherry pick" the results, they might as well throw the whole process out the window. When the results seem intuitively most uncomfortable in the short term is actually when that discipline is most needed to make the manager take the specified action.

At First Quadrant, we think we have learned a valuable lesson about the nature of a quantitative approach, namely that it should not be a black box. Someone should be able to lift the lid at any point in the process and see what is going on. The real black boxes are sitting atop the shoulders of the traditional managers who cannot say precisely why they did a certain thing. If these traditional managers take a certain type of action at Point A and a similar action at Point B, can they be sure that the way they processed the new data in their heads is exactly the same? With all the evidence of cognitive biases (and all the rest of the behavioral finance research), one could become concerned that the model may be changing in subtle ways that the individual does not realize. That person may not be processing with the same model; it may have become distorted. With a computer model, one can be sure that it is exactly the same model as last time but fresh data are being used, that the process is replicable with precision, and that new data can be incorporated quickly and reliably. Models can be changed and developed over time, of course, but the changes are done on a carefully controlled and documented basis, without the noise introduced by subjective guesses about the future.

Outline of TAA Process. As TAA managers, we first investigate what drives the markets and build models to tell us whether assets are cheap, expensive, or fairly priced. From those models, we generate a set of attractiveness numbers that we rank every day using a 0–100 percent attractiveness range for 40 markets around the world (20 developed and 20 emerging).

The attractiveness ranking scale is shown in **Table 2**. The broad band in the middle, which we call the neutral area, is where, other things being equal, not a lot is happening. When an asset's attractiveness gets beyond the neutral area—toward the top and bottom deciles—it goes increasingly quickly to the limit of the control ranges that have been set. One important issue to remember when doing TAA in a systematic way is that if a fund gives a control range, TAA will use it. If a fund has specified a +10 percent or –10 percent range and the TAA manager gets a top or bottom decile signal, the manager will use that full range, which makes the setting of those ranges much more critical than in the old style of giving a big range and then not expecting the manager to use it.

Table 2. Ranking Asset Attractiveness

Asset Attractiveness	Decile
Attractive	1
Moderately attractive	2–3
Neutral	4–7
Moderately vulnerable	8–9
Vulnerable	10

Those attractiveness numbers are the same no matter what fund we are applying them to. For example, we can have only one attractiveness number for German equities on any given day. But when we apply it to the fund's own particular benchmark and its set of ranges and other constraints, it produces a recommendation unique to the particular fund. With TAA, managers can get a variety of results for different funds that have broadly similar benchmarks. The control ranges that are used for each asset class and that are based on the fund's constraints are an absolutely critical control function for the risk–return profile of the whole program. Every fund will have its own views on exactly what it wants, and some will want big ranges for big markets. Thus, TAA can give different results for different funds for entirely justifiable reasons.

Two facets of our implementation phase warrant mention: We implement exposure changes relatively efficiently and economically with index futures, and we are adamant in keeping judgment out of the implementation process. Also, we constantly remind ourselves that the place for judgment is in deciding what goes in the model at the front end, not in modifying what comes out of the model or in implementing selectively that output.

TAA Pros and Cons

TAA does have its advantages and disadvantages. Perhaps the biggest advantage is that a manager can assess the attractiveness of a wide range of markets on a day-by-day basis, even on a real-time basis. Emotion saps performance, and with TAA, emotion is removed from the investment decision-making process. TAA also allows a manager to take advantage of a substantial diversification effect. Finally, a manager can capture finer nuances of difference between valuation fundamentals with TAA than by using a subjective approach.

TAA does have drawbacks. First, as has been the case in recent years, the value added may be modest when markets are generally strong. Second, this type of approach is generally contrarian in nature. Being contrarian usually means being early, and being early can be uncomfortable. If a manager is out of step with the crowd, that may not be a popular place to be. If the opportunity set is large, however, then the discomfort can be kept at a level that is within the pain threshold of the client. From time to time, the discomfort level may move outside that pain threshold, and the manager has to be able to nurse a client through that period.

Third, equilibrium levels of key variables sometimes change. TAA may take some time to recognize a real regime shift, but the quantitative approach is not necessarily much of a disadvantage in this regard compared with a traditional one. Finally, some sponsors are still uncomfortable using derivatives, but the advantages of using index futures for asset allocation are so compelling that those fears will gradually fade away.

Conclusion

The answers to three questions can determine whether an asset allocation process is real or whether it is some warmed-over form of balanced management. First, is it based on fundamentals? It should be, and the quantitative models are merely a better tool kit to address those fundamentals than a subjective approach is. Second, is it contrarian? If it is momentum based, then it is following trends rather than going against them. Third, is implementation mandatory? If the person implementing the process can decide not to take an action that is indicated, then the process is not that different from a subjective one. An interesting test of whether a manager has been using a TAA process is to look back at the fund and see if the manager has used the ranges given.

TAA is a useful activity. Huge opportunities exist in the markets, but those opportunities are quite hard to capture. A manager, however, has to capture only a small piece of them to do better than the crowd. TAA is an effective way to capture those opportunities.

Question and Answer Session
William A.R. Goodsall

Question: How sensitive to particular time periods is your conclusion from Table 1 that simple quarterly rebalancing easily outperforms the WM average fund?

Goodsall: At the end of 1996, the picture was even more stark than shown in Table 1; over an 11-year period, the average manager was actually below drift and the quarterly rebalancing was even further ahead. A broad rule of thumb is, if equities are compounding annually at a rate that is 4 percent higher than another asset class (e.g., bonds), then in terms of raw returns, drifting will give a higher return than rebalancing. If equities are compounding below that 4 percent threshold, then rebalancing will probably give as good or better return.

Of course, we can find past periods in which equities have been above that 4 percent differential and drifting would have been better. Going forward, however, it seems unlikely that the 4 percent threshold will be exceeded, so rebalancing will probably be a better choice than drift. I should also note that we have found no period in which drifting beat rebalancing on a risk-adjusted basis.

Question: Can you comment more on the point you made that a successful investor pares back recent winners and favors recent disappointing markets?

Goodsall: An investor who goes with the flow or drifts entirely will have maximum exposure to markets at the peak and minimum exposure at the trough, which is not the optimum thing to do. One might think the best thing to do is to have minimum exposure just before the peak of the market and vice versa. But, of course, that stance is not practical, and you are probably not going to be able to time the market that well anyway. If you can be somewhat contrarian, then you can do quite a bit better than the crowd. But being contrarian does have a cost in terms of discomfort because stepping away from the crowd is hard to do. If a market has become completely hammered, everybody has losses and the news looks terrible, so stepping up to the plate and going heavily into that market is hard to do. The cost if you are wrong, if the market goes down some more, can be huge; however, that is exactly the time you should be looking at buying that market.

Question: What do you think is the probability of global TAA (GTAA) outperforming quarterly rebalancing in the long run?

Goodsall: Whether GTAA can outperform rebalancing depends heavily on the quality of the forecasting process. If you do not have a good forecasting process, then periodic rebalancing is probably the best choice. But if you have a good forecasting methodology that works, then there is opportunity to add value with GTAA because the quarter end or the month end will not necessarily be the optimum moment to rebalance.

Question: Are there alternatives to time-based rebalancing?

Goodsall: If you mean some sort of range or threshold rebalancing, the answer is yes, but the results are not substantially different from periodic rebalancing. The basic approach is to set a range, typically 3–5 percent, then rebalance when the exposure reaches that range away from the central exposure point. The size of the range is obviously important for the results, but the critical point in any rebalancing is that once you reach your threshold—whether your time point or your range limit—you come back to the center point. Beyond that, the important fundamental decision is whether or not to rebalance; the methodology that is used is simply a refinement.

Uses of Futures and Index Funds

James R.C. Woodlock
Managing Director, Quantitative Division
Barclays Global Investors Limited

> Implementing a global asset allocation strategy can be accomplished by purchasing an equities basket, futures, or index funds, but each alternative differs in terms of costs and benefits. Although using futures does not involve trading commission, custody costs, and tax withholding, it does involve an annual roll commission, margin financing costs, and basis risks. In contrast to futures contracts, index funds reduce basis risk and transaction costs and are readily available. As a result, investors could easily achieve global equity market exposure at a low cost and avoid expensive withholding taxes and stamp duties by using index funds.

Investors can be rather inflexible when thinking about global asset allocation. They usually see global asset allocation only as a matter of Germany versus France or Japan versus the United States, for example. The myriad investment objectives and constraints of today's investment environment demand a more creative view of asset allocation decisions. This presentation examines three possible asset allocation choices—an equity basket, futures, and index funds—and illustrates the construction of a global equity fund.

Asset Allocation Choices

A U.K. institution intending to buy exposure to U.S. equities could do so via three main vehicles:
- an equity basket (i.e., an actively managed, diversified basket of U.S. shares),
- futures, and
- index funds.

The three choices can all achieve the desired asset allocation objectives but differ in terms of costs and complexity.

Equity Basket. The total cost to a U.K. fund of acquiring a standard U.S. equity basket is about 34 basis points (bps). The bid–ask spread on that basket is about 22 bps. The commission cost is about 9 bps. The custody and market impact costs are small, about 2 and 1 bps, respectively.

Suppose a U.K. investor bought a basket of equities to replicate the S&P 500 Index. The dividend yield of the S&P 500 is about 1.7 percent. For U.K. investors, dividends are withheld at 30 percent, but 15 percent of that can be reclaimed. So, the cost, or the loss of return, is about 0.26 percent, and the net yield for this U.K. investor would be about 1.4 percent.

Futures. Futures are a way for the investor to obtain quickly the desired exposure. Compared with an equity basket, futures offer return and cost advantages, but the investor also must face margin financing, benchmark, and basis risk issues.

■ *Return advantage.* A futures contract does not receive any dividends; therefore, it does not pay any tax. As a result of that lack of taxation and also the fact that contracts are priced by the domestic investor, the return to a U.K. investor from using a futures contract on the S&P 500 does not suffer that 0.26 percent cost that the equity basket does. So, U.K. investors are better off using futures than buying a basket of shares.

■ *Costs.* For futures, the initial trading commission is low, about 2 bps, but a futures contract lasts for only three months. Thus, every three months the investor has to roll that exposure forward, which means that the initial trading commission of 2 bps becomes 4 bps, and because that contract has to be bought and sold every three months, over a year, the commission cost eventually rises to 16 bps. The market impact is small, about 1 bp, and fair value misalignment is zero on average. So, the total annual cost is about 19 bps, versus 34 bps for the equity basket.

■ *Margin financing.* Margin financing is an issue for investors using futures. At the moment, the initial margin is about 3.5 percent of the amount

©Association for Investment Management and Research

invested. Sometimes futures are used as an overlay strategy, which means that the investor does not have actual funds to back that margin position and may have to finance the position, thus incurring explicit financing costs. More often, however, futures are used as part of a broader strategy, whereby the investor has assets that can be used to provide the margin. In this case, the investor has an opportunity cost, but the lost T-bill return is partially offset by the deposit interest at the clearinghouse. The net effect is that the investor probably incurs another 2 bps of cost.

■ *Benchmarks.* Most money managers are accustomed to operating against benchmarks. When it comes to the United States, the typical benchmark for a U.K. manager is the U.S. component of the FT/S&P Actuaries World Index, not the S&P 500. But unfortunately, the U.S. component of the FT/S&P does not have a futures contract. So, to gain exposure to the U.S. market using futures, a U.K. manager would have to use the S&P 500 as a proxy.

The question is whether the S&P 500 is a good proxy. In one sense, the answer is yes. **Figure 1** shows the divergence in returns between the S&P 500 and the U.S. component of the FT/S&P. The amount of movement away from each other, as shown in the figure, is generally quite small, suggesting that the two are highly correlated. In another sense, however, they are definitely not the same index. The S&P 500 is somewhat narrow in scope, excluding mid- and small-capitalization stocks and being considerably smaller than the FT/S&P U.S. component's 640–650 stocks. Furthermore, the S&P 500 is exchange based, not market based, and actually contains Dutch companies and Canadian companies, whereas the FT/S&P U.S. component is market based and includes only U.S. companies.

■ *Basis risk.* The fact that the two indexes are close but not the same leads to basis risk. In fact, the tracking error of the S&P 500 against the U.S. component of the FT/S&P is about 0.57 percent, which, although small, is an extra risk for U.K. investors. This risk might be acceptable given the prospect of higher return, but there is no reason to believe that one of those indexes will continuously outperform the other over the long run. So, one should not have an expectation of a higher return from either index. One way of looking at the impact of the extra risk, without a higher return expectation, is by using an information ratio approach. Assuming an information ratio of 1:2, the performance opportunity cost for taking the extra risk of 0.57 percent is about 0.29 percent. Using the futures contract in effect means reducing part of the risk tolerance in the total portfolio, and the cost of that lost risk tolerance, or more specifically the cost of basis risk, is 29 bps.

■ *Total costs.* The total costs (the profits and losses, so to speak) for the use of futures can now be calculated. A total of 57 bps of profit accrues to the

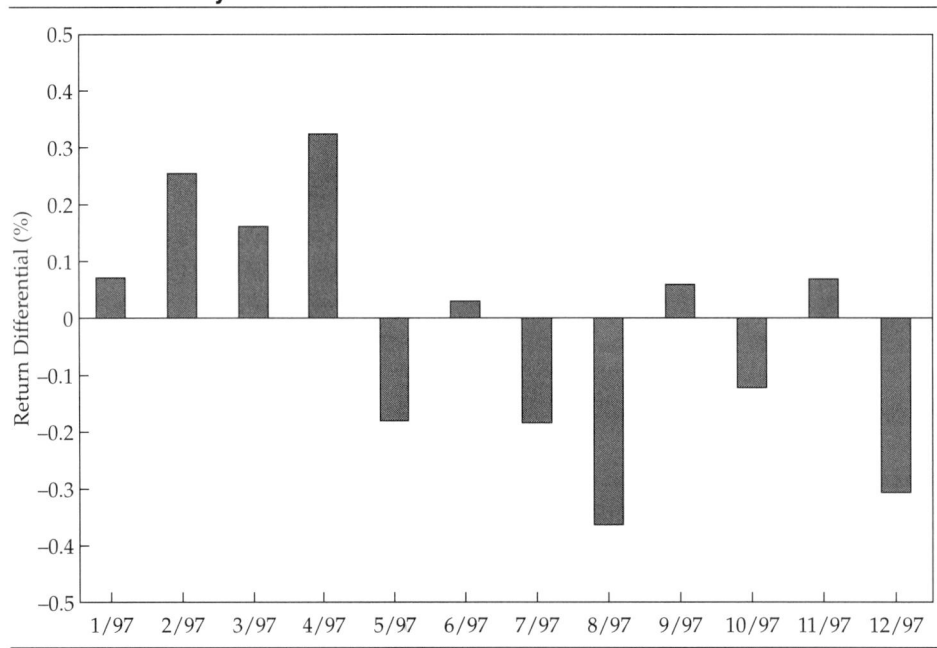

Figure 1. Divergence in Returns: S&P 500 versus U.S. Component of FT/S&P, January 1997–December 1997

Source: Datastream International Ltd.

use of futures because the total trading commission drops from 31 bps for the equity basket to 2 bps for futures (net 29 bps), the custody cost of 2 bps for the equity basket is eliminated with futures (net 2 bps), and the tax cost of 26 bps incurred with the equity basket does not exist with futures (net 26 bps). The futures position, however, incurs 47 bps of additional costs: 16 bps in annual roll commission, 2 bps in margin financing cost, and 29 bps in basis risk. **Table 1** shows that the net result is a 0.10 percent advantage for the use of futures compared with a basket of equities. So, futures contracts are still advantageous, but the difference between an equity basket and futures is only 10 bps annually. This finding actually detracts from the futures position because investors using futures will have to continue to pay roll commissions going forward, whereas they would not for the equity basket exposure.

Table 1. Benefits and Costs of Futures versus Equity Basket: Net Savings

Cost Benefit	Profit/Loss
Lower commission	0.29%
Lower custody	0.02
Tax benefit	0.26
Roll commission	–0.16
Margin financing	–0.02
Basis risk	–0.29
Net savings	0.10%

■ *Additional factors.* Using futures is advantageous for any strategy that is likely to change rapidly and frequently, as would be the case in some overlay approaches. Most asset allocation strategies are long term, but for those with a shorter-term orientation, futures are the fastest way to lose or gain exposure.

One problem with using futures is that many plan sponsors and trustees are uncomfortable with them, so the manager has to go through a long education process of teaching the benefits and raising the client's comfort level. Other intangibles, particularly accounting, risk management, and cash management issues, also fall on the loss side for futures, not so much for clients but for the managers who are deciding how to gain desired exposures for their clients. Accounting for futures is quite complex and requires very specialized knowledge. Risk management cannot be overstated: If the manager gets the futures contract wrong at any point in time, the result can be terribly expensive. And the manager must have a well-designed and strongly supported cash management function in place to support any serious ongoing futures strategy.

Finally, one of the problems with using futures is that futures do not exist in some parts of the world and are somewhat questionable in others. The S&P 500 and the U.S. component of the FT/S&P may be decent proxies for each other, albeit not perfect, but futures contracts elsewhere around the world, such as for the German DAX or the French CAC, are actually built on very poor proxies. So, basis risk becomes an even more serious and costly problem.

Index Funds. Index funds are the third choice for achieving desired asset allocation exposures. Relative to equity baskets and futures, the chief advantages of using index funds are elimination of basis risk, reduced transaction costs, and ready availability.

■ *Basis risk.* The index funds that are available around the world are generally consistent with the benchmarks that most managers are being measured against. Thus, the basis risk is minimal. **Figure 2** compares a U.K. fund that tracks the U.S. market with the underlying index. The daily tracking error of the fund

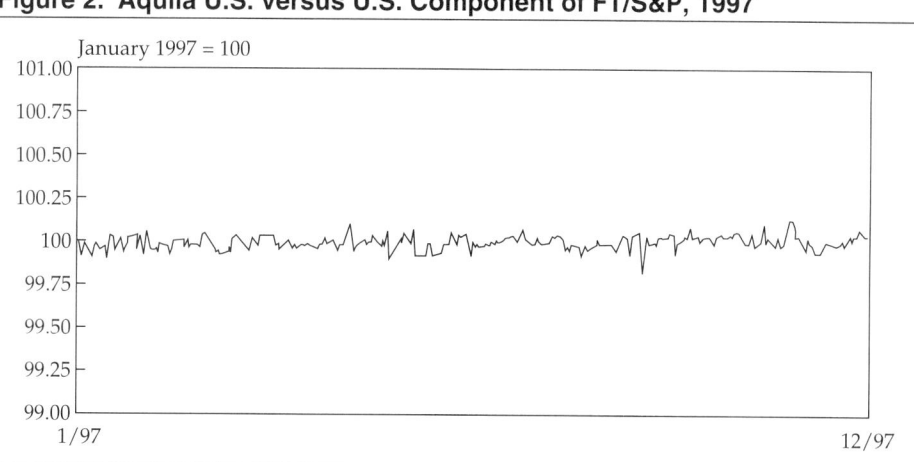

Figure 2. Aquila U.S. versus U.S. Component of FT/S&P, 1997

relative to the index is very small. Furthermore, a graph of the 100-day moving average of these data would be a straight line. So, the basis risk between the index fund and the benchmark is essentially zero.

■ *Transaction costs.* Compared with equity baskets and futures, index funds generally have lower transaction costs, including commissions, spreads, and especially market impact costs. Actually, because index funds operate in a vast global network, market impact costs are eliminated. At almost any time, if a manager wants to buy a Japanese index fund, he or she is likely to find somebody who wants to sell one, as long as the manager has the technology or the reach to find it. Granted, the manager does have to give up some timeliness with index funds; the manager might have to wait a week, even a month, to get the needed exposure. Remember that with futures, the manager can get immediate exposure, so using futures entails ready and ample liquidity.

■ *Availability.* Index funds are not much use to anybody unless many and varied index funds are readily available on a global basis. Indexing, which was pretty well unheard of in the United Kingdom in 1984, has grown to nearly 21 percent of the market, as seen in **Table 2**. The United States has about 30 percent of the institutional market in index funds. Index funds have grown to quite substantial proportions around the world, so the supply is plentiful.

Table 2. Prevalence of Indexing as a Percentage of Total Market

Country	Market Share
United States	30%
United Kingdom	21
Australia	10
Netherlands	10
Canada	8
Hong Kong	5
Japan	3

Note: Market share determined by value of funds under management.

Global Equity Fund

By using index funds, an investor can allocate assets and get market exposure quite cheaply. The following example illustrates the process of using index funds to build a global equity fund.

In January 1998, we at Barclays Global Investors had a U.K. client with a substantial portfolio that was all in cash. The client wanted to create a global equity portfolio. The client was frightened about market impact around the world and wanted to proceed on a gradual basis. In other words, the client did not want exposure tomorrow but over the following six or eight weeks. By using our contacts around the world, we were able to accomplish the following to create a global equity fund.

- *Crossed U.K. equities with a life insurance company.* A life insurance company that was moving to active equity management from index funds provided the U.K. equity exposure that this particular client wanted.
- *Crossed Swiss equities with a retail unit trust.* A retail unit trust had a big redemption, so Swiss equities were picked up in this cross.
- *Crossed U.S. equities with a U.S. public fund (S&P 500 plus smaller companies).*
- *Crossed a non-U.S. with U.S. corporate pension fund that was moving to active management.*
- *Crossed U.K. equities with a U.K. segregated fund moving from U.K. equities to bonds.* A U.K. segregated fund was moving from U.K. equities to bonds because of the minimum funding requirements of the Pensions Act 1995.
- *Crossed Japanese equities with a pension fund in the Netherlands.* Crossing Japanese equities with a pension fund in the Netherlands was the client's asset allocation decision.
- *Crossed Japanese equities with a U.S. public fund.*

This series of index-fund-based crosses enabled this client to achieve 97 percent of the desired exposure. The resulting fund had about US$2 billion of acquired assets, with minimal market impact and costs.

Conclusion

The possibility exists that index funds could replace futures as an asset allocation tool, but they probably will not for several reasons. First, index funds are best transacted at the unit level. In other words, investors do not really want to buy or sell 640 individual stocks, but if those stocks have been packaged into a fund, then those units can actually be exchanged between the various counterparties in a single transaction, like purchasing a futures contract. Sometimes, unfortunately, because of regulatory barriers around the world, index funds cannot be invested across borders, and the investor has to go below the unit level and actually exchange the securities. Having some kind of globally recognized investment vehicle for transferring index funds across borders would be beneficial, but that vehicle is going to be some time in coming.

Second, creating a global equity fund with index funds is not an instant process. In the example given earlier, the client was more than willing to wait. Unfortunately, finding the appropriate counterparties around the world takes time. Technology will improve the timeliness. The process is like a giant order board at the end of the day, and eventually, technology will enable all the bids and all the offers around the world to be known.

Third, cross-border differences still mean that investors have to deal with potential short-term tax disadvantages, such as withholding taxes and stamp duties.

Despite these hurdles, billions of pounds are now being transacted in this way. These transactions are not going through markets but rather are being exchanged between counterparties. Companies are rushing to become global fund managers because one of the great advantages of being a global fund manager is reach; global fund managers can find counterparties who are willing to exchange exposure around the world.

Question and Answer Session

James R.C. Woodlock

Question: Who benefits from stock lending within an index fund?

Woodlock: Stock lending is a big business in itself. Index funds effectively hold the universe of stocks, and because they are passive, they have no demand to sell at any point in time. So, index funds are the obvious first choice for a borrower of stock.

Index funds are also attractive from the fund company's point of view. Barclays, for example, earns about one-third of its total revenue from stock lending. The arrangement generally is a split between the client (two-thirds) and ourselves (one-third). So, stock lending is a known, commercial practice that we undertake on behalf of our clients.

Question: How do you measure the risk of stock lending in an index fund?

Woodlock: Unfortunately, we cannot measure the risk of stock lending because there has never been a failure. All the lending programs we have are fully collateralized. So, should anything go wrong, the client is not at risk because the collateral stands behind the whole arrangement. In recent years, we have found that it is better to sell a complete portfolio to a borrower and in return receive an assurance backed with a sufficient credit rating so that should anything go wrong in the lending process, the loan will be made good by the borrower. Therefore, the risks are covered.

Question: What are your thoughts on performance measurement for index funds?

Woodlock: The way performance measurement should work is that investors should look at the invested proportion. So, for example, if you are measuring the performance of a U.K. passive fund manager against a U.K. active manager in U.K. equities, only the amount that the passive fund manager has in U.K. equities will be actually measured. The decision to go into cash is an asset allocation decision and should be measured separately. All the evidence that I have seen indicates that if the stock selection decision is carefully separated from the cash/liquidity decision, index funds perform very well. Unfortunately, that careful separation does not always occur, and a good deal of noise is introduced into performance measurement as a result.

Question: What is the cost of buying an index fund with a bid–offer spread?

Woodlock: Inevitably, the buying and selling of index funds is done on a cross transaction, which is typically done at mid-market price. So, there is no bid–offer spread on the index fund. That arrangement might evolve but does not now exist.

Rebalancing the Portfolio

Stephen Lowe
Principal, Global Policy Group
Gartmore Investment Management PLC[1]

> Rebalancing a portfolio is an integral part of the portfolio management process. Avoiding the rebalancing decision can result in drifting from the strategic asset allocation, a mismatch between assets and liabilities, and shortfall risk. Periodic, trigger, and specific rebalancing can help managers reduce shortfall risk and enhance returns, but managers still need to consider such practical issues as turnover costs, administrative considerations, and changes in the degree of risk aversion and time-varying risk premiums.

Various approaches can be used to rebalance a portfolio, but the standard, or conventional, approach is to first use mean–variance optimization, or some variation thereof, to determine the desirable strategic portfolio. That strategic portfolio (the indicated optimal portfolio) is generally constructed based on investor (e.g., the plan sponsor or the plan sponsor's trustees or fiduciaries) expectations about the central tendencies of return and risk for the portfolio. By their nature, mean–variance optimization models assume some kind of normality in the distribution of the risk–return pattern around those central tendencies. The distribution does not have to be absolutely normal; it could be lognormal or near normal. Essentially, the conventional approach uses mean–variance optimization, requires inputs of return and risk, and assumes a normal distribution.

The second step is the actual rebalancing decision. Although rebalancing might sound like a boring peripheral topic, in fact, it is absolutely essential to the long-term development of a portfolio of assets. The assumptions and the logic behind the decision about how to rebalance the portfolio are essential to the entire strategic arrangements of the plan.

The third aspect of portfolio construction and of management of the arrangements for the portfolio over the long term is a tactical one. I am not simply talking about tactical asset allocation, although TAA might be one aspect of the process. Tactical decisions involve such issues as how and when the strategic portfolio will be implemented. The exact timing of portfolio rebalancing can matter greatly. For instance, suppose a U.K. plan sponsor decides to allocate 55 percent of its assets to U.K. equities. The sponsor then conducts a manager search and spends some time deliberating before implementing the portfolio. If the sponsor has cash to start with or is waiting for contributions, the opportunity costs of deciding to go slow with the implementation can be enormous. No one could have avoided noticing the importance of small tactical timing decisions after going through the kind of market conditions that existed in the 1997–98 period, when global developed markets, excluding Japan, returned more than 60 percent. Clearly, timing matters a great deal.

Tactical decisions are not simply a question of start-up. Obviously, once the portfolio is under way, various issues—such as how active managers are appointed; the precise way in which managers are reviewed; how managers are hired and fired; and how the transition between managers, the transition between rebalancing weights, or the transition between changing the optimal mix of the portfolio is handled—require tactical decisions that can make a big difference in the eventual return of the portfolio.

This presentation focuses on the rebalancing aspects of strategic planning that investors need to consider. Within the conventional framework, this presentation reviews the theoretical justification for deciding to rebalance a portfolio back to the original strategic portfolio, examines the practical considerations that arise and go into the conditions that promote successful (and unsuccessful) rebalancing in terms of return or risk or both, and finally, provides an alternative approach for making the decision about the strategic allocation of a portfolio.

---

[1] Mr. Lowe is now Executive Director, Account Management and Business Development, UBS Brinson Limited, London.

Theoretical Justification

A portfolio might need to be rebalanced back to the original mix for two reasons: risk reduction or return enhancement. Rebalancing can be designed simply to reduce the risk of the portfolio relative to the liabilities with which the portfolio is matched and designed to defray. Additionally, rebalancing can be designed to exploit systematically the assumed likelihood that the assets in the strategic portfolio will deviate from their central tendencies. For example, by selling assets that are being overbought and buying assets that are being oversold, the portfolio can be rebalanced to enhance returns. Depending on why the plan wants to rebalance the portfolio (risk reduction, return enhancement, or both), the plan can use one of three approaches: periodic rebalancing, trigger rebalancing, or specific rebalancing.

Periodic Approach. Periodic rebalancing is primarily done to reduce risk but can be used to enhance returns. The most common period used is quarterly, although monthly, weekly, and occasionally even daily periods are used. In the case of daily rebalancing, which means virtually a constant rebalancing, the rebalancing is clearly designed to minimize risk and keep the plan's asset portfolio absolutely in line with the assumed stationary liability portfolio.

Empirical research done by actuaries at Watson Wyatt Worldwide, which has been published by the *British Actuarial Journal*, shows little difference in results of models that were rebalanced on a daily, weekly, or monthly basis for benchmarks in which two asset classes were the components of the strategic portfolio.[2] Similar evidence is also cited in one or two other published studies. For those benchmarks that were studied, the empirical evidence suggests that no huge difference existed between a monthly periodic approach to asset rebalancing and one in which the plan simply decided to rebalance constantly.

The following example illustrates rebalancing done at a three-year time interval. **Table 1** shows an optimal portfolio with a simple initial asset mix, one that is quite common to risk-averse U.S. plans: 35 percent in U.S. equities, 60 percent in U.S. bonds, and 5 percent in cash. Suppose that something outrageous happens, such as the annual returns from those assets in the mix deviate substantially from the long-run expected returns that were used to determine the ideal mix. So, for a three-year period, the compound annual rate of return of those assets becomes 30 percent for the equity portion, 13 percent for the bond portion, and 5.8 percent for the cash portion. All else being equal, if the plan does not rebalance the port-

Table 1. Drift Portfolio

Asset	Initial Mix	Three-Year Compound Average Growth Rate	Ending Mix[a]
U.S. Equities	35.0%	30.0%	45.4%
U.S. Bonds	60.0	13.0	51.2
Cash	5.0	5.8	3.4
Total	100.0%		100.0%

[a]Three years after implementation of initial mix.

folio, it ends up with a very skewed mix: 45 percent in equities, 51 percent in bonds, and 3 percent in cash.

That example is actually not so outrageous. It reflects almost exactly what happened in the United States from 1995 to early 1998. Thus, if a plan uses an asset rebalancing rule of revisiting the drifting mix of the portfolio at an interval of every three years, then the plan could quite easily have a very different portfolio from what it started out with, have a potentially risky mismatch of assets and liabilities, and have exposure to shortfall risk.

Rebalancing at three-year intervals could be looked at from various points of view. First, the plan might be deliberately trying to exploit the expected tendency of the equity components of the portfolio to do well. Although the plan is basically a risk-averse investor, which explains why a low-return asset (i.e., bonds) has the biggest allocation in the portfolio, it is really quite conscious of shortfall risk and wants to try and play it both ways—maintain low risk but achieve high returns. That is, it wants to try to exploit the trend of equities to do better than bonds, which the plan hopes to accomplish by rebalancing every three years rather than more frequently. Second, the plan may not have a lot of confidence in the inputs it uses to determine asset allocation, so it is quite happy to go with the unexpected, which may be what happens in practice. In the United Kingdom, actuarial reassessments of a portfolio's position are commonly done roughly every three years. So, no one expects that trustees will decide to rebalance the portfolio any time before that interval of three years is up.

If the plan rebalances the portfolio constantly back to the original mix, it will miss out on all the differential returns, but taking advantage of differential returns might not be the plan's goal. The plan might have decided that it did not know what was going to happen to returns, so it uses central tendencies that it believes in to estimate return and risk. The plan believes that for its level of risk aversion and aversion to a plan shortfall in the long run, adhering to that original risk-averse mix of 35 percent in equities, 5 percent in cash, and 60 percent in bonds is best. So, the plan is happy to rebalance constantly back to the long-term strategic asset allocation. Obviously, in

---
[2]*British Actuarial Journal*, vol. 2, no. 4 (1996):975–1001.

that case, the ending mix will be the same as the initial mix, but the plan will have kept the portfolio in line with its desired level of risk at all times.

Trigger Approach. Another approach for rebalancing the portfolio is the trigger approach. One particular trigger might be a threshold that is required to activate the rebalancing for risk reduction purposes. Say a plan's asset portfolio is 50 percent in U.K. equities. Once U.K. equities reach 52 percent of the portfolio's total assets, the plan rebalances back to 50 percent. That 2 percent threshold above or below the strategic allocation can apply to all the other assets in the portfolio as well. Of course, the drawback with this approach is that some assets will need to move an awful lot more in value terms than others to activate the rebalancing. For example, an asset category that constitutes 10 percent of the total allocation would have to increase or decrease in value much less than one that constitutes 50 percent of the total allocation to trigger the rebalancing.

Another trigger approach could adjust for the different weights of constituent asset categories in the portfolio. Theoretically, this trigger approach should work better than the periodic approach to exploit the pure volatility of assets; no matter what the weight in the asset portfolio, the trigger will be activated by the movement of the particular asset in question, whether it is 1 percent of the equity portfolio or 50 percent of the equity portfolio.

Specific Approach. In the specific approach to rebalancing, the idea is to enhance returns by exploiting each asset specifically. For example, instead of using a time period (e.g., yearly) to initiate the rebalancing, the plan might decide to try to exploit the volatility of assets by buying low and selling high.

Take the outrageous example, shown in **Table 2**, for a U.S. multinational corporation with operations and liabilities in North America and South America. The biggest weight in this equity portfolio is the U.S. component, which is the least volatile asset (10 percent asset volatility in terms of the variability of the return). One of the smallest weights in the portfolio is Venezuela, but it is also the most volatile (46 percent). Periodically rebalancing the portfolio at fixed intervals—rebalancing the Venezuelan weight at the same time as the U.S. weight—would not make sense if doing so would conflict with tactical strategies that seek to maximize return by exploiting volatility.

If the rebalancing goal is return enhancement, what would make sense is to exploit the full volatility of the Venezuelan component while minimizing the amount of turnover in the volatile asset categories—Brazil, Mexico, and Venezuela—because, after all, rebalancing does have a cost. In this case, the obvious decision is to use a specific trigger based on the differences among asset volatilities in the portfolio mix. The plan could also use a volatility-based approach, not just in terms of monitoring the asset category—Venezuelan equities, for example—on a percentage of the portfolio basis but in some way triggering rebalancing according to the price behavior of the asset category.

Table 2. Sample Equity Portfolio for a U.S. Multinational Corporation

Country	Weight	Volatility
United States	70.0%	10%
Chile	5.0	24
Mexico	10.0	37
Brazil	10.0	38
Venezuela	5.0	46
Total	100.0%	

Practical Considerations

Although one may want to rebalance the portfolio frequently to either reduce shortfall risk or enhance returns, practical considerations influence the rebalancing decision. Administrative considerations (such as turnover costs and complexity), changes in the degree of an investor's risk aversion, time-varying risk premiums, unstable correlation matrixes, and human judgment can have a significant influence on the rebalancing decision.

Administrative Considerations. When rebalancing a portfolio, turnover costs can be considerable. For example, if a portfolio has a big component in emerging markets or a big component in a market such as the United Kingdom or Switzerland, where stamp duty or securities taxes are a big consideration, turnover costs can be very high.

■ *Transitions.* Administering a plan's assets from a top-down level is complex and fraught with difficulty. The management of transitions from one manager to another, establishing initial exposure to new asset classes or new markets, and transitions that are caused by rebalancing—all are very complex: Frequently, misunderstandings and miscommunications occur. The management gets easier if the plan has a global custodian and if the global custodian is heavily involved in the administration of the assets. In practice, a number of funds do not use global custodians, and even if they did, they might not involve the global custodians in the asset allocation process.

■ *Combining rebalancing with TAA.* Rebalancing can be combined with TAA. Clearly, once plan sponsors have decided that they want to rebalance their portfolios, then frequently, they also have decided that they want to manage their long-term arrangements with tactical decision making. These tactical decisions are made by managers who try to arbitrage the tendency for assets to get at least temporarily mispriced. Thus, plan sponsors may use the TAA manager to manage the long-term strategic allocation and to rebalance the portfolio. Clients may ask managers to do both strategic rebalancing and TAA at the same time, which is complex to administer. The more the manager who is responsible for the strategic rebalancing of the plan back to the original mix has to work with other managers of separate asset classes, the greater the chance for complications. Reporting relationships are quite difficult when multiple managers are involved, and managerial issues arise that have to do with the responsibility that people have for following instructions and how the instructions will be given. Therefore, in practice, the rebalancing decision is not an easy one, especially if the plan uses a number of managers who manage different specialist components of the portfolio.

■ *Derivatives overlay.* The plan could use a derivatives overlay program to rebalance the portfolio without incurring turnover costs. The problem, of course, is that not all markets have derivatives, such as venture capital, private equity, or emerging markets. If a portfolio has a large allocation to those assets, the plan is condemned to leaving them out of the derivatives overlay (and not rebalancing them) or rebalancing them in rather costly or in less frequent ways than the assets that can be rebalanced with a derivatives overlay. The question is: Who does the derivatives overlay? But that question is really related again to the issue of using an outside manager, an internal manager, or a global custodian to do the overlay.

■ *Performance measurement.* Rebalancing can also result in performance measurement implications, which can get quite severe. Suppose, for instance, a plan has a U.S. small-capitalization manager and that U.S. small-cap stocks have done well, going from a 5 percent initial allocation to 7.5 percent. As a result, the plan wants to rebalance back to its original mix. The plan may not want to force the small-cap manager to sell assets, which would be costly if the portfolio is big. Small-cap stocks are fairly illiquid assets, so the plan would like to use available OTC derivatives. The problem is, the plan still has to deal with the residual because the portfolio's manager is still managing 7.5 percent of the portfolio in U.S. small-cap stocks on a cash basis, which is producing a stock selection variance from the benchmark. At the same time, the plan actually has only 5 percent in its strategic portfolio and (net of derivatives) in its actual asset allocation portfolio, so a residual results. Whatever variance the stock selector generates over or under the benchmark return will not be attributable at the asset allocation level, and it should not be attributable at the stock selection level either. It is neither one nor the other, but it is a residual that has to be accounted for somewhere in the plan, which complicates the analysis of how returns are generated for the plan.

Constant Risk Aversion. Another consideration, which is unrelated to the return aspect of the rebalancing decision but is relevant to the risk aspect, has to do with portfolio drift. At some point in time, the plan sponsor established the optimal portfolio as the strategic portfolio, considering the plan's level of risk and its anticipated liabilities. The problem is, if the asset portfolio's drift is not matched by the liability portfolio's drift, then the result will be a difference in net wealth—the net worth of the plan or, alternatively, the surplus of the plan, however determined. Of course, net wealth can be determined in many different ways—actuaries vary their approaches, the regulations and laws vary—but in principle, unless assets and liabilities are perfectly matched, a variation in net wealth will result over time.

The problem with the change in net wealth is that it might change the plan's degree of risk aversion and, therefore, the strategic asset allocation. Table 1 can be used again as an example of a risk-averse U.S. plan that has quite a large allocation to bonds and cash, not much to equities, and periodically rebalances every three years. The plan ends up with a net worth that is a lot more than what it started with when it determined its strategic mix. If net wealth varies significantly over time, the risk aversion of the investor may also vary considerably. The plan may not be as risk averse at the end of this three-year period as it was at the beginning. This example may be extreme, but the principle is valid for all cases: After a change in net worth, a plan might find that running an optimization exercise results in a different strategic asset allocation because the portfolio's appetite for risk has changed.

Return Relationships. A problem may arise if the plan's long-term expected returns are related to fundamental variables that affect the return-generating process. If these fundamentals in the return-generating process are related to the plan's liabilities, then the way in which valuations fluctuate may influence the plan's optimal portfolio in one period relative to the optimal portfolio in another period.

Take, for instance, a U.S. pension plan that has as its primary source of liability the earnings of the employees in the plan because the benefit payout is a function of the participants' final salaries. **Figure 1** illustrates the long-term relationship between the S&P 500 Index, or a proxy for the index prior to the 1920s, and the level of wage earnings. The figure graphs the average wage earnings in the manufacturing sector in the United States (which are not much different from those in the whole economy and is the best series for which data are available). This ratio is far from being stable and does not exhibit a central tendency with a long-term variability. A statistician would find basically nothing stationary about the relationship between stock returns and wage earnings. The ratio may be periodically stationary but, if so, on a time-varying basis.

So, if anything in the return-generating process depends on the relationship between the assets used to generate returns and the liabilities the plan is trying to manage, then the inputs that are being used to come up with the optimal portfolio are subject to revision. Essentially, if a relationship exists between stock valuation and future returns, fluctuations in that ratio may explain why the optimal portfolio could vary from one period to another. For example, Figure 1 shows incredible variation in the ratio of stock prices to wage earnings. In 1980, the ratio was less than 0.4. At the end of 1997, it was way above 1.8—almost a fivefold change in eight years. It is a massive change that is likely to cause some concern if the approach for framing the strategic arrangements for the plan is dependent on a notion of the value of what the plan is buying.

Covariance Matrix Stability. Another risk-related problem is the stability of the variance of the returns in the portfolio. **Figure 2** illustrates that during the past 10 years, the monthly variance of stock returns on a five-year average basis in Germany, the United Kingdom, Japan, and the United States has moved around quite a bit. Similarly, the variance of the bond returns exhibits instability. As **Figure 3** shows, in the late 1980s, the volatility of U.S. and U.K. bonds dropped sharply. Clearly, a plan that used U.S. or U.K. bond volatility data in the early 1980s to construct its optimal portfolio would have a dramatically different portfolio from that of a plan that used data from the late 1980s.

The correlation between assets, another key aspect of the covariance matrix, can also change over time. Take a simple example between two assets—Japanese equities and U.S. equities—shown in **Table 3**. Again, the inputs used for determining the optimal portfolio have shifted around quite radically over five-year periods in the past 25 years. In this case, the

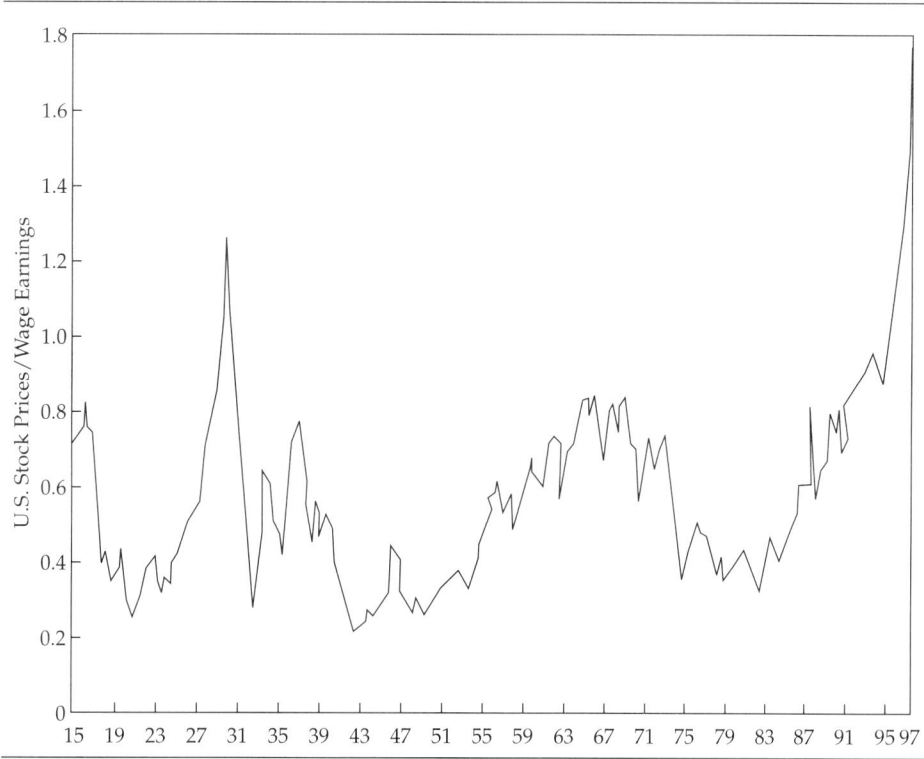

Figure 1. Relationship of U.S. Stock Prices to Wage Earnings, 1915–97

Source: Based on data from Sanford C. Bernstein & Co., Inc.

Figure 2. Equity Market: Rolling Five-Year Standard Deviations of Monthly Returns in Local Currency, 1987–97

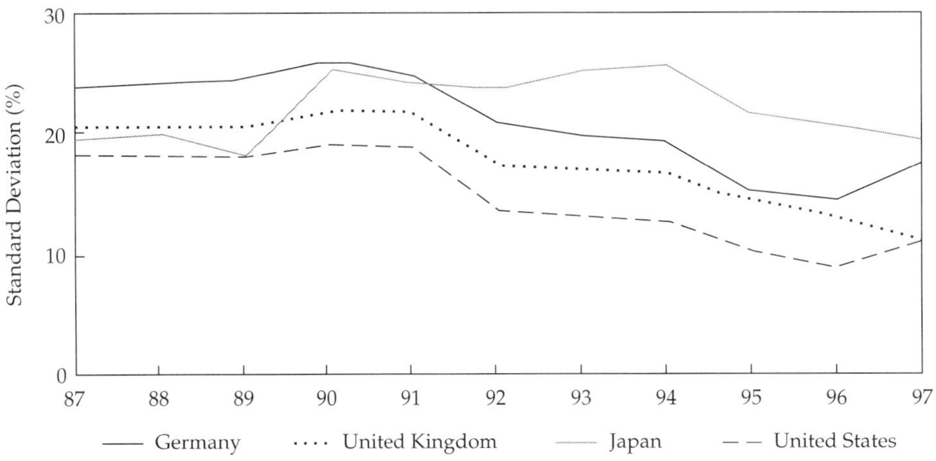

Source: Based on data from Barclays Capital.

Figure 3. Bond Market: Rolling Five-Year Standard Deviations of Monthly Returns in Local Currency, 1987–97

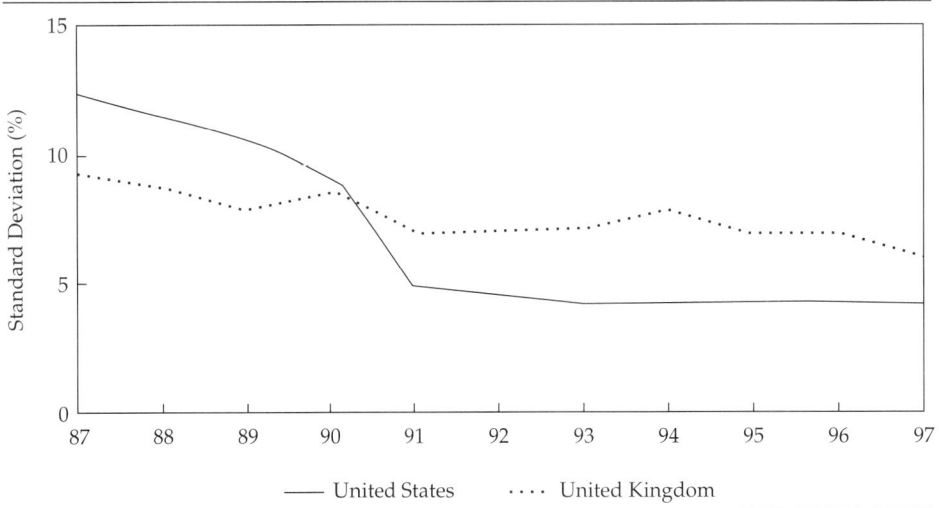

Source: Based on data from Barclays Capital.

correlation between two assets has gone from 0.38 in the early 1970s, to 0.14 in the late 1970s, then up to 0.29 in the late 1980s.

Therefore, the inputs used to determine the optimal portfolio can vary over time, which means that the optimal portfolio can vary depending on when the calculations are made.

Judgments. The governance of a plan's strategic portfolio to meet a liability is critical. That governance is basically about how the decision makers interact, what sort of decision-making process they use to make their judgments about the strategic portfolio, and how they choose to rebalance back to that portfolio or not rebalance back to that portfolio. All those judgments, in the end, involve human decisions—human judgment. Those people need to select original inputs when they form the original optimal portfolio, and they have to revalidate and revise those inputs over time. The revisions might be small, such as considering whether one manager can add value as an active manager in U.K. equities relative to another, or they might be big, such as deciding that they were wrong about the strategy they implemented.

Recent experience is particularly influential. For example, five years ago people thought about the risk premium quite a bit differently from how they do now because of the recent market fluctuations. In addition, previous to the current market environment, many people thought that dividends were meaningful as a valuation input. In the 1995–98 bull

Table 3. United States versus Japan Equity Correlation in U.S. Dollars

Period	Correlation
1972–77	0.38
1977–82	0.14
1982–87	0.25
1987–92	0.29
1992–97	0.20

Note: Monthly correlations for the five-year periods. Correlations are calculated using the FT/S&P World Index – United States (net income reinvested) versus FT/S&P World Index – Japan (net income reinvested).
Source: Based on data from QUANTEC, Ltd.

Table 4. Global Equity Portfolio Benchmark: Equal Expected Returns

Market	Allocation
United States	30.0%
Europe	30.0
Japan	30.0
Pacific	10.0
Total	100.0%

market, many people think that dividends are a less important valuation input than they were in the past. Alternatively, of course, many people still believe that dividends are just as important now as then—that nothing has really changed and others are fooling themselves if they think that dividends do not mean as much. The point is that recent experience makes a difference. If not actually clouding judgment, it certainly informs judgment.

The conclusion that must be drawn from all these practical considerations is that the optimal strategic portfolio for any given liability is likely to vary over time.

Optimal Rebalancing Conditions

Rebalancing works best when returns and risk remain stable around assumed means. In addition, rebalancing is most effective if the plan's net wealth is constant or if the strategic portfolio itself is flexible and changes with the plan's level of risk aversion. That is, if the strategic portfolio responds to alterations in the plan's return and risk assumptions, then rebalancing can work. It will not work, however, when the plan is rebalancing back to a strategic portfolio for which it has lost confidence in the original inputs.

The following example helps to illustrate when rebalancing works best. **Table 4** shows an optimal equity portfolio that has similar expected returns for the markets in which it invests. (This framework is different from the one in Table 1, in which the investor was risk averse and had deliberately, as a result of risk aversion, adopted a portfolio of assets with different expected returns.) If the plan's confidence in the similar expected returns is high, the plan will be attracted to rebalancing the portfolio to exploit the central tendencies of the returns. Therefore, when assets depart from their central tendencies, they should be bought or sold, depending on whether they are expensive or cheap.

Figure 4 graphs the returns of the rebalanced and drift portfolios for the initial portfolio outlined in Table 4. The rebalancing approach used a threshold of 5 percent. What this analysis shows, which is no great surprise, is that a rebalancing approach for portfolios of global equity assets in equal mixes, or in a mix that is fairly equal, such as this one, worked well in the late 1980s. The reason that rebalancing worked is that assets, in general, appeared to exhibit a mean-reverting tendency during that time. If the U.S. equity market got expensive, it became cheaper again. If the Japanese equity market did badly, it did better again. If the European markets did badly, they recovered to some kind of mean tendency. As a result, the rebalancing approach generated a good return relative to the drift portfolio (10.6 percent versus 11.1 percent) and generated that return with a slightly more moderate level of volatility of the portfolio's value from period to period (15.54 versus 15.57). The turnover for the rebalanced portfolio was 10.6 percent versus zero for the drift portfolio.

In recent years, something strange has happened: Assets have not exhibited any kind of mean-reverting tendencies, in valuation terms, in a number of stock markets. That phenomenon has been evident in Japan, for instance, where the gap between bond yields and equity yields has become extraordinarily different from what it used to be. At the same time, the yield gap has widened in markets such as the United States and Europe. So, perhaps not surprisingly, the drift portfolio has started to significantly outperform against the rebalanced portfolio in the 1995–98 period. In addition, the rebalanced portfolio's variability has been about the same as, not lower than, the performance of the drift portfolio.

Those non-mean-reverting conditions are the type of conditions under which rebalancing decisions are unlikely to be satisfactory, such as when net wealth is highly sensitive to the behavior of assets. A plan that is conscious of its market value from month to month or from quarter to quarter, for regulatory reasons or for actuarial reasons, will be much more sensitive to its market value than a plan that uses an actuarial smoothing approach, such as the one used in the United Kingdom.

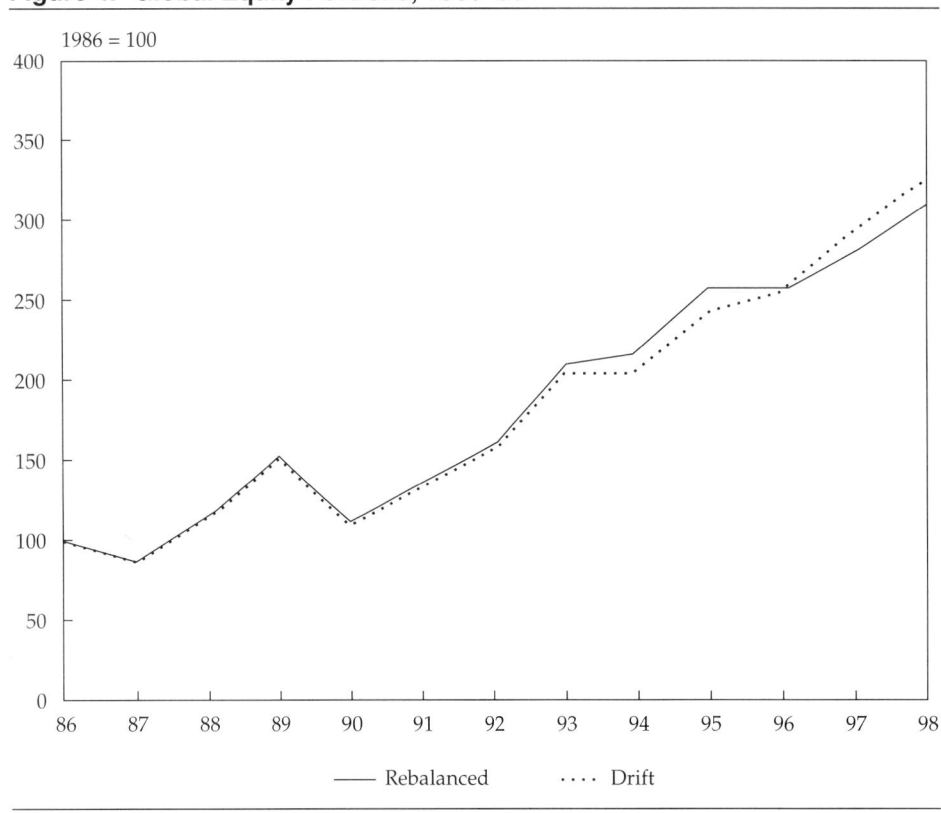

Figure 4. Global Equity Portfolio, 1986–98

Alternative Approach

Because those non-mean-reverting conditions are the type of conditions under which rebalancing is unlikely to be satisfactory, one might wonder whether TAA is a partial solution. Can a TAA manager be employed to temporarily adjust the strategic portfolio so that the trustees do not decide to permanently adjust the strategic portfolio? Assuming that U.S. assets are expensive, the plan could hire a TAA manager who would underweight U.S. equity assets against a strategic portfolio to moderate the risk. Alternatively, the plan could abandon a strategic approach altogether, in the sense that it could actually change the inputs, constantly update its strategic model, and allow the portfolio to drift. Or the plan could just give up the decision entirely and use the naive approach that Don Ezra mentioned.[3]

Of course, an entirely different approach would be to use, for instance, what in the United Kingdom is usually called the "peer-group balanced approach." In this approach, the plan does not determine a strategic portfolio. The plan determines a strategic benchmark, but it is not a fixed benchmark. The composition of that benchmark can change considerably over time. Essentially, the plan decides to go with the consensus: the universe of funds run by balanced managers (i.e., the peer group). The manager's job is to manage the overall plan with regard to certain ranges, such as aiming for performance in the first quartile.

The peer-group balanced approach is a unique approach for managing a plan's strategic affairs to meet a liability. The plan delegates the asset allocation decision in two ways: first to the peer group itself because the plan's assets are going to drift with the changes in the peer-group consensus portfolio and, second, to some other group of people (i.e., managers) to make decisions against that benchmark on the plan's behalf.

So, it is not a true strategic portfolio, but it is not drifting. It is reflexive in the sense that it reflects changing return and risk assumptions. Managers within the peer-group universe make decisions based, to some extent, on their changing perceptions of conditions in the world—how potential returns are changing and how risk is changing. In some sense, they make the decisions that the plan sponsor or the trustees might have had to make. Basically, the plan is letting the "market" make those decisions.

Peer-group managers also try to exploit asset volatility. They not only change their return and risk

---
[3]See Mr. Ezra's presentation in this proceedings.

assumptions, but they also tend to make decisions on the basis that assets are expensive or cheap—overbought or oversold. So, managers sell out of, or reduce, assets that have done well recently and buy assets that have performed badly.

Even in this approach, the plan sponsor's interests should be identical to those of the peer-group managers, in the sense that the utility function is constant. That is, both parties should put the same utility on the information ratio that the portfolio will generate. The ratio should be specified in advance, and both parties should understand what its utility is.

Some may think that the peer-group benchmark is a way for fund managers to manage their own business risk. That would be true if balanced fund management were an oligopoly and all of the major managers decided it was mutually in their interest to minimize their risk rather than maximize their returns. So, if that oligopoly were to put a higher utility than the client did on a low information ratio, the peer-group benchmark would be a way for fund managers to manage their own business risk. Some people think that an oligopoly of that kind has existed in the U.K. pension market, at least temporarily. Obviously, in practice, that claim would be extremely difficult to prove statistically. It is also difficult to understand how an oligopoly could be perpetuated in a market as competitive and open as the U.K. pension business.

One can conceive of circumstances in which these advantages of delegating the asset selection decision could turn into disadvantages. For instance, this peer group might have a great concentration of managers. As a result of this large concentration, the peer group could find that it has become less flexible in a couple of ways. One is that with scale, managers might become more risk averse. They may, for instance, no longer necessarily see their best interest as maximizing returns for the plan in the same way that they did when they were a small firm. This issue of size versus returns does not apply only to large managers. For example, someone starting up a fund management firm in the United Kingdom might want to attack the U.K. balanced management marketplace. That start-up firm may believe that its best interest is to make a big splash, which might mean being risk seeking, not risk averse. The firm considers that its best chance of building a business from scratch is to dramatically outperform the other balanced managers. This firm wants to move away from the peer group to build its own business.

A lot of criticism has been directed at the large managers in the U.K. balanced universe because of the fact that they may have become more risk averse. They have a nice big business, so why rock the boat? Size can also influence transaction costs. When a manager becomes very large, even if it wants to change its mix, it may not be able to simply because it manages too many assets.

Conclusion

The decision as to how a plan sponsor rebalances its portfolio, if at all, is integral to the decision the plan sponsor makes for how it will meet its liabilities. Rebalancing is not a peripheral decision, and the plan sponsor cannot avoid it. If the plan does not acknowledge that it has to think about rebalancing, then it is going with the drift portfolio by default.

The practical difficulties of rebalancing are immense, and as a result, when one looks at those practical difficulties, no obvious solution presents itself for how and when to rebalance. Although no simple or entirely satisfactory solution exists, this presentation has touched on a few of the considerations for putting together the framework in which a plan's ongoing management arrangements have to be decided.

Risk Allocation Instead of Asset Allocation

Ronald G. Layard-Liesching
Partner and Director of Research
Pareto Partners

> The unrewarded allocation of investment risk is leading to a revolution in U.K. pension fund management—a movement away from balanced fund management toward specialist management. Pension fund trustees are realizing that asset managers may be managing their own business risk rather than the pension fund's risk. The realization that forecasting returns is difficult in large efficient markets and that market timing does not add value is leading to a new portfolio management framework—risk allocation.

A revolution in thinking and practice is taking place in the most sophisticated global funds worldwide. The old mantra that the key decision is asset allocation is being replaced by a new and revolutionary framework—risk allocation. The electronically integrated global financial village in which investors live offers little informational advantage for consistently forecasting returns within a market. So, pension fund management is returning to the real goal—the allocation of risks relative to liability structures. This approach provides a very different view of the investment process compared with the traditional asset allocation perspective. This presentation examines the changes in asset management in the United Kingdom. It illustrates why forecasting returns is so difficult, discusses the problems with mean–variance analysis, and finally, looks at the profound revolution in theory that is occurring within the United Kingdom.

Changes in Asset Management

In the United Kingdom, a large-scale move away from balanced management toward specialist management is under way. Because no single firm can be the best at all specialist activities, balanced management has been viewed by pension fund sponsors and trustees as an easy solution to get some expertise in all asset classes. On average, a U.K. pension fund employs 1.9 balanced managers.

Recently, balanced managers have substantially underperformed in the core investment activities—in U.K. stock selection, in the fund's equity/cash split, and in country allocation. This underperformance is forcing a reappraisal of the "two balanced manager" norm in the United Kingdom. About a dozen very large, sophisticated funds around the world are leading the move toward the new paradigm of risk allocation. Several are in the Netherlands, and many of them are in the United States, where some of the most sophisticated work is being done in investment management. Unfortunately, the United Kingdom is just beginning to move toward specialist management; it is almost 10 years behind the rest of the world.

In the United Kingdom, specialist management is a minority activity, albeit a very rapidly growing one. Roughly half of all the assets managed externally for U.K. pension funds in the past decade have been managed by just six fund management companies. In contrast, in the United States, more than 2,500 fund management firms compete for the large, institutional-sized assets.

Historical reasons explain this strange structure in U.K. pension fund management. In the past, the merchant bank acting for a U.K. company would also own a fund management company and a stock brokerage firm and handle custodial services. So, pension fund management would often be awarded on a relationship basis. The visible fund management fees charged were low, but hidden charges and stockbrokerage profits made fund management a very profitable activity for the management company. Nowadays, full disclosure of all such hidden charges is supposed to occur, which should encourage competition.

Also in the past, the oversight of the pension fund in a U.K. company was usually a part-time activity for a senior person who had other major responsibilities (e.g., in the accounting, finance, or personnel areas). Historically, U.K. companies have not provided enough resources to properly evaluate specialist investment management. Outsourcing all decisions via balanced management has been an easy solution. In addition, plan sponsors have been extremely reluctant to pay consultants to undertake proper investment reviews because of the visibility of consulting fees and the lack of visibility of fund underperformance. For example, a fund consultant might be paid only £15,000 to select a fund manager for a £50 million mandate. Committing such small resources to such vital decisions is inappropriate. Correct manager selection can be worth more than 1 percent to a fund, which dwarfs any consulting fee or cost of internal staff for undertaking detailed manager evaluation.

Peer pressure has also contributed to the prevalence of balanced management. Fund returns in the United Kingdom are usually judged versus peer-relative returns, rather than versus a liability-determined specialized benchmark. In addition, U.K. pension funds are held in trust for retirees; the assets are not viewed as a company asset in the United Kingdom. With little perceived company benefit from better absolute pension fund performance, companies have not been motivated to try to enhance fund returns.

Now, the situation is changing dramatically in the United Kingdom because of bad investment performance, the minimum funding requirement, and consultant performance analysis.

Bad Performance. Bad active management decisions by balanced fund managers have had a negative impact on the returns of some U.K. pension funds. Perverse judgments in the form of market timing, equity selection, and country allocation have contributed to the drag on the performance of U.K. pension funds. All these bad decisions have arisen from the unrewarded allocation of investment risks.

■ *Poor market timing*. For example, an overallocation to cash during an unprecedented bull market for equities was justified on "valuation" grounds. This excuse would have been valid if any academic or practitioner experience supported the validity of aggressive equity market timing. No clear evidence exists, however, that the risk associated with aggressive domestic market timing produces commensurate risk-adjusted returns.

■ *Poor equity selection results*. Some funds have recently had one-year U.K. equity returns that were nearly 10 percentage points below the FTSE (Financial Times Stock Exchange) All-Share Index return. This level of underperformance can be achieved only by taking extreme stock selection risk, which is inappropriate for the core equity investment of a large fund. Worse still, performance measurement shows that at some investment firms, different pension fund clients have had markedly divergent U.K. equity returns.

If the underperformance were isolated, or just a short-run phenomenon, it could be discounted. But based on long-run data, 65 percent of U.K. funds with managers actively selecting equities underperformed the FTSE All-Share Index. A few large U.K. managers have good long-run stock selection records; however, the level of underperformance provides a strong argument for abandoning active equity management and conventional stock selection methods within a balanced format.

■ *Poor country allocation*. U.K. funds went into international equity markets decades before funds in other countries did, which may explain the comfort with the extreme deviations from capitalization-weighted benchmarks taken by U.K. managers. Peer-relative performance measurement means that U.K. fund managers react to their performance risk versus their competitors' risk. U.K. investor weightings in the U.S. equity market decreased to less than 5 percent during the 1997 bull market. I would argue that balanced management has encouraged the six largest balanced managers to manage their own risks, not their clients' risks. Fund managers should evaluate their *clients'* risks versus the fund's liabilities and should not be managing their *own* business risks versus those of their competitors. Being massively below the capitalization weight of the U.S. equity market was an extremely risky and expensive decision for U.K. funds.

Minimum Funding Requirement. The minimum funding requirement (MFR) introduced in the Pensions Act 1995 is forcing a move away from peer-relative management. Despite major differences in the maturities of different U.K. funds and in their funding positions, the fund manager often managed the funds in the same way. Clearly, a mature fund with many retirees and a poor funding position is taking on a great deal of risk by being heavily invested in equities. But because of the way in which pension returns were evaluated, a game of "financial chicken" developed. Each fund manager would increase his or her fund's equity weighting and get higher relative performance. The game reached the point that a U.K. fund, regardless of the nature of its liabilities, had more than 80 percent of its assets in equities.

From the perspective of managing assets versus liabilities, this high equity allocation was very risky, but this was an era of elastic valuation of actuarial funding status. If a fund was in difficulty, then a higher return assumption could be put in the actuarial valuation with the understanding that it would be revised down in "better times." More importantly, the equity allocation bet was successful. Despite the poor records of many managers, the funds made very high absolute returns simply from the high level of equity investment.

It was a self-fulfilling prophecy. All U.K. fund managers increased the equity weightings, and lo and behold, U.K. equities rose. The same phenomenon will likely happen in continental Europe in the coming decade. Historically, continental European funds were either dominantly invested in bonds or were funding pensions on a "pay as you go" basis. The introduction of proper asset-liability analysis is causing a rapid move into equity allocation on the Continent. Thus, these funds are moving up toward a 60 percent equity allocation, while U.K. funds are moving down toward this level.

Consultant Performance Analysis. The availability and quality of consulting services have increased dramatically in the United Kingdom. The systems that consultants have developed allow them to pick apart performance numbers. Once an investor has a consultant's performance attribution for a certain manager, the investor no longer has to listen to the manager's performance "story." Consultants can undertake performance attribution on aggregate balanced manager returns. They can identify for the pension trustees the exact strengths and weaknesses of different specialists within a large balanced fund management firm, and they can also measure which of the risks were rewarded with return.

Move to Specialization. Today, a U.K. company's pension assets are often very large. As previously mentioned, pension assets are not a direct asset of a company, but changes in fund contributions can have a major impact on a company's earnings. Hence, a company benefits by putting significant resources into getting the best investment results. In addition, the MFR is changing the structure of pension funds. Although the MFR is not as extreme as the U.S. Financial Accounting Standards Board's approach to the valuation of pension assets (Statement of Financial Accounting Standard No. 87), the MFR does force a recognition of the different maturity statuses of pension plans. In addition, trustees are becoming increasingly aware that just giving funds to the largest investment management firms may not produce the best outcome.

So, a revolution is under way in U.K. pension fund investment practice. The move to specialist management is no longer just words, and clients are increasingly willing to abandon balanced management. As **Table 1** illustrates, the recent breakdown of search activity reported by Watson Wyatt Worldwide shows a significant increase in the number of specialist managers that have been hired. Surprisingly, the number of specialist managers doubled from 1996 to 1997.

Table 1. Number of U.K. Funds Hiring New Managers

Manager Type	1996	1997
Multiasset	13	12
Specialist	33	66
Other	53	49
Total	99	127

Source: Based on data from Watson Wyatt Worldwide.

Forecasting Returns

Most active fund managers believe that their function is to forecast returns and then structure investments so that the investments are exposed to the highest returning assets. That approach does not always work—especially in large, efficient markets.

From the perspective of the total pension fund, the situation is very different from that of other market participants. The majority of a pension fund's assets are invested in large, liquid markets. Most funds have more than 80 percent of their assets in liquid equity and bond markets, which are considered to be efficient. So, rather than being in an information-privileged environment, where large investment firms might have access to data that are unavailable to the general public, pension funds are on an absolutely level playing field with everyone else in these large, liquid markets. If all the participants are getting the same data, then large institutional investors no longer are in a position to purchase superior information. They thus cannot achieve superior returns at the expense of smaller, less-informed or overseas market participants. In equities, an active manager typically has 100 percent annual turnover. With fees, brokerage, and market impact, this turnover means that the outperformance, the alpha, must exceed 1 percent a year just to pay for the costs of active equity management.

The active equity manager return data are not encouraging, and one can draw two strong conclusions from these data. First, as **Table 2** shows, 10-year performance numbers indicate no discernible evidence, in the aggregate, of value added from active management. Five-year performance numbers are even worse than the 10-year numbers. The median returns before fees for equity managers in the United Kingdom, Europe, and the United States closely resemble the respective benchmark index return. For example, the median return for U.K. equity managers was 15.77 percent versus the benchmark (the

Table 2. Active Manager Equity Returns, December 31, 1987, to December 31, 1997

Measure	United Kingdom	Europe	United States	Japan
25th percentile	17.19%	18.93%	19.03%	2.78%
Median	15.77	15.72	18.32	0.26
75th percentile	14.75	14.88	16.87	−1.43
Benchmark index	15.71	16.20	18.04	−2.48

Source: Based on data from Frank Russell Company.

FTSE All-Share Index) return of 15.71 percent. These results do not mean that investors should index investments, but what they certainly do mean is that investors should not take risk in the conventional way. If an investor does the same thing as everyone else, then he or she will earn median returns. If that investor reconfigures the use of risk differently (e.g., if the investor allows managers to hold short positions as well as long ones and then equitize the positions), then he or she can get 100–300 basis points (bps) more than the benchmark index.

Second, in most countries, excluding the United Kingdom, a large fund has multiple active equity specialist managers. With multiple managers, it is an arithmetic impossibility for the actions of an individual manager engaging in stock selection to add significant value at the total fund level. As a firm's business grows and the number of stocks in a portfolio increases, outperformance decreases. Often, the firm starts to manage its own business risk and simply wants to be on the right side of the index. That is, the firm becomes a closet indexer. At best, the returns hug the benchmark; at worst, the result is underperformance. What I am suggesting is that returns cannot be consistently forecasted in a large, liquid market. Return inefficiencies can be exploited, however, between markets or in less liquid, more inefficient markets. A problem still persists for the large funds, because they cannot put that much money to work in less efficient, small markets.

Impact of Technology. One reason for the reduced opportunities to add value within one country is technology. Technological innovations mean that compared with the past, financial data are disseminated more rapidly. The implications of any new information can be calculated more rapidly and efficiently, a much enlarged group of market participants exists, and execution of trading can be carried out more rapidly and at lower cost. Using the Internet, investors now can trade and get real-time information, which can be immediately downloaded and analyzed. This ease of obtaining and analyzing data implies increased market efficiency—especially in major markets. Less evidence of systematic active outperformance is found when risk is taken in a conventional investment format. The impact of technology is irreversible. No one should expect the financial markets to revert to a less efficient era, when the "first call" from an informed analyst provided outperformance. Technology is making beating the market harder than before. All participants are getting all the data and all the analytical tools at the same time.

The time to reconsider the whole investment process is now. Bear in mind that almost all the short-term analyses and forecasts are paid for by participants who have short-term time horizons and incentives to induce a fund to trade. These "short-term" participants create all the return forecasts, the noise, that bombard investors. To tune out the noise, investors must go back to the starting point, the original purpose of pension funds—to pay retirees' pensions.

Revolution in Theory. Fifty years ago, Harry Markowitz introduced his Nobel Prize winning work on mean–variance analysis. For the past quarter of a century, the mean–variance approach to asset allocation has dominated institutional investing. Every major institutional investor uses mean–variance analysis in asset allocation, but a revolution is occurring that now brings new tools to investors.

The revolution has been taking place on many levels. On the level of theory, leading academics have been questioning the core beliefs—initially, the capital asset pricing model and now even efficient market theory itself. At the technology level, available computational power and communication speed have been increasing dramatically. In addition, new mathematical and artificial intelligence techniques are being developed. These techniques permit researchers to solve much more complicated questions than they have been able to in the past. But the biggest revolution in investment management is actually quite simple: All large funds are now undertaking detailed performance attribution. Investors can now identify the separate components of return and measure the risks associated with accessing these return streams. They can then budget their use of risk.

Mean–Variance Analysis Problems

Performance attribution calls into question the basis of conventional investment thinking and mean–variance analysis. Using return forecasts, variances, and correlations to establish "optimal" investment strategies is not optimal. Indeed, some call the optimization process "error maximization." Optimization is merely a technique that reveals the implications of the assumed inputs. Mean–variance analysis is an extremely powerful tool, and those who have used this technique for the past 20 years in practical asset allocation applications have learned to manage its inherent problems.

Non-Normal Distributions. Return distributions are not normally distributed. Most of the time nothing happens. Then all hell breaks loose, and the return distribution becomes skewed. In 99 percent of financial research, the distribution of financial returns is assumed to be normal for three reasons. First, many asset return distributions can be closely approximated (in a chi-squared sense) with a normal curve. Second, the central limit theorem states that if random events with bounded second moments are combined, then a normal curve will emerge. And third, with the normal curve, applying a very large body of associated theory is straightforward; the math is simple.

For asset allocation, applying a normal curve can be dangerous. Any active asset rebalancing strategy will induce—or has the aim of inducing—asymmetrical returns. Investors seek to reduce downside risk and increase upside risk, which produces return distributions that are nonsymmetrical and cannot be modeled by a normal distribution.

Another problem is that, although the normal curve fits the empirical distribution of returns "in the middle," the normal curve poorly fits the tail of the distribution of financial returns. Many academics seek to address this issue by using a normal curve that has changing variance, which is the approach taken in the GARCH (generalized autoregressive conditional heteroscedasticity) and stochastic volatility literature.

The problem is that the distribution of financial returns is *fat tailed* not thin tailed. The probability of an extreme financial market move declines to zero in a polynomial fashion, not in the exponential fashion of a normal curve. Hence, a normal curve is incapable of describing observed financial return distributions. This flaw may appear to be a minor error in the tail of the distribution. Unfortunately, all of the cumulative return in a financial series lies in the tail of the distribution. For example, the return of the U.K. equity market since 1970, graphed in **Figure 1**, shows an apparent powerful excess return from assuming equity risk. But the cumulative outperformance of U.K. equities over cash disappears if the largest 4 percent of monthly returns is eliminated, as shown in **Figure 2**. In summary, the normal curve fits the monthly observations well, but the entire outperformance of equities over cash lies in the tail, where the normal curve fails to fit. This lack of curve fitting is a problem if the aim is to capture outperformance.

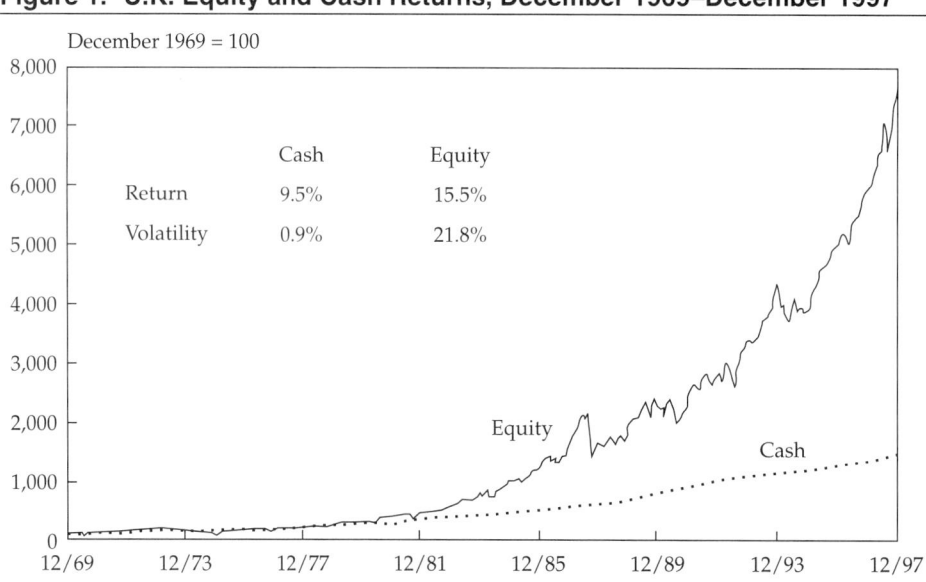

Figure 1. U.K. Equity and Cash Returns, December 1969–December 1997

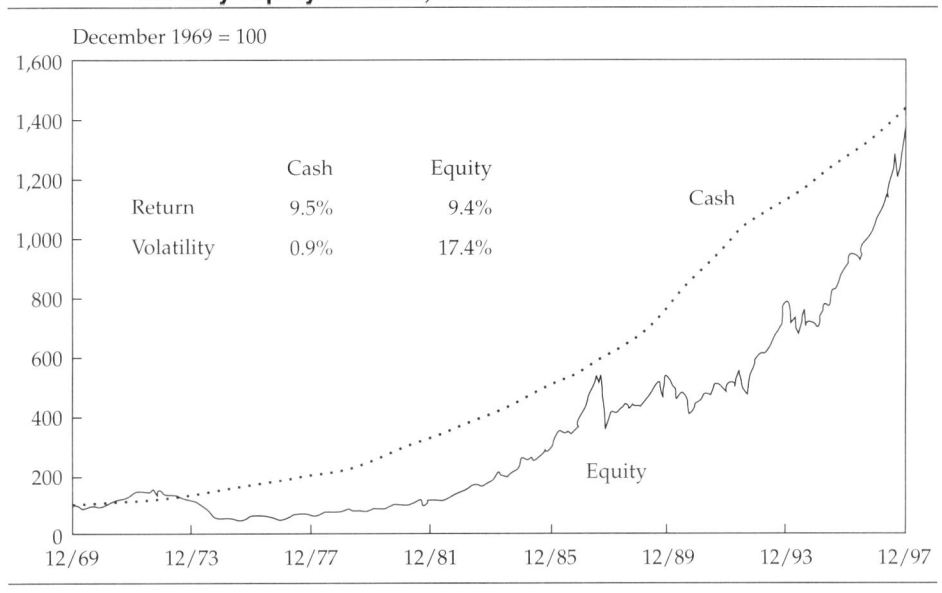

Figure 2. U.K. Equity and Cash Returns Excluding the Top 4 Percent of Monthly Equity Returns, December 1969–December 1997

Ineffectiveness of Market Timing. Outperformance of U.K. equity returns over cash was concentrated in 4 percent of the time periods in the monthly returns analyzed. Different investments can be compared in terms of the extent of the time concentrations of the return streams. For equal total returns, one would prefer to have investments in which the outperformance is not time concentrated. But no academic evidence exists to support market timing.

The more that the cumulative return is compressed into in a very brief period of time, the more difficult it is to time markets. Thus, timing the bond market is less difficult than timing U.K. equities, which, in turn, is less difficult than timing international equities. Currency market timing is the most challenging of all.

This time concentration of returns explains the poor experience that managers have had with value-based, single-country equity market timing—domestic tactical asset allocation (DTAA). An insurmountable degrees-of-freedom problem arises when DTAA is attempted using conventional statistical modeling. The reason is that the outperformance, or excess returns, will be concentrated in less than 20 observations for a model that is fitted to 20 years of monthly historical data (240 observations). The number of possible variables that can be legitimately fitted to these 20 observations, and the number of possible transformations of these variables that can be considered, make statistically based market timing extremely difficult.

The conclusion is that a statistical approach to DTAA is extremely difficult to validate. In any form of investment activity, many years (generally more than a decade) are needed to evaluate statistically whether the manager results are caused by chance. If all the difference in returns occurs in just 4 percent of the periods, then separating skill from chance will require much more than 10 years of data—it could even take a manager's entire career to distinguish between real skill and mere chance.

Note that the conclusion is not that attempting to time markets is wrong but that the risk allocated to this activity should be set in relationship to the confidence of returns from this information source. At Pareto Partners, we believe that a fund should allocate little risk to aggressive market timing within a single country; the risk for a long-term investor is that of missing out on those few periods when risky assets outperform cash.

Unreliability of Low Correlations. The fundamental tenet of investing is diversification. The correct, intuitive statement is, "We do not want all the eggs in one basket." In trying to express this insight in a mathematical form, quantitative analysts measure diversification using the Pearson product moment correlation of monthly asset returns. This standard formula for measuring correlation was developed almost a century ago by Karl Pearson.

Measuring diversification in this way creates three problems. The first is a statistical issue. The Pearson correlation measure is easily distorted by outliers. For example, the apparently low correlation between Dutch and Italian equity returns rises sharply from 0.516 percent to 0.724 percent once outlying "noise" observations are downweighted, as shown in **Figure 3**. The question for investors is whether they

Figure 3. Effect of Noise and Extreme Observations on Dutch versus Italian Equity Market Correlations

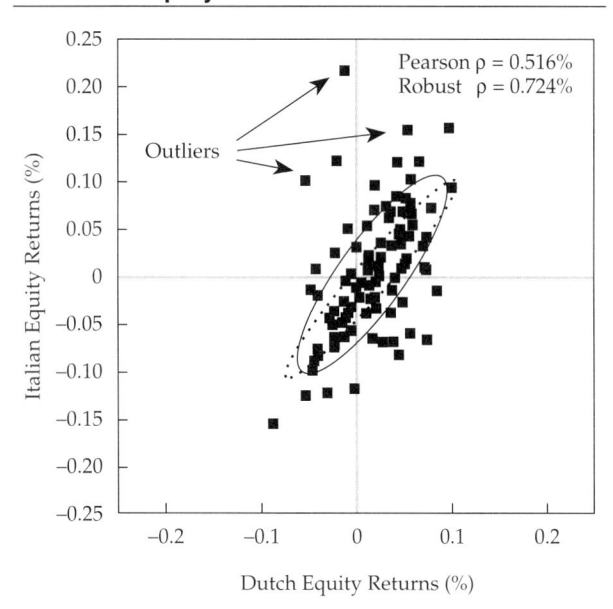

Pearson ρ = 0.516%
Robust ρ = 0.724%

want to be diversified with noise or whether they want to be genuinely diversified. After the 1987 stock market crash, financial research reported that diversification was gone because all the correlations had risen. But if October 1987 is eliminated from the data, correlations remain unchanged.

The second issue is that a low correlation is not intrinsically desirable. Investors are concerned about correlations only during declines, not rises, in markets. Unfortunately, mean–variance analysis cannot let researchers express the fact that investors love correlation on the upside.

The third issue is that correlation measures diversification across returns, but diversification across information is also needed. The apparent diversification of using multiple active managers can be completely annulled if they all access the same information. Diversifying across information sources is as important as diversifying across assets. If all the individual managers underweight U.K. utilities in their stock selections, or underweight the U.S. equity market in their asset allocations, then the fund may end up taking unacceptably large aggregate risk. In this regard, consultants can be very helpful in verifying that the managers are actually accessing diverse information sources for the fund. The key is to find experts who can see how to garner value added, understand why they added value, and systematically encode those insights so they can be tested and can achieve added value in the future.

Allocating Risk

Since the landmark study by Brinson, Hood, and Beebower, observers have universally accepted that asset allocation is the key determinant of long-run returns.[1] Although this claim has been questioned recently in Jahnke,[2] asset allocation has been important because returns relative to downside risk have been dramatically different among assets. **Table 3** shows the returns, volatilities, and risk of loss over a three-year period for four asset classes. Although a three-year period is not a long time to measure the risk of loss, if the historical risk of loss is minimal, then more money will inevitably be allocated to the highest returning assets.

Equity returns have been dramatically high in real terms. Real equity returns are much higher than either forecasts made a decade ago or theory would suggest. For example, equity returns are too high to be consistent with the consumption-based capital asset pricing model. This phenomenon is referred to as the "equity return premium puzzle." If these dramatic differences in returns did not exist, then asset allocation would not be critical to long-run return. Theory, and common sense, states that returns relative to downside risk should not be permanently out of line. But they have been out of line for decades.

The conventional asset allocation approach examines an efficient frontier. The implication is that a fund manager can select an "optimal" trade-off to

---

[1]Gary P. Brinson, Randolph L. Hood, and Gilbert L. Beebower, "Determinants of Portfolio Performance," *Financial Analysts Journal* (July/August 1986):39–44.
[2]William W. Jahnke, "The Asset Allocation Hoax," *Journal of Financial Planning* (February 1997):109–113.

Table 3. Returns, Volatilities, and Risk of Loss, January 1977–February 1998

Measure	Cash	U.K. Bonds	U.K. Equities	MSCI World Index ex-United Kingdom
Return	9.7%	13.0%	18.2%	13.8%
Volatility	0.9	11.4	17.0	15.5
Risk of loss	0	0.5	0.5	6.2

Note: Risk of loss is measured over three years.
Source: Based on data from Datastream International Ltd. and MSCI.

meet a fund's particular goals. Mean–variance analysis is typically used to establish a strategic asset allocation, and then returns are measured relative to this allocation mix. A fundamental problem with this analysis, however, is that both risk and return change rapidly over time. Thus, a fixed strategic allocation will not embody a fixed risk appetite. Unfortunately, no evidence suggests that investors can consistently forecast returns in the large, liquid markets. **Table 4** shows how the risks and returns across asset classes fluctuate markedly in successive three-year periods. The very wide range of numbers for returns and volatilities is technically known as nonstationarity—that is, the values are changing continuously. **Figure 4** highlights the fragility of the mean–variance optimization process in the face of nonstationary risk and return for the three-year period ending January 31, 1998. For example, the risk–return relationship for U.K. equities changed dramatically between January 31, 1995, and January 31, 1998. The volatility of U.K. equities dropped from about 14 percent to about 9 percent, while returns significantly increased.

In asset allocation, the analyst pretends that the returns, variances, and correlations are known with total certainty. According to this assumption, if the forecasts are correct, the resulting allocation will be optimal.

In contrast to the acute nonstationarity of an asset's returns and risks, the liability profile of a fund is relatively stable, although the net present value of liabilities will obviously alter as bond rates change and as inflation assumptions change. In the abstract, a fund would not seek to match relatively stable liabilities with assets that have rapidly changing returns and risks. At a minimum, a fund would want to have some stability in the asset risks.

Although returns cannot be forecasted, strong evidence shows that risk can be forecasted. In addition, managers can control the risks simply by altering the exposure to risky assets. As Peter Bernstein puts it so eloquently, "You cannot manage outcomes; you can only manage risks." Maintaining a fixed allocation with monthly rebalancing based on a long-run risk–return analysis is equivalent to passively accepting a change in risk profile. If the actual risk of equities rises or falls, then portfolio risk will change over time.

A natural extension is to vary the exposure to the risky assets in inverse proportion to the asset volatilities. This move is to stabilize the aggregate risk faced by the fund. Of course, to do this adjustment properly, care must be taken to measure volatility robustly. As in the case of measuring correlation, a single outlying event (such as the October 1987 crash) will distort the measured volatility if a conventional fixed window for volatility measurement is used. But as **Table 5** shows, even when using a nonrobust volatility measure, the fund still experiences a substantial increase in return relative to risk at the level of the total fund. Note the subtle, but important, issue of implicit data mining, sometimes referred to as "data snooping." Investors all know that the stock market recovered from the 1987 crash. The crash caused volatility to rise. Hence, it is highly probable that robust volatility estimation will improve the risk

Figure 4. Instability of Returns and Volatilities, 1995–98

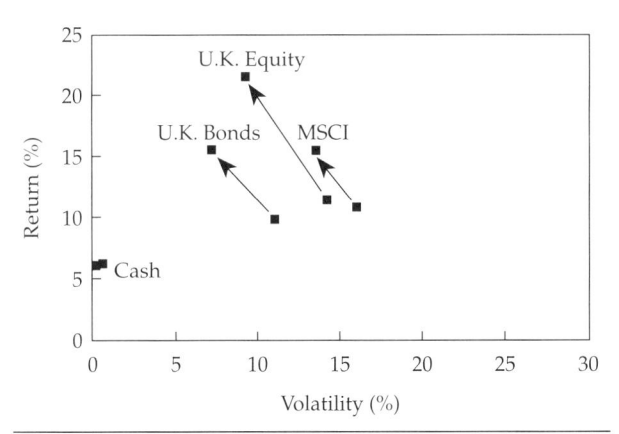

Note: MSCI is the MSCI World Index ex-United Kingdom

Table 4. Nonstationary: Risk and Returns across Asset Classes

Three Years Ending	Returns				Volatilities			
	Cash	Bonds	Equities	MSCI[a]	Cash	Bonds	Equities	MSCI[a]
01/31/80	0.92%	17.00%	16.72%	12.31%	9.80%	12.83%	18.74%	2.87%
01/31/83	0.58	13.62	18.34	14.27	13.02	17.90	21.10	22.86
01/31/86	0.39	8.25	14.30	16.14	10.27	12.52	24.29	22.55
01/31/89	0.40	11.27	25.66	20.03	9.84	13.05	17.55	17.62
01/31/92	0.49	9.57	16.39	17.34	12.66	9.10	11.85	1.70
01/31/95	0.52	10.85	15.67	13.99	6.38	10.18	10.77	11.51
01/31/98	0.14	7.20	9.19	13.44	6.29	15.53	21.70	15.58

[a]MSCI World Index ex-United Kingdom.

Asset Allocation in a Changing World

Table 5. Effect of Outliers on Return and Volatility

Measure	Nonrobust Volatility	Robust Volatility
Return	15.2%	15.7%
Volatility	12.4	11.8
Return pickup for 12.8% volatility	0.72	2.00

rebalancing results. This conclusion does not invalidate the result but means that nonrobust estimates should also be examined. Furthermore, as volatility changes, asset allocation should also change, as **Figure 5** shows. If U.K. equities become less risky, as they did in the 1977–86 and 1990–97 periods, then investors should want to increase the allocation to U.K. equities.

Researchers widely report that simple monthly asset rebalancing schemes outperform the active asset allocation decisions of conventional balanced managers by more than 100 bps a year. One reason for this discrepancy is the episodic nature of equity outperformance. As mentioned earlier, equities outperform cash only in brief subperiods. Thus, monthly rebalancing can lock in that cumulative outperformance. But if a simple price-rebalancing approach can outperform a balanced manager's active asset allocation, then the logical decision is to go further and rebalance assets based on risk in order to stabilize a fund's asset-risk exposure.

The fundamental principle is to allocate the risk exposures in relation to the level of confidence in the expected associated returns. Given the disappointing performance of U.K. active management, this form of risk allocation is worthy of consideration.

Conclusion

The essential goal of a pension fund is to take risks versus the liabilities in order to enhance retiree benefits, and the key to effective pension fund management is risk allocation.

The global financial markets have become more efficient over time in the sense that short-run return forecasting within a market is difficult to accomplish with consistency. Performance attribution is able to identify those risks that are associated with expected returns, those risks that are not associated with expected returns (and should be managed or eliminated), and those risks that must simply be accepted. Taking on conventional active security selection risk provides little expected return within the large, liquid financial markets.

For this reason, all large global funds are rethinking their process of fund management and how they deploy their management time and satisfy their risk appetite. In the United Kingdom, this reevaluation has led to the move to specialist management. Overseas, the large sophisticated funds are appointing internal risk managers explicitly to budget the fund's appetite for risks. Many funds are allocating risk to new activities, such as global allocation to exploit risk–return imbalances between markets, long–short strategies to exploit the information on overvalued securities, and private equity and venture capital investments to exploit taking on liquidity risk. Thus, risk allocation has emerged as the key discipline in managing a large fund in today's world.

Figure 5. U.K. Equity Volatility: Nonrobust 36-Month Window, December 1969–December 1997

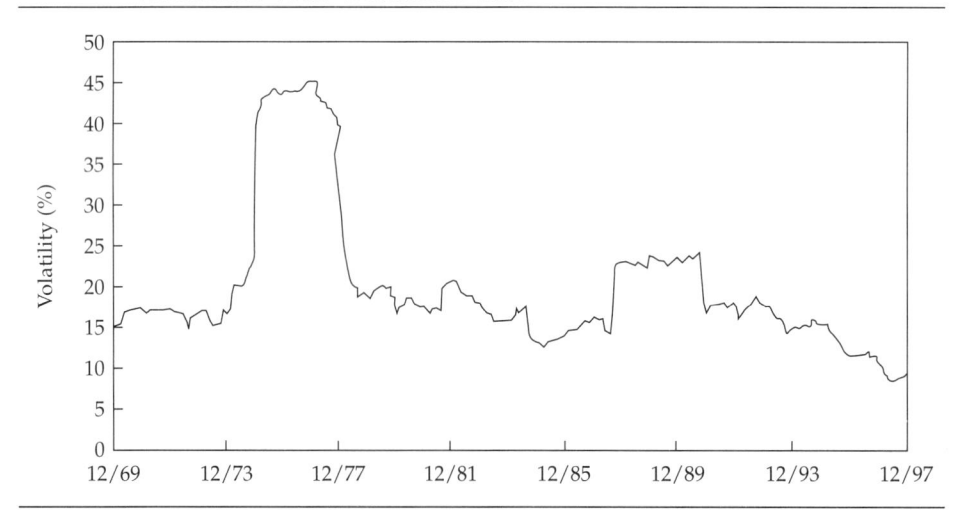

Question and Answer Session

Ronald G. Layard-Liesching

Question: Do you think that the current trustee structure in the United Kingdom is one of the reasons why the U.K. approach differs from those in other countries?

Layard-Liesching: Yes. The fact that pension assets are held in trust in the United Kingdom is obviously radically different from the situations in other countries, where the pension fund assets are viewed as an asset of the company. This difference comes to a head when a subsidiary of a U.S. company wants to restructure the fund; very difficult negotiations on the exact nature of the surplus ownership take place.

The difference is also the result of the historical relationships between the companies themselves and their merchant banks. In the old days, the company's merchant bank would naturally get the fund management mandate. Now, an increasing number of consultants are offering pooled funds themselves. In other words, if the company itself doesn't have the resources to do the correct manager evaluation, then consultants can put together a pool of managers to bring together these focused resources so that the activity can be outsourced. Indeed, in the United States, some companies are thinking of totally outsourcing their entire pension schemes. So, these legal differences are important in how funds are structured in different countries.

Question: Are extreme values that important for analyzing the effectiveness of market timing?

Layard-Liesching: Extreme values are very important. Conventional analysis focuses on the 95 percent of usual outcomes. This approach is irrelevant because you're basically getting cash-like returns from equities, and then 5 percent of the time, you're getting huge returns. If you could forecast these extreme values, you would be very well off. Unfortunately, there isn't much evidence that you can forecast these extreme events consistently. I am not a great proponent of market timing within one market; the return-to-risk ratio is too low. But by market timing across 10 markets, you can take slight risks in all of them and get some return advantages.

Question: How can one measure the success of risk managers for big, sophisticated funds?

Layard-Liesching: It is difficult to measure their success because you are looking across the entire gamut of risks. Their job is to identify the range of risks and opportunities that funds should be looking at because a lot of the risks are hidden. For example, a lot of funds are now looking at their credit risk. With the arrival of the European Monetary Union, we're going to have an explosion in the credit markets. Credit risks will grow very dramatically in the next few years, when banks as we know them disappear, and we will be left with credit risk directly on investors' balance sheets.

Question: What is your opinion of value at risk (VAR) as a risk management tool?

Layard-Liesching: Everyone has picked up on VAR. It is the magic bullet. But should we be using daily or monthly risk numbers for VAR if we are long-term investors? If I have a decades-long investment horizon, what do I care about daily risk?

I am concerned that the whole VAR concept has been oversold to the point that if the market falls, everyone will say their VAR has increased and they will simultaneously cut their positions. Just as with portfolio insurance, this selloff can create a rather sharp fall. It is not that VAR is wrong, but the real risk is the extreme environments. Saying that three standard deviations is my risk point fails on two counts: First, you have the issue of fat tails in the distribution of returns, and second, when you get into a crisis, you have serial dependence on returns.

So, my concern is twofold. First, VAR is being used by people who should have long-term time horizons. Second, VAR is being used in the belief that it can actually measure your risk of loss, but it can't. So, it is not of much use for long-term investors.

A Different Approach to Benchmarks

John Morrell
Chair
John Morrell and Associates

> Although the investment management industry has done a number of things very well during the past 10 years, the tendency to avoid risk has led many investors into a consensus trap. The solution to this strategic error involves reexamining how one views such things as equity allocation, risk, investment style, benchmarks, and market equilibrium. The path to top-quartile performance requires focusing on equilibrium fair value and incorporating this "neutral" concept into a customized strategy benchmark.

"I'm mad as hell, and I'm not going to take it anymore!" The movie *Network* depicts an aging television newsman, played by Peter Finch, who is driven to a nervous breakdown by short-term performance pressures, a ratings war, and the fact that the industry he had grown up with and loved had become instilled with values that he did not respect. These changes drove him to a state of nervous exhaustion and breakdown and led him to make the famous statement quoted at the beginning of this paragraph. The final irony was that his news program became very popular because nobody knew what was going to happen next.

I sometimes feel more than a little sympathy with the Peter Finch character. The use of benchmarks in the United Kingdom, as part of a consensus type of management, is undergoing similar changes to those seen in *Network*: What was once a valid and respected approach is no longer. This presentation reviews some of the problems with the investment management industry, discusses the implications of the consensus trap into which so many investment managers fall, and proposes some remedies. The presentation also attempts to provide an answer to the question of what represents an equilibrium fair value and how best to incorporate this concept of "neutral" into a strategy benchmark. Finally, it offers various ways to improve conventional investment management.

Industry Problems

The consultancy profession has been responsible for a great many improvements in techniques, in discipline, and in inquiries into many areas of investment management that were previously only dimly perceived. On balance, consultancy has been a thoroughly good thing, and the advances that have been made have been material and worthwhile. But as with all rapid change, there is good and there is bad. The hand of the consultant has been steady in situations in which arithmetic measures are involved, but it has been less sure when it comes to the art, rather than the science, of investing.

■ *Risk.* Many investment managers think that standard deviation equals risk. Does it? At John Morrell and Associates, we do not think so. We think that the ability of a share price to fluctuate should be seen as much, if not more, from the perspective of opportunity as from that of risk. Because share prices advance over time more than they fall, taking the long-term view, we believe that we should call standard deviation more opportunity than risk. We have developed an alternative to the classic graph that shows return on the vertical axis and volatility on the horizontal axis; we have simply added a third dimension, time through a cycle. Depending on the whereabouts in the cycle, there is a time to expand opportunities and a time to reduce liabilities. This three-dimensional model seems to be a much better model for active investment management than the traditional risk/return model. It represents an envelope of opportunity that should be exploited most of the time. Of course, our model requires judgment of the cycle, which is perhaps the most difficult problem of all; nevertheless, it still seems to us a much better model for investors than the classic one.

■ *Emerging markets.* Emerging markets are generally seen as a separate investment category from developed markets, thus dividing global markets into two categories. We think it is much more reasonable to think of emerging markets merely as small markets on a global continuum from large to small.

■ *Specialized management*. Managers are often grouped by specialty and not allowed to move outside that specialty area. We believe this practice is not in the best interests of the industry.

■ *Book value*. One of the errors of consultancy has been to say that book value, or cost, does not matter. Back in the 1950s, the book value of investments in an investment trust was the only thing shown in the annual report. Then suddenly, consultants said that book value does not matter at all. But book value does matter. Book values determine the size of an investor's bet and will be a reference point for scaling back or adding an investment.

■ *Benchmarks*. A lot of poor advice has been given on the subject of benchmarks. People tend to avoid risk. By calling volatility "risk," it becomes something to be avoided. So, to avoid risk, investors either get in line with what everybody else is doing (e.g., follow the peer-group universe) or get in line with what everybody else thinks (i.e., follow an index); either way, they fall into the consensus trap.

The Consensus Trap

The investment management industry is its own worst enemy. It has unquestioningly accepted a flawed investment methodology—the idea that the consensus is a good neutral benchmark. Books such as *Extraordinary Popular Delusions and the Madness of Crowds* by Charles MacKay illustrate that consensus is a false philosophy. Indeed, active managers need to be reminded that their fees are justified by betting *against* the consensus, not with it.

The consensus can be seen from two perspectives: the consensus of every participant in the market, which is the index, and the consensus of the professionals in the market, which in the United Kingdom is The WM Company or CAPS universe of pension funds. The index represents the market consensus about the appropriate values put on companies' capitalizations. It is the consensus of all market participants (i.e., what everybody thinks). By contrast, the WM or CAPS universe of pension funds is the consensus of what the professionals think. Both the index and the universe serve as standard measures of past performance, although in the United States, the market-capitalization index has become the predominant standard. The WM and CAPS universes are based on peer-group actions, which are always of great interest to managers. Both the index and the universe can be useful in identifying value added and performance attribution, but the truth remains that the appropriate neutral strategy benchmark is neither the index nor the universe.

Origin of Consensus Following. The popularity of consensus following has come about because of four interrelated influences.

First, trustees are generally happy to stay close to the consensus to avoid the risk of being wrong vis-à-vis their peers. In addition, in the United Kingdom, the Pensions Act 1995 made them think about responsibilities that they were not equipped to address, so they turned to the experts—the actuaries and consultants.

Second, by their nature, actuaries and consultants like to deal with facts. But facts are history. Actuaries and consultants proposed a methodology that addresses the past with numerical certainty. Their recommended methodology centered on the numerical certainty of the index—a representation of consensus.

Third, senior business managers in investment organizations identified their major risk as losing business to a competitor. Their "defense" has been to respect the consensus by staying in line with it.

Fourth, chief investment officers (CIOs) were told by consultants that 70 percent of the return from international investments comes from the country decision and only 30 percent from the security selection decision—a questionable piece of data in my opinion. The CIOs concluded that a top-down investment process was the solution. This conclusion acted to put top asset allocators and strategists in the driver's seat and confined portfolio managers to the back seat. The consultants also told the CIOs that all their accounts had to show the same results to demonstrate that they used a disciplined investment process, which led to investment by committee. Investment by committee, in my experience, is dull, unexciting, and likely to produce an index-type result.

Consequences of Consensus. Each of those four decisions was rational given the problems that each group faced, but each response can be questioned. For example, trustees are responsible for setting an appropriate investment strategy. Consultants tend to think in terms of historical data, but their job is to devise an effective strategy for future asset management. Business managers who thought they could get protection from staying in line with their local competitors failed to notice that they now live in a globally competitive world. Although the CIOs responded logically, they turned their firms upside down as a result of their decisions. Portfolio managers, who previously had absolute responsibility in picking stocks for their portfolios, now were in a secondary position.

Consensus is a deadly trap that is difficult to escape. Wrong decisions are not made right by being shared. In our view, consensus, in any form, is inappropriate for setting the neutral weight of investment opportunity, which is, or should be, the purpose of a strategy benchmark. The decision to heavily underweight the United States four years ago has cost U.K. pension funds an estimated £20 billion in opportunity cost (i.e., the profit forgone).

So long as the "universes" and the "indexes" command respect, any deviation raises the likelihood of incurring tracking error, which consultants and trustees abhor. Tracking "increment" is a less emotive phrase than tracking "error" and is properly neutral because variations may be positive as well as negative. Those few U.K. managers who doubled the weight for the United States compared with the WM universe were well rewarded.

Remedies

Something can be done about the consensus trap. The remedies we propose involve changing the way one thinks about equities, risk, investment style, benchmarks, and market equilibrium.

- *Equities.* We believe wholly in the long-term value of equities and that every fund should have the maximum that it can hold in equities. Equity is ownership, and a world of difference exists between being an owner and being a creditor. International equities increase opportunity and reduce risk.

- *Risk.* We do not agree with the classic definition of risk. With the regionalization and the globalization of markets, we believe that political risk will be less important and that industries and sectors will become progressively more important.

- *Investment style.* Certain investment managers have skills that should be encouraged, but they need to be closely monitored. We believe that active management will produce better results for the economy and for the client than passive management—providing it is based on sound methodology. The vitality of the capitalist system, after all, depends on people being prepared to bet on success and being willing to risk failure.

- *Benchmarks.* We believe that benchmarks have two distinct roles: as a measurement tool (historical focus) and as a strategy tool (forward-looking focus). These are clearly two very distinct and different approaches to the use of a benchmark.

InterSec Research Corporation published some figures showing that in the United States, about 20 percent of new international mandates were customized in 1997, up from 3 percent in 1996. The notion that a client's needs are best met by a customized strategy benchmark that is specific for the client's purposes is the most natural belief in the world. One solution, "off the rack," for all pension funds is an absurd oversimplification.

- *Equilibrium.* A natural desire exists to find some form of equilibrium, or neutral position, from which to decide whether values are excessive or not. All free markets are given to overshooting and undershooting. Recent developments have exaggerated this phenomenon. Instant dissemination of investment intelligence, short-term performance pressures, consolidation among brokerage houses, and consolidation among investment management houses have all tended to build consensus, which undermines the variety of opinions that is essential to the efficient working of a market.

The key question remains, "Overshoot or undershoot what?" It cannot, after all, be market cap because that is the measure that overshoots. It cannot be the universe because that is not known at the time. Against this background is a critical need for a respected measure of fair value. Such a measure can be used for setting strategic benchmark neutral weightings, which can bring a positive performance bias.

The Morrell Method

An effective alternative to the consensus trap is a value-based investment method. This method offers investors the opportunity to improve performance significantly under all principal mandates, especially emerging market mandates.

First and foremost is the realization that the backward-looking consensus has little relevance for setting strategy. What is needed for setting strategy is a neutral-weighted benchmark that is rooted in the absolutes of wealth and wealth creation as reflected in companies' financial statements. For active managers, the strategy benchmark should be changed from the present backward-looking stock market index, or from the WM consensus, to a measure based on firm fundamentals common to all capitalist enterprises. Such a strategy benchmark could then be given to outside management firms by the boards of trustees of pension funds.

The values in the strategy benchmark become the set of neutral values from which the manager overweights or underweights according to his or her tactical judgments. This substitution introduces a positive performance bias into the portfolio and removes the tendency of a market-cap index or consensus-based index to raise the neutral weight for assets that have gone up and lower it for those that have gone down.

Such a method is productive in any market but is particularly productive in markets that are "less efficient" (in the modern portfolio theory sense). The volatility of exchange rates makes the Morrell method particularly valid for international investment mandates. To arrive at our market-neutral international strategy benchmark, we make adjustments for overvalued and undervalued currencies by using purchasing power parity (PPP) values.

Methodology. We start by removing "price" from the concept of a strategic benchmark—both the price of currency and the price of stock. We focus instead on the fundamentals, which produces a stable set of values for international and domestic allocations and reduces transaction costs.

The Morrell method is based on a fundamental approach to defining neutral. This methodology has the merit of transferability. Portfolio managers are trained to overweight or underweight sectors, industries, and stocks. The new strategic benchmark sets a neutral weight from which the same tactical judgments are made.

The essence of the method is to use the information available from the published financial statements of the companies that make up any particular investment universe. We have filtered the information down to what we believe to be the key appropriate measures of wealth and wealth creation. Capitalistic enterprises are about creating wealth, and the numbers by which that process is addressed are available through the audited accounts of the companies. Every capitalist enterprise has a measure of wealth on the balance sheet (i.e., a measure of static wealth). It also has a measure of wealth creation, which is in the operating statement. This measure is the dynamic of wealth creation. Nothing is more factual than the audited financial accounts of companies—not perfect perhaps but preferable, dare I say, to Street estimates.

We identified what we consider to be the seven measurable common elements of wealth and wealth creation in a company and extracted those numbers from the available data to build company-based financial statements. These data take us all the way through to a sector, to an industry, or to a country on a logical basis. The elements have nothing surprising in them, being measures used by financial analysts the world over. The proprietary analytics underlying the Morrell method consist of identifying and combining those key elements in what we believe to be a formula of universal application. PPP values of currencies are used to remove the distortion of overvalued and undervalued currencies. Such a formula drives the neutral values of country, industry, and sector. These values are updated as each new set of financial statements is released.

Currency. One has to be mindful of the currency distortions to international allocations in terms of market cap. Huge losses were incurred by investors in Japan who followed the market cap as their benchmark. By this measure, the U.S. market was at one time smaller than Japan. Quite apart from the dramatic rise in the Japanese stock market itself, the yen appreciated from ¥360:US$1 in 1973 to ¥80:US$1 in 1997. On this measure alone, an international index used for setting strategy would have encouraged U.S.-based investors to invest five times as much in Japan as in their "neutral" and would have encouraged Japanese investors to invest one-fifth in the U.S. market—the very opposite of investment wisdom. U.S. pension funds that were persuaded that an investment in the MCSI Europe/Australasia/Far East market-cap-based index was a low-risk investment lost a fortune when the Japanese bubble finally burst—an expensive lesson.

Country Weights. Our country weightings reveal the extent to which the market-cap basis has distorted international asset allocation decisions. Market cap makes no allowance for interest rates of 0.5 percent in Japan versus 5 percent in the United States, no allowance for P/Es of 75 in Japan versus 25 in the United States, no allowance for the cross-holdings of Japan, which are phantom capital and may account for as much as 50 percent of the market cap of Tokyo, and no allowance for overvalued or undervalued currencies. Small wonder then that Japan (which at one time represented 38 percent of the market-cap-based MSCI World Index versus 29 percent for the United States) was, by our reckoning, never more than 12 percent of an international measure and is currently 10 percent, just one-fifth of the importance of the United States.

So far as emerging markets are concerned, attaching a label to a group of 29 countries designated "emerging" on the basis of lending criteria set by the International Finance Corporation and the World Bank was, to say the least, naive. It led to serious misallocation of capital and unnecessary market disequilibrium and introduced systemic risk to the whole group so that trouble in one part infected the whole. Investing in emerging markets should be a highly selective process, as London discovered 100 years ago. This situation speaks to the need for customized benchmarks for emerging markets. Some urgent revision will be necessary when investor interest returns—as it will.

We are enthusiastic proponents of responsible investing in small markets, but the truth is that international markets are a continuum from very large to very small. Because liquidity is crucial, investments in countries that are appropriate for a small fund may not be appropriate for a large fund. Addressing emerging markets requires a customized approach to constructing an appropriate strategic benchmark.

Being competent in addressing 29 markets (i.e., the MSCI emerging market universe) is a considerable commitment for any investment firm, but the class of emerging markets is an investment category of considerable potential and, as such, investment firms have to be able to respond to demand. We believe that our allocation system incorporated into the class of emerging markets via a pooled fund provides a better answer than other alternatives. Backtesting our formula suggests an outperformance of the MSCI Emerging Markets Index of 300 basis points (bps) net of rebalancing transaction costs. This is a formula-driven active/passive approach to the emerging markets. Compared with market-cap-based systems, it stabilizes the allocation to both the class of emerging markets and to the recipient countries. Furthermore, it has a stabilizing effect on the markets themselves by encouraging managers to sell high and buy low, which reverses the bias of market cap that is reflected in the index.

Performance. What this new thinking means for both clients and managers is that they can now break out of the box in which they have allowed themselves to be corralled. Consultants who warn of tracking error should study the possibility of adding value rather than the possibility of losing value. The tracking deviation of a wealth-based, value-based strategy benchmark gains more than it loses.

A strategy benchmark clearly deviates from market-cap-based measurement indexes by representing an objective neutral position that is based on fundamental values. The whole purpose of such a strategy benchmark is to outperform the consensus in either manifestation (index or universe).

We have comprehensively back tested our formula and had it audited to verify that it has been unchanged throughout the 27-year period. Backtesting shows that for a global mandate, we added more than 200 bps a year for the most recent 10 years and 100 bps a year for the past 20 years. For emerging markets, we added as much as 350 bps (gross) a year for the seven years that we have been able to make comparisons with the MSCI Emerging Markets Index.

Summary

The Morrell method provides a way out of the investment management industry's self-imposed problem of how to escape the grip of the index. The solution is to embrace the concept of the strategy benchmark.

Customization. First, a mandate is agreed on between the client (the owner of the fund) and the investment house (the investment manager). This mandate should be based on the client's needs and is reflected in the appropriate strategy benchmark. A value basis, such as that of the Morrell method, serves as a sounder basis for constructing a custom-built strategy benchmark than either the index or the universe. The result is a purpose-built benchmark reflecting the needs of the client and matched by the investment skills of the manager. Customizing may appropriately be modified to reflect the particular skills of each investment firm. A firm that has a particular strength in the Far East or a particular strength in emerging markets could, in conversation with the client, tilt the strategy benchmark in the direction of the firm's expertise. So, the customization is not only to meet the needs of the client but also to meet the skills of the provider.

The essence of customization is to make the "suit" fit. Customization is also important in light of the worldwide trend away from defined-benefit to defined-contribution plans. Defined-contribution plans are being created with extremely diverse investment strategies because the time horizons, degrees of risk aversion, and expectations of people are different. That situation is not much different for a defined-benefit pension fund because each defined-benefit pension fund faces constraints that are similar to those of a defined-contribution plan. Our view, naturally enough, is that the Morrell method provides a sounder basis for a customizing process than any other.

Advantages. Having the right strategic benchmark offers important advantages. First, it prevents any major long-term misallocation of capital. The client's capital is appropriately allocated around the world to where wealth is being created. Avoiding misallocation prevents errors such as U.S. pension funds overweighting Japan in the late 1980s to early 1990s and U.K. pension funds underweighting the United States in the mid- to late 1990s. Reratings and deratings that take place over time are much more easily identified if the manager has a solid basis of value against which to make judgments.

Ten years ago, our equilibrium formula gave the United States a weight of 43 percent globally when the market cap of the United States was only 27 percent. It gave Japan a global weight of 11 percent when the market cap was 43 percent. In other words, the Japanese market was hugely inflated above real values, and the U.S. market was very cheap against real values. Today, these values have moved in line with our values. At the end of July 1998, the Morrell method gave the United States a value of 45 percent when the market cap was 49 percent. Only recently has the U.S. market become fully valued in our view. Our equilibrium for the United States is equivalent to about 7,800 on the Dow. We currently put the value of Japan at 9.5 percent of the world against a market cap of 11 percent. So, we think Japan is still moderately overpriced in terms of international comparative wealth creation. Bearing in mind that yen profits from industry were lower in 1997 than they were 20 years ago, one can see that our wealth creation formula correctly penalizes Japan.

A second advantage of our system is that it exploits the volatility of fashion. Emerging markets, which are notoriously volatile, are particularly susceptible to our improved methodology. The inclination to increase allocations at the top and reduce allocations at the bottom is exaggerated by the volatility that is characteristic of emerging markets. For example, Malaysia, prior to its crashing, was 1.4 percent of the world market. After the crash, it went as low as 0.3 percent of the world market. If that 0.3 percent is thought to represent the neutral weight against which bets are made, one sees immediately the buy high/sell low bias. Our value remained around 1 percent before and after the crash. The market was overvalued before the crash and then became very undervalued. The reversal of the tendency for market-cap benchmarks to give buy high/sell low signals is the essence of what we are proposing as a better method.

Another advantage of our system is its universality. Our system allows clients to reintegrate emerging markets into the main spectrum—based on the value being created in those markets. Instead of having to have two separate mandates (one for emerging markets and one for developed markets), they can have one fund based on the universal fundamental values that cover all markets. Similarly, building from the bottom up as we do (i.e., using company data), we can apply our framework constructively within the European common market. Once the euro comes in, we can go to sector weighting and industry weighting within the 11 countries in the European Monetary Union. As globalization proceeds, we can use the same process globally and internationally. The ability to integrate is one of the advantages that we can offer.

They say that the best is often the enemy of the better. The Morrell method may not be the best investment methodology, but we believe it is a better methodology than consensus following, whether the consensus is an index or the peer universe. We see it as a logical step forward for investment pragmatists that leads to better allocation decisions. Used as a benchmark for managers, it introduces a positive bias to investment operations by having a better neutral position. We believe that it is the way to beat the measurement benchmark. It is, in that sense, a system to beat the system.

The Way Forward

By adopting the following suggestions, conventional practice can be changed for the better.

- Trustees must be encouraged to add experienced investors to their boards of trustees. This action is necessary if trustees are to accept the responsibilities imposed on them by the Pensions Act 1995 in the United Kingdom and ERISA in the United States. Only then will they be equipped to adopt a proactive role in designing a customized benchmark suitable for their particular circumstances.
- Trustees need to accept that index-based benchmarks are not the true and only gospel. They are counterproductive to performance. A customized strategy benchmark based on fundamentals, such as the Morrell method, can improve performance and reduce volatility.
- Investment firms owe it to their clients to develop their own investment methodology. They need to develop strategy benchmarks that reflect their perceptions of investment opportunity and their management strengths. Investment firms have become too accommodating to consultants and too subservient altogether. They need to reassert themselves.
- Consultants and actuaries have key roles to play. They should help their clients in matching liabilities to assets, in developing appropriate investment strategies and mandates, and in devising appropriate customized strategy benchmarks. The consultant can then identify investment managers whose approaches best match their clients' needs.
- Trustees have a duty to address all investment opportunities. The artificial distinction between emerging markets and developed markets should be dismantled. The world stock markets should be seen as a continuum from largest to smallest.
- Business managers of investment firms need to appreciate that collective misjudgment is still misjudgment. In a globally competitive world, a local consensus offers no security. The consensus approach of U.K. asset allocation has been a missed opportunity in relation to the U.S. market, which threatens London's credibility as the world's leading international investment center.
- Balanced managers in the United Kingdom have pursued a highly successful strategy in maximizing exposure to equities, but they need to adopt a customized-benchmark approach to better match their talents to client needs.
- Investment firms need to redefine internal roles. Asset allocation and country allocation decisions should be part of the responsibilities of portfolio managers, "advised" by economists and strategists. This traditional relationship worked. Top-down country allocation has largely failed.

Question and Answer Session

John Morrell

Question: Because your approach is based on the size of companies and the ability of companies to create wealth, how does the allocation differ from a GDP-type of benchmark?

Morrell: GDP was something that we initially investigated as an input for our formula. We were looking for stability, away from price, and GDP provides that stability. But we rejected it in our formula because you can't buy GDP and because it produced many distortions. For example, when comparing Germany and the United Kingdom, you'll find that the U.K. market cap is 140 percent of GDP and the German market cap is about 35 percent. GDP, in our view, produces more problems than it solves.

In the customization process, we include an *aide-mémoire* column for GDP, particularly for emerging markets. So, we are saying that it is a factor, and when you customize your benchmark, you should keep it in mind. If privatization programs are running strongly, there is a strong case for keeping in mind the GDP weight as well as the market-cap weight and our weight. All three are relevant. One of the advantages of customization is that everybody can look at all the key factors and make their own judgment as to relevance.

As to how the numbers differ, our country allocations differ substantially from GDP-derived allocations.

Question: Can you clarify the basis of your wealth-creation benchmark? Is it essentially a country's total corporate profits?

Morrell: Wealth is reflected in two measures: static wealth and dynamic wealth. The static wealth numbers come from the balance sheets, and the dynamic wealth measures come from the operating statements. Clients get a handbook that describes the composition of our strategy benchmark in detail. But rather like Coca-Cola, the formula is secret, but the ingredients are known and described in detail. There is a high degree of transparency.

Question: How do you handle countries, such as Germany, where the available capital and the size of the market are dysfunctional?

Morrell: As I said, GDP is a background factor that should be kept in mind. It is a question of judgment. The GDP of Germany compared with the market cap of Germany and compared with our value for Germany are three components that need to be carefully assessed by anybody who is customizing a benchmark. But note that with the advent of the euro, the domestic market for Germany will be 11 countries, not just 1.

Question: Any comments on style-specific indexes?

Morrell: The style question is important. We need to recognize that managers have natural styles, and they should be encouraged to follow those styles. If they are good at what they do, it shows up in the results. At the same time, they do need to be monitored carefully to see that they are true to their mandate.

We offer a proprietary monitoring service for that purpose. We measure large cap, medium cap, small cap, and growth and value in a whole portfolio because the qualities that belong to stocks belong to the whole portfolio too. We look at how the manager is moving among large cap, small cap, and growth and value. We want to make sure that that style manager is giving the client what the client expects the manager to give.

Question: How do you adjust for different accounting standards around the world when looking at company financials?

Morrell: The short answer is, "We don't." Unfortunately, accounting standards are not yet universal. Nevertheless, probably 85 percent or 90 percent of our country indexes include companies that have accounts audited by internationally acclaimed auditors. It is only in the bottom 10–15 percent that you get into tough accounting problems. Part of the reason why we take cash flow more seriously than earnings is because it tends to smooth out accounting differences.

Question: If market cap is not the basis of the benchmark, what is?

Morrell: The elements include PPP for international comparison. The static items are gross balance sheets and net balance sheets. The dynamic items are cash flow, earnings, and dividends. As I said, these are the tools familiar to all investment analysts.

Self-Evaluation Examination

1. According to Urwin, which of the following is the first step in forecasting returns?
   A. Select an appropriate risk-free rate.
   B. Examine the current yield structure.
   C. Estimate future inflation rates.
   D. All of the above.

2. According to Urwin, which of the following provides evidence of portfolio disinvestment of domestic equities by U.K. pension funds?
   A. Many U.K. funds have an increasing appetite only for emerging market equities.
   B. As U.K. pension funds move toward becoming eurozone investors, they will off load some of their domestic stocks in search of eurozone equities.
   C. U.K. pension funds are relatively immature, so a high allocation to domestic equities is actually very appropriate given the long investment horizon.
   D. None of the above.

3. According to Ghayur and Dawson, international equity and bond market return correlations are _____ over time, global equity market return correlations _____ when markets are _____, and international equity and bond market return correlations _____ when volatility increases.
   A. Stable, increase, rising, decrease.
   B. Unstable, increase, declining, increase.
   C. Increasing, decrease, rising, decrease.
   D. Decreasing, increase, declining, increase.

4. According to Ghayur and Dawson, correlation and volatility data suggest that the asset-class risk of equities is increasing.
   A. True.
   B. False.

5. According to Merciai, which of the following statements are correct?
   I. Correlation data for world markets indicate that world financial markets are integrated.
   II. From a theoretical standpoint, currency gains and losses balance out over the long term, but in the real world, currency depreciation or currency appreciation can extend throughout short periods.
   III. The base currency does not have a significant impact on risk–return relationships and efficient frontiers.
   IV. At the world level, market timing is even more important than at the domestic level because major financial markets experience distinctive periods of overperformance and underperformance.
   A. I and II.
   B. II, III, and IV.
   C. I and III.
   D. II and IV.

6. According to Duncombe, using hedged versus unhedged correlation and volatility data makes very little difference to the final portfolio allocations for both U.S. and U.K. investors.
   A. True.
   B. False.

7. According to Duncombe, which of the following styles do currency overlay managers use to capture market inefficiencies?
   A. Dynamic hedging or option replication.
   B. Volatility smiles.
   C. Currency surprise.
   D. Variance ratio.

8. According to Hole, which of the following explain the high equity allocation of U.K. pension funds?
   A. The measurement of liabilities in real terms because of inflation concerns.
   B. The use of consensus or peer-group asset allocation in benchmarks.
   C. The use of asset and liability smoothing.
   D. All of the above.

9. According to Hole, which of the following will happen assuming that the United Kingdom joins the European Monetary Union?
   A. Cash returns will diverge.
   B. Bond returns, from a government-debt perspective, will converge to reflect simple credit risk.
   C. Sector factors across Europe will become less important relative to country factors.
   D. None of the above.

10. According to Witschi, which of the following factors contribute to the small equity allocation for European pension funds?
    A. Accounting standards.
    B. Funding rules.
    C. Portfolio regulations.
    D. All of the above.

11. According to Tapley, which of the following best explains the asset allocation differences between U.K. and European pension funds?
    A. Cultural reasons.
    B. Structural reasons.
    C. The size of the pension surplus.
    D. None of the above.

12. According to Ezra, which of the following modeling approaches can best take real-life problems into account?
    A. Simulations.
    B. Mean–variance optimization.
    C. Multistage stochastic programming.
    D. Generalized autoregressive conditional heteroscedasticity (GARCH) models.

13. According to Goodsall, tactical asset allocation removes emotion from the investment process.
    A. True.
    B. False.

14. According to Woodlock, index funds will probably replace futures contracts as the global asset allocation tool of choice.
    A. True.
    B. False.

15. According to Lowe, which of the following are optimal conditions for rebalancing a pension plan's portfolio?
    I. When returns and risk remain stable around assumed means.
    II. When the plan's assets increase monotonically over time.
    III. When the strategic portfolio has a constant level of risk aversion.
    IV. When the strategic portfolio is flexible and changes with the plan's level of risk aversion.
    A. I and II.
    B. I, II, and IV.
    C. II and III.
    D. I and IV.

16. According to Layard-Liesching, which of the following is leading the movement away from balanced fund management toward specialist management among U.K. pension funds?
    A. Poor market-timing ability of U.K. money managers.
    B. Poor equity selection results.
    C. The unrewarded allocation of investment risk.
    D. Poor country allocation.

17. According to Layard-Liesching, which of the following statements is true?
    I. Peer pressure has contributed to the prevalence of specialist management.
    II. Financial engineering has led to reduced opportunities to add value through active management.
    III. The more that cumulative returns are compressed into very brief periods of time, the more difficult it is to time markets.
    IV. Strong evidence exists that forecasting risk is possible.
    A. I.
    B. III and IV.
    C. I and II.
    D. II and III.

18. According to Layard-Liesching, varying the exposure to risky assets in inverse proportion to asset volatilities stabilizes the aggregate risk faced by the fund.
    A. True.
    B. False.

19. According to Morrell, the tendency to avoid risk has allowed many investors to avoid losses during market downturns.
    A. True.
    B. False.

20. According to Morrell, which of the following represent the origin of the consensus trap?
    A. Pension trustees trying to avoid risk of being wrong vis-à-vis their peers.
    B. Actuaries and consultants centered on past performance of the index.
    C. Senior business managers defining risk as losing business to a competitor.
    D. All of the above.

Self-Evaluation Answers

1. B. According to Urwin, the initial step in forecasting returns is to look at the current yield structure, which provides a reasonable amount of information about future returns.

2. B. According to Urwin, given the maturity of U.K. pension funds, many such funds have an increasing appetite for equities in general.

3. B. According to Ghayur and Dawson, international equity and bond market return correlations are unstable over time, global equity market return correlations increase when markets are declining, and international equity and bond market return correlations increase when volatility increases—just when investors need the benefits of international diversification the most.

4. A. Their data show that if the U.S. market falls sharply and precipitously, all other markets are likely to fall as well, and some markets that are more volatile than the U.S. market are likely to decline even more than the U.S. market. So, a portfolio is subject to asset-class risk—the risk of being in equities.

5. D. Although financial theory suggests that the world financial markets are becoming more integrated, correlation data do not clearly indicate such a trend. The base currency does have a significant impact on risk–return relationships and efficient frontiers.

6. B. According to Duncombe, using hedged versus unhedged correlation and volatility data makes a significant difference to the final portfolio allocations for both U.S. and U.K. investors. Although the use of hedged versus unhedged data does not appear to change correlation data much (see Table 3 in his presentation), portfolios constructed using mean–variance optimization provide different results—higher overall allocations to foreign equities for U.K. investors and significantly different individual foreign holdings for U.S. investors.

7. A. Duncombe notes that currency overlay managers basically use two styles: dynamic hedging, or option replication, and forecasting the direction and/or magnitude of currency returns.

8. D.

9. B. According to Hole, in anticipation of EMU, cash returns will converge, bond returns (from a government-debt perspective) will converge to reflect simple credit risk, equity returns will continue the marked convergence already experienced, intra-European correlations will increase, and sector factors across Europe will become more important relative to country factors.

10. D. In addition, the structure of fund management, higher taxation, and *ex post* asset returns will also influence the equity allocation of European pension funds.

11. C. According to Tapley, cultural explanations are unsatisfactory explanations for asset allocation differences. Structural explanations—legislative, regulatory, and contractual—are much more interesting, but the missing link in most explanations of asset allocation differences is the pension surplus. Investors with small surpluses foster loss aversion, which leads to asset allocation policies with asymmetric or option-like payoffs; investors with large surpluses hold more of their assets in risky assets, such as equities.

12. C. Multistage stochastic programming provides multiple measures of good and bad outcomes and guidance as to optimal asset allocation, has less error-maximizing potential than simulations and mean–variance optimization, can incorporate different degrees of risk aversion, and can take real-life problems into account.

13. A. Emotion is removed from the investment decision-making process with TAA. TAA allows a manager to capture finer nuances of differences among valuation fundamentals than by using a subjective approach, and it allows a manager to take advantage of a substantial diversification effect.

©Association for Investment Management and Research

14. B. Woodlock states that index funds will probably not replace futures contracts as the global asset allocation tool of choice because index funds are best transacted at the unit level, because regulatory barriers prevent index funds from being invested across borders, and most importantly, because creating a global equity fund with index funds is not an instant process.

15. D. According to Lowe, rebalancing works best when returns and risk remain stable around assumed means, when the plan's net wealth is constant, or when the strategic portfolio itself is flexible and changes with the plan's level of risk aversion.

16. C. Perverse judgements about market timing, equity selection, and country allocation have contributed to the drag on performance. These bad decisions have arisen from the unrewarded allocation of investment risk.

17. B. According to Layard-Liesching, peer pressure has contributed to the prevalence of balanced management; technology has led to reduced opportunities to add value through active management; the more that cumulative returns are compressed into very brief periods of time, the more difficult it is to time markets; and strong evidence exists that risk can be forecasted.

18. A.

19. B. According to Morrell, the tendency to avoid risk has led many investors to follow what everyone else is doing (the peer-group universe) or to get in line with what everyone else thinks (following the index).

20. D.

Selected Publications

AIMR

AIMR Performance Presentation Standards Handbook, 2nd edition, 1997

Alternative Investing, 1998

Asian Equity Investing, 1998

Credit Analysis Around the World, 1998

Deregulation of the Electric Utility Industry, 1997

Derivatives in Portfolio Management, 1998

Economic Analysis for Investment Professionals, 1997

Equity Research and Valuation Techniques, 1998

Finding Reality in Reported Earnings, 1997

The Future of the Investment Firm, 1998

Global Bond Management, 1997

Implementing Global Equity Strategy: Spotlight on Asia, 1997

Investing in Small-Cap and Microcap Securities, 1997

Investing Worldwide VIII: Developments in Global Portfolio Management, 1997

Managing Currency Risk, 1997

Standards of Practice Casebook, 1996

Standards of Practice Handbook, 7th edition, 1996

Research Foundation

Blockholdings of Investment Professionals, 1997
by Sanjai Bhagat, Bernard S. Black, and Margaret M. Blair

Company Performance and Measures of Value Added, 1996
by Pamela P. Peterson, CFA, and David R. Peterson

Controlling Misfit Risk in Multiple-Manager Investment Programs, 1998
by Jeffery V. Bailey, CFA, and David E. Tierney

Country Risk in Global Financial Management, 1997
by Claude B. Erb, CFA, Campbell R. Harvey, and Tadas E. Viskanta

Economic Foundations of Capital Market Returns, 1997
by Brian D. Singer, CFA, and Kevin Terhaar, CFA

Initial Dividends and Implications for Investors, 1997
by James W. Wansley, CFA, William R. Lane, CFA, and Phillip R. Daves

Interest Rate Modeling and the Risk Premiums in Interest Rate Swaps, 1997
by Robert Brooks, CFA

The International Equity Commitment, 1998
by Stephen A. Gorman

Sales-Driven Franchise Value, 1997
by Martin L. Leibowitz